PLACES OF DESTINY

THE LANDMARKS OF WORLD HISTORY

PLACES OF DESTINY
THE LANDMARKS OF WORLD HISTORY

BEN DUPRÉ

Quercus

CONTENTS

Previous page: The Battle of Waterloo.

Below: A detail from the Bayeux Tapestry.

INTRODUCTION

You do not have to be exceptionally sentimental or superstitious to feel the hand of history in certain places. Only the hardest heart could fail to be moved by the pathetic sense of waste in the long lines of white marble crosses and gravestones neatly set out in cemeteries along the Somme; no one who visits the gas chambers at Auschwitz can fail to sense a palpable aura of human evil. The fact that Manhattan in September 2001 and Dallas in November 1963 are indelibly etched in the memories of those old enough to remember them is due both to an acute sense of human loss and tragedy and to a more intangible feeling that the world changed, that the course of human affairs was wrenched from one path and set forcibly on another. It is the object of this book to tell the stories of such places: places where history was made.

History, as Gibbon observed, is *'little more than the register of the crimes, follies and misfortunes of mankind'*. It is inevitable, therefore, that in the current selection of places there is a bias towards the darker aspects of human nature; there are plenty of bloody defeats and bloody victories, and there is certainly no shortage of cruelty, violence and death. It is not true, however, that the devil has *all* the best tunes, and there are generally some uplifting interludes, in Philadelphia, for example, where the US Declaration of Independence was signed, and in the Galapagos Islands, which inspired Charles Darwin to devise one of the most momentous theories in scientific history. Frequently, of course, extreme adversity produces a rich soil in which exceptional human qualities can blossom, and often great suffering and resolution give rise to more or less unqualified good: the extraordinary bravery and sacrifice of ordinary Soviet soldiers at Stalingrad, for instance, were arguably the single most important factor in the defeat of Nazism. Usually, however, places have a more ambiguous complexion and their legacies are open to fascinatingly different interpretations. Did the bombing of Hiroshima bring an end to the Second World War and save tens of thousands of lives, or was it a cynical flourish of realpolitik that ushered in the fears and neuroses of the nuclear age? Were the European landings in the Bahamas in 1492 and at Botany Bay in 1770 expansions or degradations of civilization – or both?

In choosing just three dozen places of particular prominence in history, I have attempted to produce a selection that has a broad span in both time and place. The articles are arranged in chronological order and extend over two and a half millennia, from fifth-century Greece to 21st-century USA, while geographically they cover every point of the compass, from Europe and the Americas to the Middle East, the Pacific and Australia. In the end, however, the principal criteria have always remained historical significance and narrative excitement. Every place chosen witnessed a great climax or watershed in human affairs; an era-defining moment without which the progress of events in the world would have been very different. And in every case there is a cracking tale to tell that casts a fascinating light on various facets of the human condition. These are places that will forever resonate with the tremor of great or ghastly deeds; places where, as Yeats said of Dublin in 1916, *'a terrible beauty is born'*.

In writing this book I have been fortunate enough to enjoy the unfailing support of my editor, Richard Milbank. Researching it has transported me, in imagination at least, to many wonderful and exotic places. Nevertheless, the love and toleration shown by my wife, two daughters and a dog allow me to confirm what may not be an entirely original thesis, viz. that there is, after all, no place like home.

Ben Dupré
Oxford 2008

The main trunk road between northern and southern Greece snakes its way along a strip of land defined to the east by the Aegean and to the west by the mountains that form the rugged spine of the country. As you enter the Phthiotis region and skirt around the Malian Gulf, the road is often closely confined by sheer wooded mountains on one side and sea on the other. At a point where the terrain opens out into a broad, coarsely grassed plain, there are two prominent monuments on the roadside, one featuring an ancient Greek warrior with crested helmet, spear and shield.

THERMOPYLAE

❧ *August 480* BC ❧

Greece's triumphant defence of Western freedom

If you stop here, you may find that the familiar briny scent of the Aegean has an unexpected sulphurous note. For at the foot of the mountains there is a stream fed by the hot sulphur springs that give the place its name: 'Hot Gates', or Thermopylae in Greek. This is the site of perhaps the most famous rearguard action in the history of warfare. Here, 2500 years ago, the Spartan king Leonidas – the figure on top of the monument – and a small band of loyal Greeks attempted to block the advance of the vast army of the Persian king Xerxes.

After the bitterest of struggles the Greeks were finally overwhelmed and annihilated to the last man. Trampling – literally trampling – over the corpses of their dead adversaries, the Persians marched southwards and eventually put Athens to the torch. Yet it was the almost superhuman resistance of Leonidas and his fellows that was credited, from antiquity onwards, with providing the spark and inspiration for the subsequent victories at Salamis and Plataea that finally extinguished the Persian threat. Forever afterwards Thermopylae has been portrayed not only as the quintessential act of defiance against impossible odds but also – rather simplistically – as a triumph of (liberal) West over (despotic) East. In this light Leonidas and his comrades are viewed as the saviours of Greek, and by extension Western, liberty and civilization.

A modern statue of Leonidas in Sparta. This king of the ancient Spartans is commemorated as a heroic warrior who led a small Greek force in a last stand against the Persians at Thermopylae.

XERXES' UNFINISHED BUSINESS

Greece had long been a festering sore to Xerxes, the Great King of the Persian empire, the most expansive kingdom the world had ever seen. A decade before Thermopylae, in 490 BC, his father Darius, had launched a punitive expedition directed principally at Athens, which had supported the Greeks of Asia Minor in a failed revolt against Persia. Darius' venture, however, came spectacularly unstuck at Marathon, where the Greek (mainly Athenian) army defeated a far larger Persian force. On Darius' death in 486 Xerxes inherited the crown and with it the obligation to avenge his father's humiliation. He set about launching a second and far greater expedition, mustering tens of thousands of soldiers and hundreds of ships from every part of his kingdom. This time the explicit aim was to subjugate those Greek states that had so far refused to bow to his authority.

The Greek response was, for the most part, weak and fragmented. Unable to settle age-old animosities, the majority of the Greeks either 'Medized' – went over to the Persian side – or opted to stay on the sidelines. Just 31 of the

Rocky cliffs loom over the site of the battle between the Greek and Persian armies at Thermopylae. Now a broad plateau, in 480 BC the Aegean came close up to the cliffs, forming a narrow pass.

THE LEGACY OF THERMOPYLAE

If the Greek resistance had crumbled under the wheels of Xerxes' juggernaut, the course of history would have been very different. In particular, the magnificent flowering of Athenian democracy and culture in the latter half of the fifth century would not have taken place, and the significance of that for the development of Western civilization is beyond question.

There is some oddity in Spartans being honoured as the saviours of Western values, for Sparta itself was the strangest and most illiberal of all the Greek states: a culture based on extreme militarism and underpinned by enslavement of fellow Greeks. The crucial point about the Spartans, however, as Herodotus explains, is that they were fiercely constitutional – they acted freely under their own (admittedly very peculiar) laws. Ironically, the fruit of Sparta's self-sacrifice at Thermopylae was a flourishing in other Greek states that was denied to – indeed, was in many respects anathema to – Sparta itself.

mainland Greek states agreed to set aside their differences and to unite in resisting the Persian invaders. While Leonidas headed north to hold the pass at Thermopylae, a combined Greek fleet set sail to Cape Artemisium, the northernmost headland on the island of Euboea, where they would lie in wait for the Persian warships as they sailed down the western Aegean coast.

THE PASS AT THERMOPYLAE

Anyone now surveying Thermopylae, with its broad plateau running gently down to the sea, would wonder how the Greeks could ever have hoped to stem the Persian tide at such a point. But an ancient Greek would scarcely recognize the place as it is today. Over the past 2500 years silting-up of the Malian Gulf has forced the sea to retreat, leaving the site of the fighting several miles inland. In Leonidas' day, however, the course of the modern road was washed by the surf of the Aegean. Between mountain and sea there was a strip of land so narrow in places that there was space only for a single cart to pass. Along this defile, which extended for some 3 miles (5 km), there were three especially narrow constrictions, or 'gates' (*pylai* in Greek, hence Thermo*pylae*). The gates at either end were narrowest, but while the ground at the Middle Gate was somewhat wider, at around 20 metres (66 ft), the cliffs at this point were sheer and steepled up to around 1000 metres (3280 ft), making them all but impregnable. The position was further strengthened by an old defensive wall, which the Greeks set about rebuilding. It was here that Leonidas chose to make his stand.

Thermopylae was in many respects an excellent choice. Not only did the narrow terrain largely neutralize Xerxes' strong cavalry, but – most importantly – it partly offset Leonidas' extreme numerical inferiority. Their hands tied by religious obligations (it happened to be the Olympic festival at the time), the Greeks had only sent an advance force of about 7000, to which the Spartans

had contributed just 300 of their élite warriors. The exact size of the Persian army is not known (the ancient estimates are hugely exaggerated), but it may well have been more than 20 times larger than the Greek force.

THE BATTLE FOR THE PASS

The Greeks' great strength lay in their heavily armoured infantry, or 'hoplites' (named after their large round shield, or *hoplon*), who fought in a close formation known as a phalanx, interlocking their shields and thrusting overarm with their long spears. On the first and second days at Thermopylae the fighting followed a similar pattern. Wave after wave of Xerxes' foot soldiers, with lighter armour and shorter spears, were forced by the terrain into making a series of head-on assaults on the Greek phalanx and were thoroughly outmatched. While the Greeks fought in relays to stay fresh and suffered few losses, the Persians rapidly incurred dreadful casualties (the historian Herodotus, again probably exaggerating, puts the figure over three days at 20,000).

At the end of the second day, just as Xerxes was coming close to despair, his luck changed. A local man named Ephialtes agreed at a price to guide the Persians along a track that snaked through the mountains and led to a point close to the East Gate, behind the Greek line. Xerxes' best troops, the so-called Immortals, were promptly dispatched and easily overcame the guard set by Leonidas to watch the path. It would only be a matter of hours now before the Immortals made their descent and were in a position to attack the Greek rear.

When news of the imminent outflanking reached the Greeks early on the third day, most of the army moved southwards to safety, while Leonidas and a small force including his 300 Spartans and 700 Thespians remained, facing almost certain death, to cover their retreat. '*Eat a good breakfast,*' Leonidas is supposed to have said to his comrades, '*for this evening we shall dine together in Hades.*' When at last they were surrounded, the surviving Greeks retreated to a small hill, where they reputedly fought on until their spears were broken, then with their swords, and finally with their hands and teeth. A Spartan named Dienekes had earlier responded to the news that the Persians' arrows would be so dense as to blot out the sky with a typically laconic reply: '*All the better: we shall fight in the shade.*' In the end, Dienekes, Leonidas and all their comrades fought and died in a torrent of Persian arrows.

LEST WE FORGET

In antiquity a monument in the form of a stone lion was set up at Thermopylae to honour the memory of Leonidas (whose name means 'lion-like') and his fallen comrades. Also at the site there was a tablet engraved with a celebrated epitaph in honour of the Spartan (Lacedaemonian) dead written by the poet Simonides of Keos:

GREECE

Aegean Sea

Thermopylae .

.Athens

.Sparta

Mediterranean Sea

'Tell them in Lacedaemon, passer-by,
That here obedient to their laws we lie.'

The ancient monuments have not survived but have been replaced in modern times. The large bronze statue of Leonidas stands on a marble pedestal on which are engraved just two words: MOLŌN LABÉ. This phrase, supposedly uttered by Leonidas in response to Xerxes' demand to hand over his weapons, means simply: *'Come and get them.'* The second monument at the roadside, featuring a figure representing the god Eros, is a memorial to the 700 Thespians who died in the battle. On the other side of the road is the hill on which the Greeks made their last stand; the site was plausibly identified in the 20th century by the discovery of a mass of Persian arrowheads.

Leonidas at Thermopylae, *as depicted by the French neoclassical painter Jacques-Louis David (1748–1825). The selfless dedication and sacrifice exemplified by Leonidas appealed strongly to the Romantic sensibilities of the early 19th century.*

13

The body of water known today as the Rubicon is a small river – little more than a stream – that rises in the Apennines and flows out into the Adriatic just north of Rimini. The coastal plain through which it flows to the sea has long been prone to flooding, and over the millennia the rivers in the region have continually changed their course. It is perhaps as much a philosophical question as a geographical one whether this or any other river in the area is identical to the one that bore the name Rubicon in the first century BC.

RUBICON

❧ *January 49* BC ❧

A small river that precipitated the demise of the Roman republic

As a physical feature, the ancient river was clearly no more remarkable than its modern namesake; certainly not an obvious catalyst for catastrophic political upheaval. Yet the importance of the Rubicon in Roman times was due not to its size but to its location. In the first century BC the Rubicon marked the northern border of Italy; the area north of the river, now part of Italy, formed the province of Cisalpine Gaul ('Gaul this side of the Alps'). Roman law required a provincial governor to relinquish his *imperium* – the power he exercised by virtue of his position – before leaving his province at the end of his term and returning to Italy; in his capacity as military commander-in-chief, this entailed disbanding or handing over command of his legions. For a commander to refuse to do so was an act of treason – in effect, a declaration of war on the state.

In early January 49 BC the Roman general Julius Caesar was at Ravenna, a few miles north of the Rubicon, contemplating just such an act of treason. Over the border, in Italy, his political enemies had been scheming against him. They appeared to have backed him into a corner: if he laid down his command and returned to Rome, as the law required, he faced prosecution and political ruin; if he crossed the border with his soldiers, he would plunge the Roman world into civil war.

Reaching his decision, Caesar took the road south from Ravenna. As the biographer Suetonius recounts, in his *Lives of the Twelve Caesars*:

A fanciful and anonymous 19th-century engraving showing Julius Caesar crossing the Rubicon. The phrase has since become synonymous with any irrevocable and momentous act.

'Catching up with his cohorts at the Rubicon, he paused for a moment. Appreciating the enormity of the step he was taking, he turned to those around him and said: "Even now we can turn back; but once we cross that small bridge, everything will depend on the sword".'

Finally, encouraged (so Suetonius would have us believe) by a miraculous trumpeter sounding the advance, Caesar strode forward, crying: *'Let us go where the gods' omens and our enemies' crimes summon us!* iacta alea est – *the die is cast!'*

A ROTTING REPUBLIC

Crossing the Rubicon was a moment of intense anguish for Caesar and it was certainly a grave shock for the Roman state. With hindsight, however, we can see that the trauma that precipitated the collapse of a system of government that had endured for 450 years was the predictable result of more than half a century of social and political violence and unrest.

The pillars that upheld Rome's republican constitution were built on deep loathing of the monarchy that had preceded it. The overthrow of the kings of Rome in the late sixth century BC – the last monarch was the tyrant Tarquinius Superbus – was a totemic event in Roman history (the title *rex* – 'king' – remained taboo throughout the republic and beyond). A range of constitutional safeguards was aimed at preventing anyone ever again attaining such autocratic powers. So, for instance, the highest office of state, the consulship, was held jointly, each incumbent having equal powers, and its tenure was limited to one year; similar restrictions, including minimum age requirements, were placed on lower offices. In general, a system that had evolved over hundreds of years proved highly resilient. Exceptions to the rules were made in times of emergency, but always for the good of the republic; and normal procedures were restored once a crisis had passed.

Corrosion began to set in as soon as concern for the common good started to give way to the aspirations of individuals bent on winning wealth and power for themselves. As the first century progressed, virtually every inhibition was swept aside as political and social advancement became the goal at any cost. Within the ruling élite, young hopefuls would stake their future on making it to the top, often getting caught in a spiral of debt as they borrowed heavily in order to bribe voters to elevate them to positions in which they could recoup their losses. Provincial governorships were seen as the opportunity for unbridled plunder, while accusations of extortion and electoral bribery were seized on by political rivals, making fear of prosecution an ever-present menace. Inevitably there were big winners, who would accrue enormous wealth and influence, and equally big losers, who would countenance any course of action that offered a prospect of restoring their fortunes.

THE TWO RIVALS

Within this volatile political climate, it was the conflicting ambitions of two men in particular that brought matters to a head: Gaius Julius Caesar and Gnaeus Pompeius Magnus (Pompey). Talented, ambitious and ruthless in

THE TROUBLED BIRTH OF AN EMPIRE

The title 'Caesar' was adopted by the emperor Augustus and many of his successors, but Julius Caesar himself was not emperor of Rome. While he may have lacked the title, however, he enjoyed much of the power and privilege. Just a few weeks before his assassination on the Ides of March (15 March) 44 BC, Caesar had been made *dictator perpetuo* (dictator for life) – and this was merely the latest of a string of extraordinary powers that a fawning senate had bestowed on him. By the time of his death the republic had already become a feeble pretence – transparent to all but the most die-hard republicans. Brutus, Cassius and the others who conspired to kill Caesar did so in the name of the republic, but at most they managed only to prolong its death throes by sparking a further cycle of civil war.

Within two years they too were dead, defeated at Philippi by the Second Triumvirate of Marcus Lepidus, Antony and Octavian, who had assumed effective control of the Roman world from 43 BC. It was Octavian, Caesar's adopted son and heir, who finally became sole ruler of the Roman empire after his victory over Antony at Actium in 31 BC. He took the title 'Augustus' in 27 BC, somewhat ironically at the same time as he formally restored many of the trappings of the republic. But these were a mere fig leaf: his new title (combined with the designation imperator, 'emperor') set him above the state; his power was immense and absolute.

A statue of Julius Caesar erected in 27 BC by his adopted son and first emperor Augustus.

pursuit of their interests, both were classic products of the age. Each had established himself on the basis of military genius: Pompey's finest moment had come in his eastern campaigns of the mid-60s BC, in which he had defeated Mithridates VI of Pontus and annexed Syria; Caesar's in the Gallic Wars of the 50s BC, by the end of which he had brought Gaul under Roman control. Such victorious campaigns brought huge wealth, popularity at home, and the loyalty of veteran legions, who not only profited from plunder but also looked forward to generous land settlements in the future. Powerful on their own, these two political giants had formed, in 60 BC, an informal coalition (later called the 'First Triumvirate') with the plutocrat Marcus Licinius Crassus. In this way they ensured (as Suetonius observed) that *'nothing in the republic could be done that displeased any one of the three'*: they conspired together to push through legislation and to gain extraordinary appointments that increased their already enormous influence.

Such was the stellar rise of Pompey and Caesar that it was inevitable that before long friction would start to build up between them. From the mid-50s BC, the bonds began to loosen, first with the death in 54 BC of Caesar's daughter Julia, whom Pompey had married to cement the coalition, then with the death of Crassus at the Battle of Carrhae in 53 BC. A real firebrand in his younger days, prepared to bend all the rules, Pompey had gradually moved closer to the conservatives in the senate – the so-called *optimates* – who included such eminent figures as the redoubtable Marcus Cato (Cato the Younger) and the orator Marcus Cicero. An incongruous and often reluctant bedfellow, Pompey became (as the historian Sallust sarcastically observed) *'moderate in everything save in seeking domination'*. It was natural, therefore, that most of the senate should look to Pompey in dealing with the sensitive and potentially inflammatory matter of Caesar's return from Gaul.

SHOWDOWN

Caesar's time in Gaul had massively increased his standing, bringing him wealth, popularity and the loyalty of his battle-hardened legions. But his absence from Rome had also allowed his many and powerful enemies to scheme against him. Enraged at his growing influence, they eagerly prepared to prosecute him, alleging various illegalities in his consulship of 59 BC and in his conduct of the Gallic campaigns. To escape their clutches, Caesar's aim was to win the consulship in 48 BC, which would give him immunity from prosecution. However, he needed to do so without losing the protection afforded by his legions, which would happen if he followed the customary procedure and presented himself in Rome as a candidate.

A solution seemed to have been found in 52 BC, when a law was passed allowing Caesar to stand for the consulship *in absentia*. But his opponents were now blocking this route. Pompey, adopting an increasingly tough stance in support of his new-found allies, was asked what would happen if Caesar wished to become consul while retaining his army; *'What would happen if my son wished to attack me with a stick'* was his ominous reply. Increasingly fevered negotiations were carried on between the senate and Caesar's proxies in Rome – principally two tribunes of the people, Gaius Scribonius Curio and the soon-to-be-eminent Mark Antony. Caesar's final offer was to retain only the minimum force required to ensure his safety – an offer that Pompey, apparently, was prepared to accept – but it was now too late. The consul Gaius Claudius Marcellus, one of Caesar's most inveterate enemies, requested that Pompey *'defend the republic'*. Caesar was given an ultimatum, demanding that he lay down his command or become *hostis* – a public enemy. Caesar had been backed into a corner. He was, in effect, being asked to trust in Pompey's

goodwill to save him, and that he was unwilling to do. Left with no other way of defending his *dignitas* – his honour and status – he made his fateful decision to cross the Rubicon on 10 or 11 January 49 BC. To an astonishing degree, a civil war that spelt the end of the republic was the product of the pride and vanity of two men. As the poet Lucan deftly put it: *'Caesar could not countenance a superior, nor Pompey an equal.'*

KING IN ALL BUT NAME

In the ensuing civil war, Pompey soon showed complacency to match his vanity. He had earlier boasted that he had only to stamp his foot to fill the whole of Italy with armies, but it soon became apparent that most people in fact had little appetite for war. Shrewdly showing clemency wherever he met resistance, Caesar swept down through Italy and by March 49 BC had forced Pompey to abandon Italy and to cross over to Greece to recruit and regroup. After brilliantly defeating Pompey's legions in Spain – *'an army without a general'* – Caesar then turned to Greece, where he suggested (in jest) that he would find *'a general without an army'*. In this Pompey managed to disappoint him, but his success was short-lived. In August 48 BC his forces were decisively defeated at Pharsalus in Thessaly, and within weeks he was dead himself, murdered as he fled to Egypt. The fighting dragged on for a further two and a half years, until March 45 BC, when Pompey's sons were defeated at Munda in southern Spain, but in truth Caesar had long since become master of Rome, a king in all but name.

The Death of Caesar *by the French painter Guillaume Lethière (1760–1832). Caesar's increasingly autocratic attitude to power earned him the enmity of many powerful people in Rome. Sixty senators were involved in the conspiracy to assassinate him.*

19

Few places on earth can have had a richer or more colourful – and at times more troubled – history than Bethlehem. First established as an Israelite settlement some 3500 years ago, the town has at various times come under Roman, Arab, Ottoman and British rule. Perched on the Judaean Hills just 6 miles (10 km) south of Jerusalem, Bethlehem's fortunes have always been closely tied to those of its big northern neighbour. And in recent times, as Israelis and Palestinians have struggled for their national survival, the town has lain at the heart of the conflict on the West Bank, sometimes a symbol of hope, at other times an image of despair.

BETHLEHEM

⁊ 4 BC ⁊

The birthplace of a world religion

What gives Bethlehem global significance, however, is that it is the traditional birthplace of Jesus Christ. As one would expect, it is one of the most sacrosanct places of worship and pilgrimage for Christians, but it also has great religious significance for Muslims and Jews. Paradoxically, however, in spite of its manifest importance, it is at least open to question whether Jesus was born in Bethlehem at all.

WAS JESUS BORN IN BETHLEHEM?

The Nativity of Christ may well be (as Hollywood would have it) the first chapter of the 'Greatest Story Ever Told', and it is certainly one of the most familiar and frequently related. Its familiarity notwithstanding, the story of Jesus' birth is in fact a tapestry of pieces from different sources, embroidered with many later details. The main sources are the gospels of Matthew and Luke, both written within a century of Jesus' birth. They agree that Jesus was born in Bethlehem in the final days of the reign of Herod the Great, king of Judaea, but they agree about little else.

Matthew implies that Jesus' parents, Mary and Joseph, lived in Bethlehem at the time of the birth but fled to Egypt after the child was born in order to escape the Massacre of the Innocents – Herod's brutal attempt to eradicate a potential rival (the

The Church of the Nativity in Bethlehem is built over a cave
identified in the second century AD as the birthplace of Jesus Christ.
The site has been continuously venerated by Christians ever since.

TIMELINE

c.14th century BC Israelite settlement established at site of Bethlehem

10th century BC Birth of King David

4 BC Birth of Jesus

c.AD 338 Church built on the supposed site of the Nativity

1967 Bethlehem captured by the Israelis during the Six-Day War

1995 Bethlehem transferred to Palestinian control

September 2000 Outbreak of the Second Intifada

'king of the Jews' proclaimed by the Magi) by ordering the execution of all children under the age of two living in and around Bethlehem. Herod's death shortly afterwards allowed Joseph and his family to return from Egypt, but fearing the malevolent intentions of Archelaus, Herod's son and successor, they did not go back to Bethlehem but settled instead in the town of Nazareth in Galilee. There are two main oddities in Matthew's account. First, Egypt is a bizarre choice of refuge, given that there are countless places much closer to home where they could have stayed out of Archelaus' clutches. And second, there is no external evidence that the massacre that prompted the flight to Egypt actually occurred. It seems almost incredible that such a bloody atrocity would have been passed over by contemporary accounts, especially those that are hostile to Herod.

Luke makes no mention of Egypt or a massacre. In his version, Joseph and Mary already live in Nazareth but are obliged to travel from their home to Bethlehem in order to register in a universal tax census. Mary gives birth while they are in Bethlehem, after which they return home to Nazareth. But Luke's account is also beset with difficulties. The idea of a universal census is without precedent and inherently improbable, and there are in any case serious doubts about the chronology of any kind of census at the time of Jesus' birth (see Jesus' Premature Birth, p.24).

HISTORICAL AND SPIRITUAL TRUTH

It appears, then, that both gospels have to introduce awkward and inconsistent elements into the story in order to explain how Mary and Joseph came to be in Bethlehem at the time of the birth and in Nazareth after it. But such awkwardness mainly comes from taking too literal an approach to the gospels – treating them as statements of (purportedly) historical fact rather than texts written in a particular context and with a particular purpose. The writers of the gospels were evangelists: their purpose was to persuade others to share their faith that Jesus is the Christ ('anointed one') or Messiah, the saviour who will bring salvation to the children of Israel. Jewish themselves, the writers of the gospels were for the most part aiming to convert other Jews to adopt their own Christian beliefs. As a practical necessity, they had to convince their audience that their case was corroborated by the sacred texts contained in the Hebrew Old Testament. So in Matthew, for instance, it is almost a mantra that such and such happened as the fulfilment of a prophecy made by a prophet of the Old Testament.

Seen from this perspective, much of the detail of the Nativity stories begins to fall into place. An aspect of Jewish Messianic expectation was that the Messiah would be descended from David, the ideal of kingship in the Jewish tradition, whose birthplace was Bethlehem. Matthew often refers to Jesus as *'the son of David'* and, tellingly, quotes a prophecy from the Book of Micah:

> *'And you, O Bethlehem, in the land of Judah,*
> *are by no means least among the rulers of Judah;*
> *for from you shall come a ruler*
> *who will shepherd my people Israel.'*

THE MAGI

One of the most familiar elements of the Nativity is the Adoration of the Magi: the 'wise men' from the East who are guided by a star to Bethlehem, where they pay homage to Jesus as 'king of the Jews' and bring him gifts of gold, frankincense and myrrh. In fact, as in other aspects of the story, the tradition is far from simple. The Magi appear only in Matthew (Luke introduces shepherds instead), where neither their names nor number are given.

The fact that they were three in number (in the West – there are 12 in the Eastern tradition) is most likely a later extrapolation from the number of gifts, while the familiar names – Balthasar, Melchior and Caspar – are another later addition. The idea that they are kings, probably encouraged by their association

The Adoration of the Magi, *by the Sienese painter Bartolo di Fredi (1353 –1410), shows the 'wise men' honouring the infant Christ.*

with Herod but not mentioned in Matthew, of course serves to make their worship of the child all the more remarkable. Much effort has gone into identifying the so-called Star of Bethlehem – suggestions include various supernovae, comets and planetary conjunctions – but it is impossible at this distance to move beyond speculation. The chief role of the Magi, as usually understood, is to emphasize the universality of Christ's mission, in that he is an object of worship to all, including the exotic and non-Jewish Magi: '*a light to lighten the Gentiles*', in Luke's phrase.

Jesus' Premature Birth

The evangelists St Matthew and St Luke agree that Jesus was born in Bethlehem at the very end of the reign of Herod the Great, king of Judaea, and Herod is known to have died around 4 BC, i.e. four years 'Before Christ'!

This puzzle – of Jesus' birth occurring four years before he was born – isn't really a puzzle at all. Dionysus Exiguus, the Scythian monk who devised the Anno Domini, or Christian Era, system in the sixth century, calibrated his system on the basis of what he supposed was the year of the Nativity. By the time people began to suggest that his calculations had gone astray, it was too late to recalibrate. As a result, we are stuck with some apparent anomalies.

There are, however, a number of real difficulties relating to Jesus' birth date. One important case occurs in the Gospel According to St Luke. While he agrees that Jesus was born in the final days of Herod, he also states that the universal census that forced Joseph and Mary to leave Nazareth for Bethlehem was conducted when Quirinius was governor. The year of Quirinius' governorship of the province of Syria (which included Judaea) was AD 6, and he did indeed carry out a (local) census at this time. It seems that Luke has moved the event back in time in order to account for Mary's presence in Bethlehem when she gave birth to Jesus: another clue that Jesus may not in fact have been born in Bethlehem at all.

Luke explicitly identifies Bethlehem as the 'city of David' (a term which usually refers to Zion, i.e. Jerusalem) and then links it to the coming of the Messiah: '*For unto you is born this day in the city of David,*' the angel of the Lord tells the shepherds, '*a Saviour, who is Christ the Lord.*' A substantial body of Old Testament prophecy requires that the Messiah's birth takes place in Bethlehem, and it appears that Matthew and Luke have, each in his own way, answered the needs of evangelism (rather than historical truth) to square their accounts with this requirement. For Christians, supported by two millennia of religious observance, historicity is certain in any case to come a distant second to faith and spiritual truth. But whether or not Bethlehem is the birthplace of (the historical) Jesus, it is unquestionably the birthplace of Christianity and as such retains a central position in the history of humankind.

A TOWN IN TRAUMA

OPPOSITE: Smoke billows from the Church of the Nativity in spring 2002. Occupied by some 200 Palestinian militants and others, the church became the centre of world attention in a 39-day stand-off with Israeli forces.

Culturally and spiritually linked to nearby Jerusalem for most of its history, modern Bethlehem has been cruelly wrenched from the embrace of its mother city. For 28 years after the 1967 Six-Day War the town was occupied by Israeli forces, but in 1995, in accordance with the terms of the Oslo Agreement, it came under the full control of the Palestinian authorities. For the rest of the decade Bethlehem looked set to shine as a beacon of hope on the West Bank: a symbol of reconciliation between Israeli and Palestinian, between Muslim, Christian and Jew.

But everything changed in September 2000. Following the outbreak of the Second Intifada, or Palestinian uprising, Israel again occupied the town and

began to cement in place (literally) a vice-like network of
security measures. The town is now surrounded by a strait-
jacket of road blocks, checkpoints, earth mounds and – along
its northern and western sides – the massive concrete West
Bank Barrier. Cut off from Jerusalem and encircled by Israeli
settlements, Bethlehemites are subject to interminable
curfews and to severe travel restrictions. Amid security fears
and with access to the holy sites limited, the flow of tourists
and pilgrims has dried up, severing the town's main economic
lifeline. There has followed an exodus from the town of near-
bankrupt business people, especially of Palestinian Christians
– once forming a majority in the town, they have now
dwindled to about one-tenth of the population. Starved of its
economic and spiritual lifeblood, Bethlehem is now a virtual
ghost town of boarded-up shops and aborted development
projects: once a symbol of hope for a shared future, it now
stands as a bleak reminder of the heavy price
of political failure.

'In the central area there were bleached bones, scattered or in heaps, just as the men had run or stood their ground. All around lay fragments of weapons and horses' limbs, and human heads that had been nailed to tree trunks. In thickets nearby there stood barbarous altars on which the tribunes and first-rank centurions had been butchered. Some survivors who had escaped the battle or slipped their chains pointed out the spots where officers had fallen, the places where the eagles had been captured.'

ROMAN HISTORIAN TACITUS

TEUTOBURG FOREST
❧ *September* AD *9* ❧

The ambush that halted the northern expansion of the Roman empire

Such was the gruesome spectacle, as described by the historian Tacitus, that confronted Germanicus, adopted son of the emperor Tiberius and heir to the Roman empire, in AD 15, as he and his soldiers made a solemn visit to the site of the Battle of Teutoburg Forest. Deep within the German territories, midway between the Ems and Weser rivers, this had been the scene of a terrible massacre of three Roman legions: a ghastly humiliation of Roman arms, marked by the loss of the legions' eagle standards, that remained – six years on – raw and unavenged.

PROTECTING THE NORTHERN FRONTIER

Security on the empire's northern border, where the rich Gallic provinces faced the Germanic tribes across the Rhine, had remained a persistent headache for Tiberius' predecessor, Augustus, from the moment he became emperor in 27 BC. While Gaul had been conquered some 25 years earlier by his adopted father, Julius Caesar, the region bordering its frontier along the Rhine remained porous and unstable, an area subject to frequent Germanic raids and to revolts by Gallic tribes supported by their neighbours across the river. The task of pacifying these troublesome tribes became an increasingly pressing priority, and towards the end of the first century BC it appeared that conquest was the only answer.

Augustus entrusted the job initially to Drusus, Tiberius' younger brother, who conducted a series of largely successful campaigns between 12 and 9 BC. After Drusus' sudden death in that year (caused by a fall from his horse), the following two decades saw a string of commanders given responsibility for further pacification, including Tiberius himself, who took charge of the Rhine armies between 9 and 7 BC and again between AD 4 and 6. Over this period, and in spite of not infrequent setbacks, the process of subjugation appeared to be progressing steadily. Earlier gains

were consolidated by the establishment of numerous forts and garrisons and by the conclusion of treaties with a number of defeated tribes. Little by little, the emphasis began to move from military action to the usual process of Romanization, in which urban settlements, fitted out with baths and the other trappings of the Roman way of life, were built so that the natives could live and grow accustomed to the benefits and joys of *pax Romana*.

In AD 6 revolts erupted in Dalmatia and Pannonia of such severity that they demanded Tiberius' immediate presence and he was obliged to cede

Many 19th-century German painters took the Battle of Teutoburg Forest as their subject. This portrayal, by Friedrich Gunkel (1819–76), was widely reproduced in schoolbooks at the time.

command east of the Rhine. The man chosen by Augustus to consolidate and administer affairs in the fledgling German province was Publius Quinctilius Varus.

VARUS AND ARMINIUS

Most of the blame for the ensuing catastrophe fell on Varus, who was uniformly pilloried in contemporary accounts. The historian Velleius Paterculus, for instance, a cavalry officer himself, paints a picture of a man who was both avaricious and complacent, *'slow-witted and lazy, more accustomed to the leisure of camp than to the conduct of war'*. Yet at the time of his appointment,

Varus must have appeared the ideal man for the job. A well-connected member of Augustus' inner circle, Varus was vastly experienced: a man in his early 50s, he had a fine record of service as proconsul in Africa and as governor of Syria. He was certainly an able administrator; and if he spent much time implementing the less palatable aspects of *pax Romana* – imposing Roman laws and taxes – that is precisely what a governor was supposed to do.

The architect of Varus' doom was a young man known to the Romans as Arminius. A high-born member of the Cherusci tribe, who were allied to Rome by this time, Arminius seemed to be the model of a well-integrated provincial chieftain. Becoming a Roman citizen and attaining equestrian status, he served in the Roman army as commander of a Germanic auxiliary corps. It was in this capacity that he served under Varus, whose complete trust he seems to have enjoyed. Indeed, the Roman commander had even received intelligence that his subordinate was plotting against him, but fatefully he chose to disregard it.

NIGHTMARE IN THE FOREST

At the end of the campaigning season, in September AD 9, Varus set out from the area around the River Weser at the head of three legions, plus cavalry and auxiliaries, to march west to his winter camp on the Rhine. Travelling, as he thought, through friendly country, Varus had allowed his long, straggling column to march in loose order, with wagons, mules, slaves and other non-combatants shuffling along with the fighting units; and things only grew more chaotic as the rain lashed down, making feet and wheels alike slip and sink in the boggy ground.

Arminius and his auxiliaries were given leave to move ahead, supposedly to scout and reconnoitre but actually to link up with their fellow conspirators – at least three tribes, including Arminius' own Cherusci. Varus' route would take him through the Kalkriese region, a little way north of modern Osnabrück, and it was here that Arminius chose to set a deadly trap. Between the thickly forested Kalkriese Berg rising to the south and vast impenetrable marshland spreading out to the north there was a narrow corridor of ground – waterlogged here, crumbling sand there – around 3 miles (5 km) long and just a few hundred metres wide. At the foot of the hills, where the covering of oak and beech thinned out, the Germans had spent the previous few weeks

FROM ARMINIUS TO HERMANN

At the time of the Battle of Teutoburg Forest Arminius was a young man in his late 20s, and within another ten years or so he was dead – murdered, it seems, by his own people when he became too greedy for power. Whatever he may have achieved in his short life, however, is nothing compared to his posthumous deeds.

From the first stirrings of German national consciousness in the 15th century, Arminius was enlisted as a potent and soon-to-be-much-embellished symbol: a heroic figure of honour and integrity who had emerged from the forest (always a powerful German fetish) and unified Germany to cast out the perfidious Romans. The Cheruscan's elevation was assisted by Tacitus' assertion in the *Annals* (first published in modern times in 1515) that he was *liberator haud dubie Germaniae*, 'unquestionably the liberator of Germany' – in spite of the fact that the concept of Germany as a unified entity would have been quite alien to him. The picture became even more complicated as Arminius – often now Germanized as 'Hermann' – was adopted by the Lutherans, in whose hands Roman–German opposition was subtly morphed into the conflict between Catholicism and Protestantism.

By the early 19th century, 'Roman' had been not-so-subtly broadened to 'non-German' and especially 'French', thereby allowing Hermann to do good iconic service in the Napoleonic Wars. As German nationalism scaled new heights of confidence and assertiveness in the 19th century, Arminius too reached his peak – literally – with the erection in 1875 of a vast statue in his honour, the *Hermannsdenkmal*, on Grotenburg Hill in what is now called the Teutoburg Forest. Within 60 or so years Hermann had sunk to his nadir, as he predictably cast his spell over the Nazis,

Hermann of the Cherusci *(1839), a highly romanticized depiction of Arminius by the German artist Wilhelm Lindenschmidt.*

who were particularly struck by Tacitus' comment that the Germanic tribes were *'unsullied by foreign marriages ... a distinct, unmixed race unlike any other'*.

Understandably, since 1945 Hermann has largely retreated to the forest.

THE WRONG FOREST

An oddity about the Battle of the Teutoburg Forest is that it was almost certainly not fought in the Teutoburg Forest – not, at least, in the range of low, forested mountains south of Osnabrück that now bear that name. In the 19th century many scholars believed that these hilly woodlands, then known as Osning, were the site of the historical battle; and following the nationalist sentiments of the time, the area was renamed Teutoburger Wald, or Teutoburg Forest. The erection of the *Hermannsdenkmal* – the monumental statue in honour of Arminius – in the area in 1875 both reflected the scholarly (but false) identification and reinforced it in popular imagination. The name itself comes from Tacitus, who states that the battle took place at *saltus Teutoburgiensis*. The Latin word *saltus*, usually translated as 'forest', can also mean 'pass', which is better suited to the area around Kalkriese Berg where the final stages of the battle are now thought to have occurred. Archaeologists were first alerted to this site in 1987, when Tony Clunn, a major in the British army, used a metal detector to discover the first of many Roman coins, all dating to the final years of Augustus' reign. Major excavations have since uncovered a treasure trove of weapons and other objects connected to the fateful battle.

The Hermannsdenkmal *on Grotenburg Hill, long (and erroneously) thought to be the site of the famous rout of Varus' legions.*

heaping up sand and turf into a line of earthworks that were a metre or two (3.3–6.6 ft) high and topped by wooden palisades. Behind these they now lay in wait.

By this time – the third day after they left the Weser – the Romans had already been severely harried on the march and had suffered heavy casualties as they tried to ward off wave after wave of guerrilla attacks. So when Varus' surviving men dragged themselves into the narrows beneath Kalkriese Berg, they were already bedraggled and exhausted. As Arminius gave the signal, shrieking German warriors – swords, javelins, shields in hand – leapt through gaps between the makeshift ramparts and swept down in frenzied waves on the Roman line. Unable to form any kind of defensive formation, trampled on by their own terrified horses, boxed in on all sides, the Romans had no chance against the agile, lightly armed Germans and were cut down in their thousands. When all was lost, Varus himself – *'showing more courage in dying than in fighting,'* as Velleius caustically notes – fell on his sword. Of his original force, perhaps numbering around 15,000, only a few hundred escaped death or capture. For the rest, a grisly ritual of slaughter was now played out: eyes put out, tongues cut out, officers burnt alive on altars, heads nailed to trees. Varus' own body was found and mutilated, the head cut off and sent as a trophy to a neighbouring warlord.

AFTERMATH

In the wake of the massacre Germanic tribes that had stayed on the sidelines swiftly flocked to join Arminius. A spectacular victory quickly exploded into a full-blown rebellion in which virtually every Roman settlement east of the Rhine, civilian or military, was overrun. Horror swept through Rome, and there was genuine alarm that the city itself might be threatened. The immediate dispatch of Tiberius to take control of the situation on the Rhine helped to settle nerves, while the campaigns waged between AD 14 and 16 by his nephew and adopted son Germanicus at least managed to retrieve two of the three lost eagles (the third was not recovered until the reign of Claudius, 41–54). In the end, though, Germanicus was recalled by Tiberius, now emperor, who thought that his progress (such as it was) was too slow and too costly. And Arminius himself was finally undone, not by Roman arms, but by intertribal rivalries – rivalries that were only able to surface because it was clear that the imperial eagle's wings had been clipped.

According to the biographer Suetonius, Augustus – an old man and his days as emperor almost done – was devastated by the disaster that had swept away Varus and three of his legions. *'Quinctili Vare, legiones redde!'* ('O Quinctilius Varus, give me back my legions!'), he is supposed to have exclaimed. Within five years he himself was dead. In his political testament he recommended that the Germans should be contained, not conquered; that Rome's armies should not venture over the Rhine, which should henceforth mark the empire's northern border. Tiberius came to recognize Augustus' wisdom, forever putting an end to Roman ambitions east of the Rhine.

TIMELINE

27 BC Augustus becomes Roman emperor

12–9 BC Drusus' German campaigns

9–7 BC Tiberius' first German campaigns

AD 4–6 Tiberius' second German campaigns

9 Arminius defeats Varus in the 'Teutoburg Forest'

9–11 Tiberius takes command of the Rhine armies

14 Death of Augustus; Tiberius becomes emperor

14–16 Germanicus' German campaigns

21 (?) Death of Arminius

31

Five months of siege had visited unspeakable horrors on both citizens and rebels within Jerusalem. In the end, with the supply of food cut off by the encircling legions, famine did much of the Romans' work for them. In desperation, half-starved wretches began to venture outside the walls to search for any scraps they could find. As many as 800 a day were captured, then scourged, tortured and crucified in front of the city walls. To relieve the tedium of the siege – and to dash any lingering shreds of hope held by the powerless onlookers – the legionaries would nail the bodies to the crosses in ever more gruesome and contorted poses. Eventually there were so many bodies that the Romans ran out of both crosses and space to put them.

JERUSALEM

⤙ AD 70 ⤚

'The most contested piece of real estate on Earth'

These and other grisly details are recorded in the historian Flavius Josephus' account of the final agonies of Jerusalem in AD 70 as it neared destruction at the hands of the Romans. Initially a Jewish commander who deserted to save his own skin, Josephus was an eyewitness as the Roman general Titus, son of the emperor Vespasian and future emperor himself, pitilessly squeezed the life out of the Jews' holy city. Finally the most sacred place of all – Herod's great temple that dominated the city from Mount Moriah (or Temple Mount, as it was known to Jews) – fell to the Romans and was put to the torch. Jewish resistance collapsed, most of Jerusalem's citizens were massacred or sold into slavery, and the city itself was all but destroyed.

For decades before AD 70, religious and political tensions had been building in Judaea, the heartland of the Jewish people. Incensed by the corruption and insensitivity of their Roman governors, the Zealots and other Jewish extremists with dreams of independence finally rose up in revolt in AD 66. The flashpoint was Jerusalem, where the rebels massacred the Roman garrison and took control; from there violence and bloodshed spread rapidly through the rest of the country. But the rebels had fatally underestimated Roman power and resolve. After initial reverses, the Romans set about systematically crushing, capturing and burning one mutinous

The apocalyptic destruction of Jerusalem by Titus' forces is vividly conveyed in this panoramic painting by the 15th-century Italian artist Ercole de' Roberti (c.1451–96).

THE THREE TEMPLES

The temple destroyed by Titus in AD 70 was not the first Jewish temple to stand on the site and, in the view of some Jews, will not be the last. After capturing Jerusalem from the Jebusites around 1000 BC and making it his capital, King David brought into the city the Ark of the Covenant, the gold-plated chest that contained the two tablets of the Law given by God to Moses. A sacred object revered by all the peoples of Israel, this stood as a potent symbol of the union of the tribes under David. As the site for a temple to house the Ark, David chose Mount Moriah, as this was reputedly the place on which Abraham had made preparations to sacrifice his son Isaac.

Completed around 960 BC by David's son Solomon, the so-called First Temple was destroyed in 586 BC by the Babylonian king Nebuchadnezzar. After an exile from Jerusalem lasting nearly 50 years, the Jews were allowed by the Persian king Cyrus I (the Great), conqueror of Babylon, to return to the city and to rebuild the temple. This Second Temple, conceived on a humbler scale than Solomon's, was comprehensively rebuilt and enlarged by Herod the Great from around 20 BC. As part of his expansion programme, he greatly enlarged the temple platform, adding the huge containing walls, the massive bases of which can still be seen today. It was this Herodian version of the temple that was destroyed by Titus in AD 70. A surviving portion of the wall enclosing the Second Temple is the famous Western (or Wailing) Wall, which remains for Jews one of the most sacred places of worship and pilgrimage.

Various Jewish observances are made in lamentation for the destruction of the temple and in hope of its restoration. Rebuilding of the temple became associated with the coming of the Messiah and a restitution of ancient glories, but for most Jews this notion has symbolic rather than literal significance. A minority of Orthodox Jews, however, are actively planning and preparing for their ministrations within the anticipated Third Temple.

town after another, slaughtering their people or selling them into slavery. Within three years Jerusalem was virtually isolated. It was then only a matter of time before the hapless city, already torn apart by months of rebel infighting, fell to the Romans, unrivalled masters of siegecraft.

THE GREAT DIASPORA

Astonishingly, in view of the dreadful trauma they had suffered in this first revolt, a little over half a century later, in AD 132, the Jews rebelled again. This time their leader was Simeon bar Kokhba, and again they were provoked in part by religious insensitivity – Roman plans to build a temple to Jupiter in the place where the Jewish temple had stood. In the three-year guerrilla war that ensued, appalling atrocities were committed and the country was ravaged for a second time. After bar Kokhba's revolt was crushed, the emperor Hadrian was determined to leave nothing further to chance: he decreed that a new Roman settlement, to be named Aelia Capitolina, should be built on the site of Jerusalem and that entry to Jews should be forbidden on pain of death.

The failure of the first revolt had cost the Jews dear – in the destruction of their temple, they had lost a central place of worship and a potent symbol of their national identity – but the repercussions of this second reverse were arguably worse and longer-lasting. Just as the Babylonian king Nebuchadnezzar's destruction of Jerusalem and Solomon's temple over seven centuries earlier had led to a period of bitter and never-forgotten exile, so now banishment from Jerusalem began a period of nearly two millennia – until the establishment of the State of Israel in 1948 – during which the Jewish people were without a homeland. This great dispersal (diaspora) of Jewish people throughout the world was destined to have the profoundest effect on their subsequent history.

CHRISTIAN AND MUSLIM INTERESTS

Over the following centuries the policy of excluding Jews from Jerusalem, while not always strictly implemented, gave other groups an opportunity to establish or strengthen their own religious and cultural roots. As the traditional site of Jesus' death, burial and ascent to heaven, the city became an important centre of Christian pilgrimage, and in the fourth century the Roman emperor Constantine the Great built the first church on the supposed site of Jesus' tomb: the Church of the Holy Sepulchre, subsequently destroyed, rebuilt and restored on numerous occasions.

This period of Christian activity and interest in the city was followed by a phase of Muslim dominance from AD 638, when the Umayyad caliph Umar I entered the city. It was at this time that Jerusalem was interpreted by some Islamic scholars as the 'further place of worship' to which the Prophet Muhammad made his night journey from Mecca, while the sanctity of Mount Moriah itself – known to Islam as Al-Haram al-Sharif, or the 'Noble Sanctuary' – was reinforced by its identification as the site from which the Prophet ascended to heaven. In recognition of the city's importance to Islam, at the turn of the seventh century two of the defining landmarks of modern

Titus' troops sack Jerusalem in AD 70, carrying off the menorah of the temple, in this Roman relief on display in Jerusalem Museum, Israel.

35

TIMELINE

1000 BC David defeats Jebusites, captures Jerusalem

c.960 BC Solomon completes First Temple

586 BC First Temple destroyed by Nebuchadnezzar

c.515 BC Completion of Second Temple

20 BC Herod starts enlargement of Second Temple

AD 66–73 First Jewish Revolt against Rome

70 Titus captures Jerusalem, destroys Second Temple

132–5 Second (bar Kokhba's) Revolt

336 Dedication of Church of the Holy Sepulchre

638 Caliph Umar 1 takes control of Jerusalem

691 Completion of Dome of the Rock

1948 State of Israel established

Jerusalem were constructed on the platform on which the Jewish temple had stood: the Dome of the Rock (completed 691), with its magnificent golden cupola, and the Al-Aqsa mosque (c.710). The former – a shrine for pilgrims, not a mosque – is the oldest Islamic monumental structure still standing and the third most sacred site for Muslims (after Mecca and Medina).

THE CAPITAL OF MEMORY

Writing in the early first century AD, the Greek geographer Strabo suggested that Jerusalem was '*not the sort of place to elicit envy, nor one over which anyone would seriously come to blows*', because it is rocky, bordered by desert and blessed with few natural resources. Yet the 'city of peace' (as the name 'Jerusalem' is often taken to mean) has been fought over ruthlessly, relentlessly and obsessively; there can be few other places on Earth that have changed hands more frequently. The complexity of its history and of its relations with the world's three great monotheistic religions has ensured that the city has remained the focus of the deepest spiritual aspirations. And at the centre of this age-old conflict lies Mount Moriah – Temple Mount or Al-Haram al-Sharif, according to indelibly ingrained taste: '*the most contested piece of real estate on Earth*', to cite the memorable phrase of Jewish American commentator Gershom Gorenberg.

Jerusalem's religious and political centrality has lost none of its edge in modern times. The city was a prime concern for the 19th-century founders of Zionism (whose very name reflects its significance), and the status of Jerusalem has always lain at the heart of the Arab–Israeli conflict that has raged almost without respite since the establishment of the State of Israel in 1948. The Israeli writer Amos Elon described Jerusalem as the '*capital of memory*', and it certainly seems that no part of its history, however remote in time, has lost – or been allowed to lose – any of its relevance or resonance.

THE ARCH OF TITUS

A magnificent triumphal arch in commemoration of Titus' capture of Jerusalem was erected by Domitian when he succeeded his brother as emperor in AD 81. Much restored in the 19th century, the Arch of Titus still stands today at the entrance to the Forum in Rome. One of the arch's two impressive panel reliefs depicts the removal of spoils from the Jewish temple. Amongst the spoils is a large menorah (seven-branched candlestick) which was used as a model for the image on the coat of arms adopted by the State of Israel in 1948.

The triumphal Arch of Titus, located on the Via Sacra in Rome, was constructed at the end of the first century AD to commemorate the capture of Jerusalem in AD 70.

In August AD 410 an army of Visigoths commanded by Alaric swarmed into Rome and subjected the Eternal City to three days of looting. Many see this as a pivotal event – arguably the defining event – in the fall of the Roman empire in the west, yet in the immediate wake of the sacking imperial fortunes recovered quickly and a succession of western emperors struggled on for more than half a century. Indeed, a second, rather more wholehearted session of pillaging, lasting two weeks, was inflicted on Rome by Gaiseric's Vandals a full 45 years after Alaric's efforts. So what was it about this earlier event that gave it such resonance?

ROME

⟨ 24 August AD 410 ⟩

The sack of Rome that foreshadowed the end of an empire

By the standards of ancient sacking, the Visigoths seem to have shown a measure of restraint in their treatment of Rome. Collaborators based inside the city admitted their comrades through the Salarian Gate, in the northeastern stretch of the Aurelian Walls. According to the historian Procopius, some houses in the immediate vicinity of the gate were set ablaze, including the house that had once belonged to the historian Sallust, but the very fact that he includes such a minor detail suggests that arson was not extensive. The marauding Goths seem to have gathered up a considerable amount of loot from private and public properties, but – as Christians themselves – apparently took care to avoid despoiling or desecrating churches. Accounts differ on the treatment meted out to the inhabitants of Rome. Many must have been in very poor shape after the privations of the siege, but there does not appear to have been the routine and widespread slaughter and enslavement that often ensued on such occasions. To judge from the silence of the ancient sources, this may be one of the rare occasions in history where pillage was carried out largely in the absence of rape.

'IN A SINGLE CITY THE WHOLE WORLD DIED'

Part of the impact of the sack in 410 was clearly due to its sheer shock value. This was the first time in 800 years that the fortifications of Rome had been breached.

Alaric, king of the Visigoths, invaded and besieged Rome in 410, as shown in this 19th-century print.

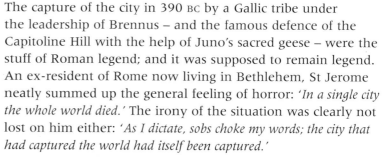

The capture of the city in 390 BC by a Gallic tribe under the leadership of Brennus – and the famous defence of the Capitoline Hill with the help of Juno's sacred geese – were the stuff of Roman legend; and it was supposed to remain legend. An ex-resident of Rome now living in Bethlehem, St Jerome neatly summed up the general feeling of horror: *'In a single city the whole world died.'* The irony of the situation was clearly not lost on him either: *'As I dictate, sobs choke my words; the city that had captured the world had itself been captured.'*

However deep the psychological trauma, what is most striking in retrospect – and what has ensured the event's historical prominence – is the extent to which it displayed many of the critical fault lines that were forming in the western empire: developments that would in time bring about its collapse.

The Hollywood portrayal of the fall of Rome requires a cast of shrieking, wild-eyed Germanic (or perhaps Hunnic) tribesmen hell-bent on mayhem. Just how far from the truth this is in the case of Alaric and his Visigoths is apparent in

This undated engraving shows delegates of the Roman republic weighing out gold as surety against the Gallic leader Brennus (centre) continuing to sack and plunder the city.

their actions in the years before 410. For it is hard to escape the conclusion that the sack itself was an act of frustration and desperation. The three days of bedlam in August 410 came only at the end of the *third* period in which Alaric had laid siege to the city. This on/off affair, starting in 408, had been preceded by more than a decade of alternating military action and negotiation, first with the eastern imperial regime, then with the western. On several occasions Alaric desisted from his hostile activities in return for some kind of payment or bribe, but his long-term ambitions seem to have remained more or less consistent throughout: he wanted land for his people and recognition of his position as their leader; he was not ultimately concerned with conquest or confrontation but with integration, or at least acceptance. In the end it was only the

duplicitous nature of the western emperor Honorius, who kept going back on his promises, that drove the Visigoths to sack Rome. To understand this curious state of affairs, we have to retrace the history of events some 35 years and to consider how the empire had developed by the second half of the fourth century.

DO AS THE ROMANS DO

One thing that had been nurtured very successfully over hundreds of years of imperial rule was a well-developed sense of Roman superiority. A deeply ingrained attitude of 'us and them' set Romans apart from the 'barbarians' who lived outside the confines of the empire. Even within the empire there was a well-marked distinction between true (aristocratic, élite, senatorial) Romans and inferior (parvenu, arriviste, nouveau riche) provincials. Unfortunately for the élite, this prejudice had become largely a figment of the blue-blood Roman imagination. For however much Romans of the old school might have

THEORIES OF THE FALL

In 1984 Alexander Demandt, a German professor with too much time on his hands, listed 210 reasons that had been advanced to explain the fall of Rome: abolition of gods, abolition of rights, absence of character, absolutism, agrarian question... The most famous answer to this most asked of historical questions was given by Edward Gibbon in his famous *Decline and Fall of the Roman Empire* (1776–88):

The decline of Rome was the natural and inevitable effect of immoderate greatness. Prosperity ripened the principle of decay; the causes of destruction multiplied with the extent of conquest; and as soon as time or accident had removed the artificial supports, the stupendous fabric yielded to the pressure of its own weight.

In tracing the decline to moral decay (induced in part by the adoption of Christianity), Gibbon gave an essentially internalist explanation, though most historians today would propose a combination of factors, internal and external. Some even claim that Rome did not really fall at all but gradually morphed into the kingdoms of medieval Europe.

To Gibbon is also due the widely accepted terminal date of the western Roman empire: AD 476. It was in this year that the Gothic chieftain Odoacer deposed the last western emperor, Romulus Augustulus, and sent the imperial trappings of cloak and diadem to Constantinople in recognition that he now ruled as king of Italy in subordination to the eastern emperor.

wished it otherwise, the empire had in fact evolved along splendidly pragmatic and relatively meritocratic lines.

Rome's most successful export – the true secret of its success and longevity – was Romanness. Over time, across a vast empire that stretched from Hadrian's Wall to the banks of the Euphrates, the indigenous peoples greedily imbibed the culture and values of the metropolis. Indeed, Romanness was exported so busily that in time the provincials became (almost) more Roman than the Romans. Inevitably, in a huge empire, life was lived most energetically on the edge – literally on the edge, on the endless frontiers that needed to be defended, where Romans, new and old, rubbed up against the barbarians on the other side of the border. It was here that battles were fought, cultures clashed, trade was done. In a world where communications proceeded at a snail's pace, Rome had receded a long way from the action; it had become something of a backwater. For the most part the vast bureaucracies needed to run an empire had moved out of town, and the imperial households and armies of courtiers had gone with them. And now there were *two* courts: everything was too big and unwieldy to be run from a single base, so in time the split into eastern and western empires had become more or less institutionalized.

The energy and dynamism along the imperial borders of course arced across the divide. Along the long Rhine–Danube frontier, a complex web of semi-tame barbarian tribes known as *foederati* ('federates') developed: traders, raiders, slavers, fodder for the Roman armies. Across these porous but fertile frontiers, client kingdoms developed with their own complex social structures

and hierarchies. It was against this background that the Visigoths –
and Alaric, the Visigoth *par excellence* – came to prominence.

THE BARBARIAN TIDE

By the fourth century the immediate Gothic ancestors of Alaric's
Visigoths were settled as agriculturalists in the region around the
Black Sea north of the Danube. The first hint of the trouble to
come came in the spring and summer of 376, when tens of
thousands of these Goths – men, women and children – suddenly
appeared on the northern banks of the Danube, pleading for
permission to cross into the Romans' Balkan provinces. The
cause of this mass migration – and of the displacement of other
Germanic populations over the next half century – was a terrifying
new threat from the east: marauding war bands of nomadic Huns
who had penetrated westwards (see '*A Race Savage Beyond all
Parallel*', p.43). The Goths – who were probably regarded as a
useful stock of army recruits – were allowed to cross but quickly
fell victim to the arrogant and corrupt behaviour of Roman
administrators. Before long, desperate for land, food and other
resources, the new immigrants were rampaging through the
Balkans. The so-called Gothic War that followed witnessed a
crushing defeat of the eastern Roman armies at Hadrianople
(Edirne, in Thrace), in 378, and was not finally ended till 382.
The treaty concluded in that year was essentially a compromise
that suited neither side.

Sporadic trouble broke out over the next decade until Alaric
emerged as a chieftain capable of leading a military (and political)
group that had already been bonded by a combination of Hunnic pressure and
Roman oppression. From 395 onwards this powerful force, now distinguishable
as Visigoths, was at large within the empire, attacking, intimidating and
extorting in order to win a suitable long-term settlement for themselves. Their
initial forays in the west, in 401 and 403, were thwarted by the Roman general
Flavius Stilicho (himself half-Vandal), who was regent for the young Honorius.
But when he fell victim to plotting in 408 and was murdered, there was no one
left capable of blocking Alaric's advance on Rome.

The Visigoths may have been the first group of Germanic peoples to burst
into Roman Europe but they were not the last. At the end of 406, also reacting
to Hunnic pressure, a powerful alliance of Vandals, Alans and Suebi crossed
the frozen Rhine and swept through Gaul, eventually settling in Spain and
northern Africa. Strong Roman leaders – first Constantius, then Aetius –
emerged who managed to bring some semblance of order, but the rot had
set in. Fledgling barbarian kingdoms had begun to take root throughout the
empire, carving out chunks for themselves and so depriving the Roman
authorities of the tax revenues they needed to raise armies and to restore
order. Local support (including, critically, rich landowners) began to drift
away from the increasingly impotent Roman overlords, who could no longer
guarantee protection. The mutual benefit that had been the glue of Roman
rule began to come unstuck; the Roman empire in the west was coming apart
at the seams.

'A RACE SAVAGE BEYOND ALL PARALLEL'

'A race of men, hitherto unknown, had suddenly descended like a whirlwind from the lofty mountains, as if they had risen from some secret recess of the earth, and were ravaging and destroying everything which came in their way.'

So the historian Ammianus Marcellinus reports the sudden surge of Huns that drove the Germanic peoples into Roman territory and so precipitated the end of the Roman empire in the west. Nomadic people whose origins lay in the vast steppe of central Asia, the Huns were formidable mounted archers. Under their most powerful leader Attila, the 'Scourge of God', they rampaged through Italy in 452 but spared Rome itself. After his death in the following year, Attila's empire was swiftly broken up and the Huns ceased to play a major role in history. Paradoxically, it was probably the Huns' indirect role as catalyst of migration in the fourth century that was more significant than their direct interventions in the fifth.

A 19th-century print showing the Huns' defeat of the Alans, a central Asian people.

In March AD 630 the eastern Roman emperor Heraclius visited Jerusalem. Decked out in purple and gold, this most exquisite of pilgrims went barefoot – though the imperial feet were kept from harm by scented carpets strewn across his path. In truth there was more triumph than humility in Heraclius' visit. After a brilliant military campaign, he had defeated the Persians and brought to an end their 15-year occupation of the Holy Land. Now it was his mission to restore in person the True Cross – the actual wood, it was supposed, of Jesus' cross, captured by the Persians in 614 – to the Church of the Holy Sepulchre, thereby signifying the return of Jerusalem to the Christian fold.

YARMUK

⟨ 16–20 August AD 636 ⟩

The battle that heralded the Muslim domination of Syria and Palestine

Neither Heraclius nor any of those present that day in 630 would have dreamed that just eight years later Jerusalem would have a second, no less distinguished visitor. Reputedly showing his humility by walking alongside a donkey on which his servant was riding, the Muslim caliph Umar came in person to accept the keys of the city from the Christian patriarch Sophronius. Here he visited the site of Solomon's Temple – the place where his friend Muhammad was supposed to have ascended to heaven and where, a little over half a century later, the magnificent Dome of the Rock would stand. The handover of the keys symbolized that the city was changing hands yet again – this time to Muslim guardianship, which would endure, with brief interruptions, till modern times.

THE RISE OF ISLAM

Heraclius could be forgiven for being caught off guard by the storm that was brewing in the deserts beyond the southern border of his realm. For more than 300 years there had been little trouble from that quarter, where garrisons in the main towns and a scattering of forts had for the most part maintained the peace. But the Byzantine empire was in a deeply vulnerable state at this time: violent dynastic strife at the top; the imperial bureaucracy in disarray; armies demoralized and depleted by years of war with the Sassanid Persians and others; treasuries all but exhausted; peoples riven by religious discord. As if that were not bad enough, a series of natural disasters, including earthquakes and bouts of plague, had further devastated the

At the top of the illumination, medieval French manuscript text appears:

uictore z tant de gés furet
occis en celle bataille que
encoies y paret les ossemés
des seignois q moururent
en celui champ. Dont il
auint q les grec qui te.r
noient la cité dantioche
furēt mlt espouétes z re

constace z la estoit la sept
ture de saint barnabe apos
tre. Et quāt il ouēt puises
les richeses de cele cité il
abatirēt les murs iusqs
as fildemēs ne onqs puis
ne fu habitee cele cité. De
la se partirēt z uindrent

Byzantine cities. This disastrous state of affairs presented the empire's southern neighbours with a unique opportunity; and it just happened that the Arab peoples were in unusually good shape to seize the opportunity, united at this time, as never before, by a new (or newly restored) faith that had recently been propounded by the Prophet Muhammad.

Most of the Arabian Peninsula had been unified under Islam by Abu Bakr, who had become the first caliph on Muhammad's death in 632. Under the leadership of Abu Bakr's most brilliant general, Khalid ibn al-Walid, these newly Muslim Arabs were now able to direct their energies northwards, to exploit the fault lines that had become apparent in the Byzantine territories. Inspired equally by religious fervour and the prospect of rich land and plentiful booty, the Arab invaders moved from minor successes to major victories, gaining a momentum that culminated in the capture in 635 of Damascus after a six-month siege. By this time most of the former Byzantine territories of Syria and Palestine (with the notable exceptions of Jerusalem and Caesarea) were in Arab hands.

Two years after the defeat at Yarmuk, Antioch fell to the Saracens. The expulsion from the city of Emperor Heraclius and his retinue by Muslim forces is shown in this illumination on a mid-14th-century Catalan manuscript.

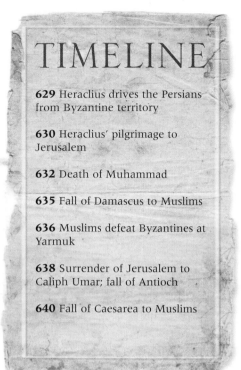

THE BYZANTINE RESPONSE

Finally coming to appreciate the gravity of the threat, Heraclius began to assemble a force to curb the Arab ambitions. Sick and exhausted after his long Persian campaign, Heraclius did not lead the army in person but entrusted the command (probably) to Vahan, a man of Armenian origin and his highest-ranking officer in Syria. The sources generally agree that the Muslim army at Yarmuk was greatly outnumbered by the Byzantines, perhaps by two to one or more, though they were well motivated and united and in Khalid clearly had the most talented commander on either side.

When the Muslim forces got wind of the Byzantine approach, they abandoned Damascus and their other gains in Syria and moved south, to the southern edge of the Golan Heights, east of the Sea of Galilee. The Golan is essentially a massive raised volcanic plateau; in the southern part of the plateau, over millions of years, a number of rivers have cut through the hard lava surface to the chalky limestone beneath, forming deep, sheer-sided gorges (wadis). One such gorge, cut by the Yarmuk, a tributary of the River Jordan, marks the southern edge of the Golan and forms the present-day border between Syria and Jordan, while two smaller gorges have been carved out by the Rivers Allan and Ruqqad, which flow north from the Yarmuk. It was in this area, in summer AD 636, that the two armies made their camps, the Byzantines a few miles northwest of the Muslim position.

THE BATTLE OF YARMUK

With the opposing armies strongly dug in, neither side was eager to make the first move and a period of attrition lasting several weeks or months ensued. The Byzantines were keen (as was their usual custom) to barter some kind of negotiated peace, but they made little headway and the delay ended up highlighting their deficiencies. Their army was heavily mixed, both ethnically and religiously, and the Christian Arabs, in particular, were torn in their loyalties. Defection and desertion became daily occurrences, while the command itself was also divided and showed signs of growing friction. The Muslim army, by contrast, remaining focused and united throughout, was boosted both by defections from the Byzantine side and by a constant flow of reinforcements from the south.

With their apparent advantage slipping away, the Byzantine command determined that it could wait no longer and in mid-August went on the offensive.

According to the sources, the battle continued for six days. Overall, the first few days seemed to favour the Byzantines, who attacked the Muslim flanks and drove them back towards their camps. It was, apparently,

MUSLIM WOMEN AT WAR

It is a surprise to modern eyes – as it was deeply shocking to Byzantine ones – to see how much women were (in Gibbon's phrase) *'prepared to wield the bow and the lance'* in the early period of Arab conquest. At Yarmuk the women at the camps were not content merely to shoo their irresolute men back into battle; they actually took up arms themselves and waded in. In his account of the battle, the ninth-century Persian historian al-Baladhuri mentions that women *'fought violently'* in the battle and singles out Hind bint Utbah, the wife of Abu Sufyan ibn Harb, who *'shouted out again and again, "Cut the arms off the uncircumcised with your swords!"'* (Formerly a Meccan opponent of Muhammad, this redoubtable woman was said by the eighth-century historian Ibn Ishaq to have cut out and chewed the liver of Hamza, Muhammad's uncle, after the Battle of Uhud in 625.) In the Battle of Marj al Suffar, shortly before Yarmuk, another doughty Muslim woman, Umm Hakim, avenged the death of her husband of one day by seizing a tent pole and – with the perfumed wedding ointment still fresh on her face – throwing herself into the battle.

only after they had been chivvied and scolded by their womenfolk that the fleeing Muslims returned to the fray. But Byzantine success was deceptive. The Muslims' highly mobile cavalry unit, positioned behind the main battle line, managed to shore up weaknesses as they appeared, while a large part of the Byzantine cavalry was apparently drawn out of position, detached from its infantry support, and forced to flee northwards. The decisive counter-attack was made against the Byzantine left and centre, where the Muslim horsemen burst through, scattering the enemy (many of whom deserted) and riding on to capture the only bridge over the Wadi Ruqqad, which lay behind the Byzantine line. With their only means of escape in enemy hands, the Byzantines were now trapped in the spur of land between the Ruqqad and Yarmuk rivers. Overnight and into the final day (20 August), desertions escalated and panic began to take hold. Before long the Byzantines were in full flight, and those that fell into Muslim hands were shown no quarter.

THE FALL OF BYZANTINE SYRIA

The defeat at Yarmuk had done as much psychological damage as physical. The Byzantines were probably too weak to regroup and raise another army in any case, but the course that the battle had taken suggested that it would be pointless. The Byzantine rulers had grown so intolerant of others – including heretical Christian groups – that they had become more hated than the Muslims. Their control of Syria and Palestine had always depended on a degree of local support. But now all that was left was isolated and disaffected garrisons, which the Muslims could easily pick off one by one. Jerusalem fell in 638; Caesarea in 640. Muslim domination of the region was complete; and it would remain, briefly interrupted only by the Crusaders, for the next one and a half millennia.

'A victorious line of march had been prolonged above a thousand miles from the rock of Gibraltar to the banks of the Loire; the repetition of an equal space would have carried the Saracens to the confines of Poland and the Highlands of Scotland; the Rhine is not more impassable than the Nile or Euphrates, and the Arabian fleet might have sailed without a naval combat into the mouth of the Thames. Perhaps the interpretation of the Koran would now be taught in the schools of Oxford, and her pulpits might demonstrate to a circumcised people the sanctity and truth of the revelation of Mahomet. From such calamities was Christendom delivered by the genius and fortune of one man.'

EDWARD GIBBON

TOURS
—⊰ 25 October AD 732 ⊱—

The victory that blocked the Muslim advance into western Europe

Such, according to the 18th-century historian Edward Gibbon was the fate that awaited Europe if the Muslim forces of Abd ar-Rahman had prevailed at the Battle of Tours in AD 732. And, according to Gibbon, the person who delivered the men of England from the circumciser's knife was the Frankish ruler Charles Martel, the 'saviour of Christendom', whose famous victory over a large army of Arabs and Berbers forever stemmed the flood of Islam into western Europe. Or so, at least (one version of) the story goes.

Before the 20th century most historians were fully in agreement with Gibbon. It was generally assumed that the purpose behind Muslim military activities north of the Pyrenees in AD 732 was conquest, pure and simple – first of Gaul and then northwards and eastwards into the rest of Europe. And the strongest reason for making such an assumption was that an expansionist policy of this kind had been energetically pursued by the Umayyad caliphate in Damascus for many decades. With astonishing dispatch, Muslim armies had wrested control of the eastern and southern parts of the crumbling Roman empire, from Palestine and Syria all along the North African coast to Morocco, and proceeded to impose Islamic customs and

Charles Martel is shown riding into battle against Muslim forces at Tours in this painting by the French artist Charles de Steuben (1788–1856).

culture on what had previously been predominantly Christian communities. Then, in the wake of a heavy defeat of the Visigoths at Rio Barbate in 711, the Visigothic kingdom had fallen under Umayyad control and most of the Iberian Peninsula had been transformed into the new province of al-Andalus, with Córdoba as its capital. And now Muslim eyes turned eagerly northwards, to the lands over the Pyrenees.

MUSLIMS IN SPAIN

From such a perspective the crushing of Muslim ambitions by Charles Martel at Tours naturally assumes vast proportions, as the victory that saved Europe (in the 19th-century German historian Friedrich Schlegel's overheated phrase) from *'the deadly grasp of all-destroying Islam'*. But, as often and inevitably in history, such a reading depends on a huge hypothetical: what would the Muslims have done if they had won at Tours? Precisely what were their intentions, forever thwarted by the Frankish victory?

When set in its contemporary context, it is immediately clear that the Battle of Tours, far from being a *'decisive trial of strength between Frank and Saracen'* (Gibbon), was neither the first nor the last of a series of trans-Pyrenean excursions made by Muslim armies in the decades following their arrival in Spain in 711. Booty is likely to have been the principal object of many of these sorties, but some, at least, were also motivated by strategic concerns. The northern frontier of Muslim Iberia had been subject to more or less continual disturbance; and of particular concern were sporadic attempts by Muslim groups in northern Iberia to extricate themselves from Andalusi control. One such, instigated by a Berber leader named Uthman ibn Naissa (known as 'Munusa' by the Franks), must have seemed especially grave when, in 729, he strengthened his hand by entering into an alliance with Duke Eudo (variously called Eudes or Odo) of Aquitaine. While Munusa's revolt was swiftly crushed in 731, it had vividly demonstrated the potential for external forces in neighbouring regions to destabilize matters within the Umayyad-controlled province. It is likely that the expedition of 732 led by Abd ar-Rahman, the governor of Córdoba, was prompted, at least in part, by the need to neutralize the threat posed by Aquitaine and its troublesome duke.

An anonymous 19th-century engraving of Duke Eudo, ruler of Aquitaine from around 700 to 735. Fiercely independent, he was forced to defend his realm from incursions by both the Muslims and the Franks.

THE FIRST BATTLE OF POITIERS?

Charles Martel's victory over the Muslim forces of Abd ar-Rahman is usually known, in the English-speaking world, as the Battle of Tours. But while Tours – and in particular St Martin's richly endowed shrine there – was the Muslim army's probable destination, some contemporary sources suggest that they had not advanced far north of Poitiers when they were confronted by Charles and the Frankish army. In French the battle is usually called, perhaps more aptly, the Battle of Poitiers, although this name usually refers in English to the Black Prince's 1356 victory over the French during the Hundred Years' War. The small village of Moussais, on the east bank of the Clain river about 9 miles (15 km) north of Poitiers, has been proposed as the site of the battle and was renamed Moussais-la-Bataille accordingly. It is unlikely, however, that the exact location of the battle will ever be known for certain, as much of the country between Tours and Poitiers consists of broad, flat pastureland, well suited to an engagement that featured a great deal of cavalry action.

BATTLE ON THE PATH OF MARTYRS

If this was indeed Abd ar-Rahman's object, he soon looked to be well on the way to achieving it, as he resoundingly defeated Eudo and the Aquitanian army at Bordeaux, apparently inflicting very heavy casualties (*'God alone knows the number of slain'*, according to a near-contemporary account) and causing Eudo to flee northwards. Driving north through Aquitaine in pursuit of the duke and leaving a trail of destruction in their wake, the Muslim forces burnt and pillaged towns and churches as they went, including the richly endowed Church of St Hilary at Poitiers. The richest prize of all lay a little further north: the famously wealthy basilica of St Martin at Tours. According to contemporary sources, it was partly in order to protect this – one of the most sacred shrines in Christendom – that Charles was moved to answer Eudo's plea for help. And it was on the Roman road between Poitiers and Tours – on what became known to Arabs as 'the Path of Martyrs' – that Charles and a rapidly mustered Frankish army came face to face with the forces of Islam.

Details of the battle itself, including the precise date and location and the strength of the opposing forces, are sketchy. Before the main engagement there were apparently several days of sparring and skirmishing in which the two armies probed and tested one another. Then, on the eighth day, possibly 25 October, 732, matters came to a head. Charles's troops, mainly infantry, formed in a large square, armed with swords and pikes thrust forward of their bucklers. Against this formation, which was *'solid as a wall, holding together like a glacier'*, the Muslim cavalry hurled themselves again and again. The issue was very much in the balance, it seems, with the horsemen crunching into the dogged Frankish lines and in places forcing a way through, until Eudo launched an attack on the Muslim rear and threatened to attack their camp. Fearful for their rich haul of plunder and their families (the Berbers, in particular, apparently travelled with their wives and children), some squadrons

broke off, giving others the impression of a general retreat. At around this time, Abd ar-Rahman himself was surrounded and killed, setting off some sort of a rout.

At this point hagiography begins to get in the way of history. In the later Christian tradition, the Frankish victory was assisted by the hand of God, so the description of it sometimes takes on a conventionally biblical tone, with Charles *'coming down on the enemy like a great man of war'* and *'scattering them like stubble before the fury of his onslaught'*. On such occasions God tends to show his vengeful side, not his merciful one, and he generally operates on a grand scale. Thus, according to one 'monkish chronicler' mentioned by the English historian Sir Edward Creasy, Muslim losses amounted to 375,000 men, while a mere (and impressively precise) 1007 Christians fell. In fact most sources agree that the fighting broke off at dusk and that the Frankish army, expecting to resume the fighting on the following morning, found the enemy had fled overnight, leaving their tents and much booty behind them.

THE BEGINNING OF THE CAROLINGIANS

Once the battle is given a fuller context, it is easy to sympathize with recent commentators who throw cold water over the more extravagant claims of their predecessors. It simply seems absurd to assert, as did (for instance) the German historian Hans Delbrück, that there was *'no more important battle in the history of the world'*. It was clearly a considerable setback for those Muslims who were set on further expansion, denying them a foothold for future campaigns and forcing them back into the peninsula. But Muslim armies had suffered serious reverses before and recovered; and they had enjoyed clear opportunities before and failed to exploit them. It is far from obvious what the consequences of a Muslim victory at Tours would have been.

Yet in making a necessary correction, some historians have perhaps gone too far in downplaying the importance of Abd ar-Rahman's 732 expedition, seeing it as little more than a glorified raid for plunder. In a different sense the Frankish victory at Tours was undeniably momentous – not so much for what it prevented the Muslim invaders from doing but for the opportunities it opened up for Charles.

The illegitimate son of Pippin II of Herstal, the governor of the eastern portion of the Frankish realm, Charles had already, by 732, demonstrated his strength and determination in consolidating by force of arms his position as sole governor of the whole of northern Francia. But he had met stiff resistance south of the Loire. It was the Battle of Tours that gave him the opportunity to demonstrate his superior power to the Aquitanians. When Eudo died in 735, Charles was quick to make his presence felt in Bordeaux, and he went on to create powerbases in Burgundy and Provence. The business of re-establishing Frankish rule in southern Gaul was still unfinished at the time of Charles's death in 741, but thanks to his tireless efforts the reunification of the realm of the Franks was well underway.

It is not known exactly when Charles earned the byname 'Martel' ('the Hammer'), but it was given in recognition of the many crushing victories that he recorded over his enemies. Exhausted at the end, Charles left it to his son,

A SYMBOL – FOR GOOD AND EVIL

On the basis of its reputation as a battle that changed the course of history, the Battle of Tours and Charles Martel himself have acquired symbolic value in the ideological conflict between East and West, between Islam and Christianity. The battle and its victorious commander had an obvious appeal in the 15th and 16th centuries, when the ambitions of the Ottoman empire, then at the height of its power, cast a deep shadow across Europe. In the 20th century Martel and Poitiers/Tours came to be used as more generalized symbols of resistance. So, for instance, during the Second World War, the French Resistance operating in the Indre-et-Loire region formed a 'Charles Martel Brigade'. More sinisterly, in the French presidential election of 2002, the National Front of Jean-Marie Le Pen was able to appeal to all sorts of deep-rooted and atavistic fears and neuroses in a succinct campaign slogan: 'Martel 732, Le Pen 2002'.

One legend surrounding Charles Martel (shown in this painting, The Mass of St Giles, *c.1500, by the Master of St Giles), was that an angel once interceded on his behalf.*

Pippin III (the Short), and his grandson, Charles the Great ('Charlemagne'), to complete the job he had started; but it is to the earlier Charles that credit should be given as the founder of the Carolingian empire. If Charlemagne (see pages 54–57) has gone down in history as being indisputably *Europae pater* – 'the father of Europe' – then Charles Martel was its earlier and essential progenitor.

For much of the year 799 Charlemagne, king of the Franks and of the Lombards, held court at his palace at Paderborn in Lower Saxony. His chief purpose was to plan yet another campaign in his decades-old struggle to subdue and convert the Saxons, but his stay had been disrupted by news of trouble in Rome. And now, amid the confusion of conflicting reports, he was expecting a most eminent – and most extraordinary – visitor: a pope bereft of sight and speech.

ROME

⋖ *Christmas Day* AD *800* ⋗

The coronation that marked the inception of the Holy Roman Empire

In the event the extraordinary was trumped by the miraculous. On his arrival Pope Leo III could both see and talk: his eyes and tongue, supposedly ripped out, had grown back. A sure sign of God's grace, he would doubtless have assured his politely credulous audience.

Some weeks earlier, at the end of April 799, the pope had been leading a procession around the churches of Rome when he had been set upon by a rival group of Roman nobles. Their plan to incapacitate the pope and so make him unfit for office clearly went awry (unless, of course, there really was a miracle), but they did manage to drag him into a church, where they apparently gave him a ferocious beating, leaving him in front of the altar *'half-dead and drenched in blood'*. There was, however, enough life left in Leo to make good his escape, and he fled north across the Alps to beg for the help of his protector Charlemagne.

In spite of the serious charges made against the pope – his assailants accused him of perjury and fornication – the king ordered that he be reinstated and sent him back to Rome with an escort to carry out his wishes. Matters were clearly far from settled, however, and towards the end of 800 Charlemagne himself set off for Rome *'to restore the state of the church which was greatly disturbed'*. It was agreed that Leo should make a public oath to purge himself of the charges brought against him. Two days after this act of purgation, on Christmas Day 800, Charlemagne was attending mass at St Peter's. As the king was rising from prayer, the pope placed a crown upon his head and, to the loud acclamation of the large congregation, proclaimed him emperor of the Romans.

THE POPES LOOK WEST

The coronation of Charlemagne has probably prompted more scholarly debate than any other event in medieval history. Yet there is little agreement over the antecedents to the event or the intentions that lay behind it. Charlemagne's court

biographer, Einhard, suggests that the king was unaware of what was going to happen and would not have gone to St Peter's if he had known, but the 'refusal of power' is a more or less standard trope in such contexts. It is much more likely that such a momentous move had been planned well in advance by the two parties, each of whom clearly stood to gain by it. Indeed, in many respects the coronation represented a formalization of trends and relationships that had developed over the preceding decades.

A page from a 14th-century illuminated manuscript showing Charlemagne being crowned Holy Roman Emperor by Pope Leo III.

TIMELINE

751 Pippin the Short seizes the Frankish throne

772–804 Charlemagne's Saxon campaigns

773–4 Charlemagne wins the Lombard crown

781 Kingdom of Aquitaine created

787–8 Bavaria annexed

796 Avars defeated

800 Coronation of Charlemagne in Rome

814 Death of Charlemagne

The papacy had generally looked to the Byzantine emperor in Constantinople for defence of its interests, but troubles in the east in the second half of the eighth century had obliged successive popes to seek assistance closer to home. Charlemagne's father, Pippin the Short, had gained papal approval for his seizure of the Frankish throne from the last of the Merovingian kings in 751; in return, five years later, he first intervened to protect the papacy from the aggressive intentions of its Lombard neighbours and then donated the territory in central Italy that became the Papal States. Following his father's example, in 773–4 Charlemagne answered the call of Pope Adrian I for protection against the Lombards; the resulting victory brought Charlemagne the Lombard crown and added their territory to the Frankish realm. By 800 there was no question that Charlemagne was the dominant force in western Europe and the de facto protector of the papacy. For the pope, the coronation served to strengthen and formalize the ties with the Frankish king while bringing kudos to his own position as bestower of the title. For Charlemagne the title brought recognition of his status in relation to the papacy and, more generally, added legitimacy to his position as sovereign of a vast empire: a domain of many diverse peoples and tongues, but one now unified under a single religion and a single king.

Predictably, the Byzantine court was less than enthusiastic about any of these developments and quite unconvinced of any legitimacy they might confer. At the time of the coronation, however, the eastern empire was facing a crisis of legitimacy of its own, as the empress Irene deposed (and blinded) her son, Constantine VI in 797 and then took over the throne herself. Such constitutional irregularity, preceded by decades of weakness, had fostered a growing sense of schism between east and west. The Frankish realm had expanded rapidly during this same period, spreading

Christianity (often forcibly) as it went. By the end of the century, Charlemagne's domain was virtually coextensive with western Christendom. Side by side with this there was a growing ideological component: a burgeoning sense of a new community – an *imperium Christianum* – taking root and flourishing under the watchful stewardship of the Carolingian dynasty. With the eastern empire in disarray and too feeble to respond, it was the perfect moment for a bold stroke of the kind delivered in Rome: one that challenged the universalist pretensions of the Byzantines and set up the Frankish king as the 'new Constantine' in the west. In a stroke he became the bulwark of those who accepted the orthodox faith of the Roman church: the temporal counterpart to God's spiritual representative on Earth.

THE GREAT CHARLES

The greatness of Charles 'the Great' – the literal meaning of 'Charlemagne' – was derived initially from his martial prowess. The essence of Frankish kingship was military

THE 'NEW ATHENS'

At the heart of Charlemagne's vision of a unified Europe directed towards the realization of God's will on Earth were programmes of religious and cultural reform. Religious reform focused principally on reinforcing the Church's hierarchical structure, standardizing the liturgy, and spreading a greater understanding and observance of the basic tenets of the faith. Central to the implementation of this programme was improved education of the clergy, which was one of the primary motivations behind the so-called Carolingian Renaissance. Driven by a group of educated clerics assembled at

A contemporary engraving of Alcuin of York.

Charlemagne's court, Latin literacy (vital for both administrative and pastoral needs) was extended and sacred texts and manuals made widely available.

At the same time there was a revival of interest in classical texts, while arts such as poetry and architecture flourished. In time the royal palace at Aachen (Aix-la-Chapelle) became the nexus of this intellectual and cultural activity. By the end of the eighth century Alcuin, Charlemagne's most influential cleric and adviser, was able to boast that Aachen was now recognized as the 'new Athens'.

success, and in this regard Charles outstripped all others, before or after. Almost every year of his long and energetic reign was marked by a campaign against one or other of his neighbours – over 50 campaigns in all, most led by the king in person. As well as consolidating the realm he had inherited from his father, he pushed out its boundaries in all directions, finally subduing the Saxons in the north, the Avars in the east, the Lombards in the south, and Aquitaine in the west.

Yet this unquenchable thirst for conquest was always allied to a greater purpose and a greater vision: the eradication of paganism and the spread of Christianity. The expansion of Christendom became both the focus and the justification for Charlemagne's territorial ambitions. His true greatness – the reason his name still has such resonance today – lay in his ability to mould and adapt the traditional function of warrior king to the changing social and spiritual needs of his day. Culminating in his coronation as emperor in 800, Charlemagne forged for himself a role that provided the essential counterpoint – sometimes harmonious, often discordant – with the papacy. At the same time he was instrumental in realigning the crucial axis between Rome and Constantinople. To a large extent it was the dynamic interplay between the pope and the Holy Roman Emperor (as Charlemagne's position was to become) that helped shape the central institutions, both political and religious, of modern Europe.

On 6 January 1066, in the newly consecrated Westminster Abbey in London, an extraordinary double ceremony took place. First, the final obsequies of the Anglo-Saxon king Edward the Confessor, just one day dead, were carried out. Then the coronation of Harold, earl of Wessex was conducted. Edward was the first king to be buried at Westminster Abbey and Harold the first to be crowned there. But Harold was also destined to be the last of the Anglo-Saxon kings and his reign was to last for less than 12 months. For on Christmas Day of the same year a second coronation would take place in the same church, as William, duke of Normandy, was crowned the first Norman king of England.

HASTINGS
❧ 14 October 1066 ❧

The battle that spelled the end of Anglo-Saxon England

In the decade preceding Edward's death, Harold Godwinson – the most influential member of the most influential family in England – had been the power behind the throne, enjoying growing dominance as the old king relaxed his hold on the reins of government. It is likely that Harold was given the childless king's blessing on his deathbed, while the Witan – the English council of elders – met on the day that Edward died and elected Harold as his successor.

Yet, in spite of his obvious qualifications, Harold lacked ties of blood with the royal house, and there were a number of powerful men quick to dispute his claim to the throne and to assert their own. The most significant of these were the Norwegian king Harald Hardrada, who traced a claim through the Viking king of England, Canute (Cnut) the Great; and Duke William of Normandy. The latter, a cousin of Edward, based his claim on a promise and an oath, both highly contentious: a promise of the throne that Edward was supposed to have made in 1051; and an oath that Harold was supposed to have sworn in 1064, to the effect that he would support William's claim. Shipwrecked on the French coast and rescued by William – all in somewhat hazy circumstances – Harold had (according

This detail from the Bayeux Tapestry shows a courtier warning Harold II of England of the appearance of Halley's Comet (top left), an event that took place on 24 April, 1066. The medieval mind construed comets as harbingers of doom and destruction.

HAROLD

to the English line) been tricked into making the oath or given it under duress. In the opposed Norman view, the oath had been made in good faith and broken by the act of Harold taking the throne: he was thus a usurper, and a perjurious and blasphemous one at that. William had shrewdly gained the support of Pope Alexander II for his position, thereby transforming his personal ambition into a crusade and winning wider European support for his undertaking. Thus fortified, the aggrieved William began making preparations to set right this wrong against himself and God.

THE THREAT FROM THE NORTH

On his accession to the throne in January 1066, Harold was well aware that he faced danger on at least two fronts. Judging the Norman threat to be the greater, through the summer he concentrated his forces on the southern coast, with a fleet ready to intercept William's growing armada. He left the defence of the northeastern coast against the Norwegian threat in the hands of the earls of Mercia and Northumbria, the brothers Edwin and Morcar, whose loyalty he had attempted to win by marrying their sister. Harold's calculations might have been vindicated if the Norman fleet had not been delayed by unfavourable weather, but in the event the northern menace materialized first. Around mid-September word reached Harold that a large Viking fleet had arrived and was ravaging the Yorkshire coast. Harold had just stood down his southern army – with the harvest at hand, manpower was needed on the land – so he now began mustering a new force as fast as he could.

Harold set off on his celebrated forced march north, covering nearly 200 miles (320 km) in just four or five days, on or around 20 September, the very day on which his northern allies were decisively defeated at the Battle of Fulford. The triumphant forces of Hardrada, now allied with Tostig Godwinson, Harold of England's disaffected brother, were still consolidating and recovering from their victory five days later, when Harold and his hastily assembled army arrived out of the blue. Caught completely off guard at Stamford Bridge on the Derwent, the Norsemen put up a valiant defence but finally crumbled when first Hardrada, then Tostig fell. But this time it was the English celebrations that were cut short, as news reached Harold that the Norman fleet had landed in Sussex.

THE NORMAN LANDING

With Harold occupied in the north, William's landing in Sussex, which was delayed for several weeks by contrary winds, was finally accomplished – unopposed – on 28 September 1066. The mass of soldiers, horses and equipment was disembarked from the fleet of 500 or more ships and rapidly moved up the coast to Hastings, where William established his base. His army then began a campaign of terror against the nearby villages, subjecting the hapless inhabitants to indiscriminate burning, looting and rape. William's aim was probably to provoke Harold into precipitate action, and in this he was entirely successful. With everything to gain from a measured response, Harold

THE BAYEUX TAPESTRY

William's conquest of England is illustrated by one of the most famous of all historical artefacts – the Bayeux Tapestry. Actually an embroidery rather than a tapestry, the piece is worked in eight coloured wools on a plain linen ground. Nearly 70 metres (230 ft) long and about 50 centimetres (20 in) high, it depicts the sequence of events between 1064 and 1066 that led to the death of Harold at Hastings. It is believed to have been commissioned by Bishop Odo of Bayeux, William's half-brother, and to have been made in England within a few years of the events it depicts. As well as being a rich source of information on contemporary customs and practices, from shipbuilding to clothing and fashion, it is one of the most elaborate pieces of political propaganda ever made, giving a very one-sided justification of William's actions following Harold's perjurious taking of the English throne.

chose instead to embark on a second forced march south, reaching London within a week, where he joined forces with his two brothers, Gyrth and Leofwin. And just five days later the patched-up army pressed on south, reaching the rendezvous point at Caldbec Hill, some 6 miles (10 km) northwest of Hastings, on the evening of 13 October.

The two forces were probably quite evenly matched in terms of numbers, at around 7500 men, but their composition was very different. Harold's army, fighting almost entirely on foot, was built around an élite core of some 1000 housecarls, the professional and highly trained personal bodyguards or household troops of the king and his brothers, who were protected by coats of mail and armed mainly with heavy two-handed broadaxes. The bulk of the army was made up of fyrdmen,

William's Norman cavalry launches an attack on the Saxon line at the Battle of Hastings, from the Bayeux Tapestry.

An Arrow in the Eye?

The one thing that everyone knows about the Battle of Hastings – that Harold was killed by an arrow in the eye – is in fact far from certain. The story is almost as old as the battle itself, derived from the scene in the Bayeux Tapestry showing the death of a knight hit in the eye with an arrow, who was (perhaps) mistakenly identified as the king. Even if Harold was struck in the eye, it is likely that the blow was not fatal and that he died later at the hands of a group of Norman knights who burst through his bodyguard and hacked him to death.

The site of the battle, Senlac Ridge, is some 6 miles (10 km) northwest of Hastings. In fulfilment of a vow, William built an abbey there, dedicated in 1095 to St Martin, with the high altar supposedly on the spot where Harold fell. Today, only its gateway (seen in the background) and isolated ruins survive.

regional militiamen called up for temporary service. The Norman army was much more diverse: around half the troops were heavy infantry, a quarter archers and a quarter cavalry. Apart from the archers, most of the soldiers wore mail armour, carried kite-shaped shields and fought with double-edged slashing swords. The knights, in addition, carried a lance, which could be thrown like a javelin or tucked under the right arm.

The battle at Senlac Ridge

Impulsive by nature and quick to action, Harold in all likelihood intended to launch a surprise attack on William's base in Hastings. In the event, however, it was his opponent – better informed than Hardrada had been in the north – who took the initiative, marching out of camp at the crack of dawn on the following morning. Caught off guard himself, Harold had little option but to deploy on Senlac Ridge, a strong defensive position a short distance south of his camp at Caldbec. Arrayed in close order over a narrow front of just 700 or so metres (2300 ft), his line was well protected by terrain that dropped away steeply on three sides, while the housecarls who formed the front rank of the line presented a wall of overlapping shields that was to prove virtually impenetrable for much of the day. Whether or not it was willingly adopted, an essentially defensive strategy was very much to Harold's purpose. For him, a draw would almost certainly have been good enough. If his army could reach the end of the day undefeated, it would only get stronger, as reinforcements flooded in from all over the country.

For the invaders – for precisely the same reason – an immediate and decisive encounter was essential. Isolated in a foreign land, their supply lines across the Channel likely to be cut and a growing army confronting them, they had no choice but to press for a swift victory. Battle began as William's archers moved into range and fired volley after volley against the Saxon shield wall – all to stunningly little effect. Following up behind, William's heavy infantry struggled up the slope, only to be driven back by a barrage of missiles. Finally the knights piled into the mêlée. Finding the Saxon line quite unbreached, both men and horses suffered grievously from the enemy axes as they tried to manoeuvre into a position to attack the wall.

This pattern of engagement, with William's forces battering themselves against the immovable English line, persisted for much of the day, and it is likely that if Harold's soldiers had been able to keep their order and discipline, they would have won the day. In the end, however, they were lured to defeat by their own successes. In the initial encounters the Breton horsemen on William's left had buckled under the incessant Saxon barrage and had finally turned and fled down the slope. Groups of Saxons, probably fyrdmen, broke from the line in pursuit but quickly became isolated and were butchered by Norman cavalry wheeling across from the centre. Harold's advantage was thus squandered by indiscipline. The same pattern of attack, retreat, pursuit and counter-attack was repeated on William's right, where his Franco-Flemish allies were deployed; and on one occasion panic took hold amid rumours that William had fallen – a crisis that he averted only by removing his helmet and shouting that he was still alive. Pro-Norman accounts later suggested that these retreats were feigned, but deliberate or not they destabilized Harold's line. Gaps began to appear in the Saxon wall and William's knights could finally start to make inroads. The disintegration was supposedly accelerated by a change in the archers' tactics, who started to aim higher and to loop their arrows into the Saxon ranks. Sensing that the tide was turning, isolated groups of English soldiers began to flee, and when news spread that Harold and his brothers were all slain, the trickle became a torrent.

AFTERMATH

It had been a desperately close-run affair, in which the biggest part had arguably been played by luck. Nor was the Norman conquest of England by any means complete: William would spend years crushing revolts and pockets of resistance, most notoriously in the brutal (and euphemistically named) 'Harrying of the North'. But if the spasms of opposition were not stilled for many years, in truth the backbone had been broken on the bloodstained battle-ground north of Hastings, where 'the flower of the youth and nobility of England' had fallen.

TIMELINE

1064 Harold's oath to William

5 Jan 1066 Death of Edward the Confessor

6 Jan 1066 Coronation of Harold Godwinson (Harold II)

20 Sept 1066 Victory of Harald Hardrada and Tostig at Fulford

25 Sept 1066 Harold defeats Hardrada and Tostig at Stamford Bridge

28 Sept 1066 Norman landing at Pevensey, Sussex

14 Oct 1066 Battle of Hastings

25 Dec 1066 William, duke of Normandy crowned William I

'A strange manner of battle, where the one side works by constant motion and ceaseless charges, while the other can but endure passively as it stands fixed to the soil. The Norman arrow and sword worked on; in the English ranks the only movement was the dropping of the dead: the living stood motionless.'

NORMAN CHRONICLER WILLIAM OF POITIERS (c.1075)

'Take warning from the fate of others and surrender your power to us. We have no pity for those who weep, nor compassion for those who protest. We have conquered the Earth, cleansing it and destroying most of its peoples. What country can give you shelter? What path can save you? There is no escape: our horses are swift, our arrows sharp, our swords like thunder, our hearts like stone, our numbers like sand. Fortresses cannot hold us back, nor armies resist. Your prayers will not be heard; only those who seek our protection are safe. Make your deliberation short and your answer swift, before the flames of war blaze up and shower their sparks upon you. For then you will lose all dignity, all solace, all sanctuary. At our hands you will suffer the most dreadful calamity and you will be swept from the Earth.'

FROM THE KING OF KINGS OF EAST AND WEST, THE GREAT KHAN
TO QUTUZ THE MAMLUK

AIN JALUT
⊰ 3 *September* 1260 ⊱

The victory that checked the westward expansion of the Mongol empire

In the early summer of 1260, the chilling message above was delivered to the Mamluk sultan of Egypt by the ambassadors of the Mongol prince Hülegü Khan. The fallout from this ultimatum would ripple through history, setting a western limit to the vast Mongol empire, extinguishing the lingering influence of the European Crusaders in the Middle East, and determining the future course of Islamic civilization and culture.

There was no bluff or bluster in the ultimatum sent by Hülegü. Grandson of the mighty Genghis Khan and brother of the fourth Great Khan Möngke, Hülegü had been given a vast army by his brother and entrusted with the task of restoring Persia to the empire and expanding the imperial borders westwards to Egypt and beyond. The decisive moment in Hülegü's campaign came in 1258, when he mercilessly crushed and burned Baghdad, the cultural heart of the Islamic world (see The Sack of Baghdad, p.68). Horror at this calamity and fear of suffering a similar fate had led, by early 1260, to the effective subjugation of Mesopotamia and Syria, including the key cities of Aleppo and Damascus.

A 14th-century Persian miniature illumination showing Mongol warriors using recurved composite bows, their principal weapons.

QUTUZ'S RESPONSE

And now, with most of the Middle East beneath his heel, Hülegü turned his gaze in the direction of Egypt. Mongol diplomacy knew nothing of velvet gloves: the Great Khan's stern ultimatum demanded unconditional surrender; anything less would be repaid with the most dire punishment. Contrary to his generals' advice – and doubtless against all expectation – Qutuz chose the path of resistance and had soon matched the Mongols in ruthlessness. He ordered the ambassadors to be arrested and chopped in half; they were then decapitated and their heads nailed to Cairo's famous (and still standing) Bab Zuweila gate. Not generally known for their consideration towards others, the Mongols were nevertheless most scrupulous when it came to diplomatic propriety. The emir of Mayyafariqun had recently responded to a demand for submission by crucifying a Mongol envoy: his reward was to witness the total destruction of his city and then to be cut up in strips and fed chunks of his own flesh, spit-roasted over an open fire. Qutuz – a Mamluk trained as a warrior from his earliest days – was clearly not easily intimidated.

At this critical moment fate conspired to add hope to Qutuz's undeniable audacity. News reached Hülegü that his brother Möngke had died, so sparking a succession crisis that demanded Hülegü's immediate presence in Mongolia. Departing with most of his army, Hülegü left a contingent of 10–20,000 warriors under the command of his general Kitbuqa, who had a fearsome reputation as *'a raging lion and fire-breathing dragon'*. His orders were to consolidate his gains in Syria and to keep pressure on the sultan in Cairo. Emboldened by this development and hoping to force the issue before Hülegü returned, Qutuz marched north to confront the remnant of the Mongol army. At the start of the march Qutuz's army, the core of which was made up of Mamluk warriors, was probably similar in size to Kitbuqa's, but as it passed through regions ravaged by Mongol raids, it was boosted by Muslim warriors of every sect.

THE BATTLE AT GOLIATH'S SPRINGS

Naturally, the 'raging lion' did not hesitate to ride out and confront the impudent sultan. Qutuz had taken up a position in the Jezreel Valley near Nazareth, at Ain Jalut (or Goliath's Springs, as tradition held that it was the place where David had slain the philistine Goliath). He sent forward an advance party under Baybars, a fellow Mamluk who had earlier fallen out with Qutuz but had sided with him to confront the Mongol threat. Encountering this advance force, Kitbuqa was for once let down by his scouts and mistook it for the whole enemy army. As the Mongols charged, Baybars gradually gave ground until he had drawn the enemy to a point where the broad valley narrowed. Kitbuqa had been undone by one of the Mongols' own favourite battle tactics – the feigned retreat. The Mamluk vanguard now wheeled round just as Qutuz gave the signal for his cavalry to swoop down from their hiding places in the higher ground on either side. The Mongols fought a valiant rearguard, nearly routing the Mamluk centre and left, but in the end they were overwhelmed by sheer weight of numbers and destroyed.

THE MONGOLS

In the space of a couple of generations the Mongols forged the greatest continuous land empire the world has ever seen, stretching from the Pacific coast of China to the shores of the Black Sea. It was also one of the most enigmatic: it seemed to spring up from nowhere and had all but vanished again within a century, leaving no monuments and few other traces of its existence. At the beginning of the 13th century a warlord who adopted the name Genghis Khan ('universal ruler') managed to unite a disparate array of nomadic Asian tribes into marauding units ('hordes') that exploded east and west in an orgy of expansion and conquest.

A Chinese portrait (1786) of the founder of the Mongol empire, Genghis Khan.

Although remembered for their acts of astonishing cruelty, the Mongols were in fact consummate and highly sophisticated warriors. Skilled horsemen and archers, they surpassed their opponents in training, discipline and mobility, and developed unparalleled systems of intelligence and communications. Everything they did – including acts of terror – was done with a purpose. A Mongol army might massacre the population of a city that resisted (impaling and flaying were favoured), but they would also make sure that the gory details spread to neighbouring cities, who would often submit without a fight – and be spared.

Nevertheless, the devastation they wrought was such that many centres of civilization were damaged beyond recovery. The Mongols' legacy of destruction and desolation is reflected in bitter contemporary accounts; the Persian writer Amir Khusrau, for instance, gives a picture of the Mongol warrior that is filled with revulsion:
'Their eyes were so narrow and piercing that they might have bored a hole in a brazen vessel, and their stench was more horrible than their colour ... Their chests, in colour half-black and half-white, were covered with lice, which looked like sesame growing on a bad soil. Their heads were set on their bodies as if they had no necks and their cheeks resembled leather bottles full of wrinkles and knots ... .'

THE SACK OF BAGHDAD

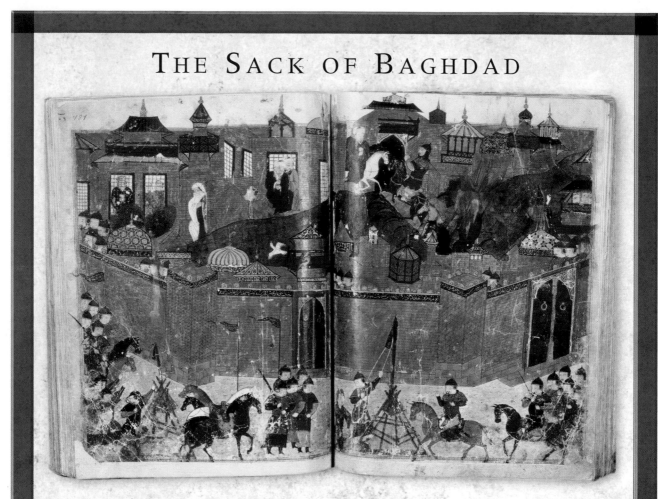

A Persian manuscript painting (14th century) of the Mongols' capture of Baghdad.

Baghdad was the jewel of the Islamic world: a city studded with magnificent palaces, mosques, libraries and colleges that were the physical manifestation of its enormous spiritual, cultural and intellectual pre-eminence. For some years before the arrival of the Mongol armies in 1257, however, Baghdad had come under the rule of a weak and ineffectual caliph, Mustasim, whose inability to marshal the city's resources against the dire threat was compounded by the treacherous scheming of his own advisers.

At first Mustasim put on a show of defiance towards Hülegü, but it soon became clear that it was all bluster. Baghdad's armies and defences had been sorely neglected, so it was little surprise when, in early 1258, the city rapidly fell to the Mongols' brutally efficient siege tactics.

There then followed seven days of sheer horror, as the male citizens were butchered (contemporary estimates ran into hundreds of thousands) while any surviving women and children, together with most of the fabulous wealth of the city, were carted off to the Mongol heartland in an endless wagon train. Mustasim – the last Abbasid caliph – fared no better. Responding to a prophecy of dire consequences if a drop of the caliph's blood touched the ground, Hülegü had Mustasim and his sons sewn in a carpet and trampled under the hooves of his Mongol horsemen. In the end it was only the stench of rotting flesh and the fear of disease that forced the Mongols to abandon the carcass of the ruined city.

No one fought more bravely than Kitbuqa himself, but eventually his horse was killed beneath him and he was captured and brought before the sultan. *'Vile creature,'* said Qutuz, *'you have wantonly spilt much blood and overthrown ancient dynasties with your broken promises. Now at last you have fallen into a trap yourself.'* *'Take no pride in this day of victory,'* replied Kitbuqa, *'for when news of my death reaches Hülegü Khan, the ocean of his wrath will well up and the earth from Azerbaijan to the gates of Egypt will quake beneath the hooves of Mongol horses.'* Infuriated, the sultan ordered the Mongol's head to be struck off. It was then sent to Cairo as proof of the Muslim victory (or, according to another account, it was taken by Mamluk horsemen, who used it as the ball in a game of polo).

TRIUMPH OF ISLAM

Qutuz's enjoyment of his victory was short-lived. He rode in triumph to liberate Damascus, but before he could reach Cairo, he was murdered by his ambitious subordinate Baybars, who seized the sultanate for himself. So it fell to Baybars to reap the benefits of the great victory at Ain Jalut. The Mongol threat did not vanish overnight, but at the same time as Mamluk power and organization were honed under Baybars' dynamic rule, the Mongol empire began to fragment. The separate khanates started to drift apart, and over the next decade the attention of Hülegü and his successors in Persia was drawn not west but north, as they became progressively embroiled in conflict with the Muslim khanate of the Golden Horde in Russia. The Mongols had their first taste of defeat at the hands of the Mamluks and it would take them more than half a century to forget it, but despite sporadic attempts they would fail to wrest control of Syria and Egypt from the buoyant Mamluks. Considering no more than the devastation caused by the Mongols in Persia and other lands that they did conquer, the arrest of their westward expansion by the Mamluks must count as one of the most momentous events in history.

The slow death of Mongol imperial ambitions was not, however, the only consequence of Qutuz's and Baybars' victory. Several of the Christian enclaves on the Levant's Mediterranean seaboard had thrown in their lot with the Mongols (many of whom were Nestorian Christians), regarding any Christian as better than a Muslim and hailing Hülegü as the champion of a new crusade against Islam. Events were to prove this a disastrous miscalculation, as Baybars and his Mamluk successors were to use their resurgent power to eradicate the last vestiges of the crusaders' influence in the Holy Land. The last crusader stronghold, the fortress island of Ruad off the Syrian coast, fell in 1302. The thwarting of both Mongol and Christian ambitions in the Middle East was the catalyst of Islamic dominance under the Mamluks that was to last over 150 years.

FROM SLAVE TO MASTER

From the ninth century onwards, Muslim caliphs adopted the practice of buying boys, often of Turkic origin from central Asia, and training them intensively in the arts of war for service in Islamic armies. These slave soldiers were known as Mamluks (from the Arabic word for 'slave'). On several occasions and in spite of their origins being neither Arabic nor Muslim, Mamluks exploited the military power vested in them to assert political control in the Arabic world. The Mamluk dynasty established in Egypt and Syria from 1250 was characterized by highly efficient (if ruthless) rule and presided over a period of great prosperity. Their power in Egypt was unchallenged till 1517, when Cairo fell to the Ottoman Turks.

'Anyone the Turks met they put to the sword, men and women, young and old alike. The butchery lasted from sunrise, when they first entered the city, till noon … In the city the blood flowed in the gutters like rainwater after a storm, while the corpses bobbed out to sea like melons in a canal… Maddened like dogs, the Turks tore through the city in search of gold and jewels. They sought out the nuns from the monasteries and all the young women, who were raped and then sold off as slaves – though some threw themselves into the wells and drowned rather than fall into the hands of their enemies… Some of the Turks climbed a tower where the flags of Saint Mark and the Most Serene Emperor were flying; these they cut down and in their place raised the flag of the Sultan.'

NICOLO BARBARO (1453)

CONSTANTINOPLE
29 May 1453

The siege that marked the transition between two great empires

Nicolo Barbaro, a Venetian surgeon resident in Constantinople, capital of the Christian Byzantine empire, left a vivid account in his diary of the fall of the city to Ottoman forces. Coming to a climax on 29 May 1453 the 53-day siege, masterminded by the dynamic young sultan Mehmet II, brought to an end the 1100-year history of the eastern Roman empire. The 'Queen of Cities', imposingly situated at the junction between East and West, would henceforth be known as Istanbul and become the capital of a new empire – the empire of the Muslim Ottomans, whose star was now rising irresistibly.

BYZANTINE DECLINE
The jewel at the mouth of the Bosphorus that was finally snatched by the Ottomans in May 1453 had already lost much of its lustre. The New Rome that had been inaugurated by Constantine the Great as his capital in AD 330 retained many of the outward trappings of greatness, but the splendid veneer was now chipped and peeling and there was little of substance beneath. Constantinople had never fully recovered from its disastrous 57-year occupancy (from 1204) by the avaricious leaders of the Fourth Crusade, the so-called Latin empire, during which time it had been shamelessly despoiled. The decline in Byzantine fortunes had then been hastened by the rise of the Ottomans, whose relentless westward expansion had already, by the 15th century, spread well into Europe, engulfing Thrace and

reaching as far as the Danube. Protected by its magnificent (if now dilapidated) walls, Constantinople had been bypassed by the Ottoman flood, but the metropolis had been all but stripped of its surrounding provinces and was now effectively an enclave – an imperial capital without an empire.

Constantinople may have been a pale shadow of what it had been, yet it still occupied a position of unique strategic and commercial importance, commanding the channel that linked the Black Sea and the Aegean. It is no surprise, then, that it had long been a tantalizing prize for a procession of conquering armies. Forever under the longing gaze of their enemies, the final emperors, always cash-strapped, were obliged to spend much of their time as

A 16th-century fresco painting of the siege of Constantinople in 1453, which brought an end to the Byzantine empire after more than a millennium.

7 1

TIMELINE

330 Inauguration of Constantinople by Constantine I (the Great)

1054 Start of Great Schism between Roman and Orthodox Churches

1204–61 'Latin Empire' of Constantinople established by Fourth Crusade

1448 Accession of Constantine XI, the last Byzantine emperor

1451 Accession of Ottoman sultan Mehmet II

1452 Mehmet begins naval blockade of Constantinople

Apr–May 1453 Siege of Constantinople

lobbyists and fundraisers, touring the European courts, cap in hand, trying to form useful alliances and to drum up financial and other support. Probably their best – and virtually their last – gambit was to represent Constantinople as the last outpost of Christianity, the final bastion against the Muslim tide from the East. The force of the argument was, however, much diluted by the deep schism that had divided the Western (Roman) Church and the Eastern (Orthodox) Church since the 11th century.

THE EMPEROR AND THE SULTAN

Such was the grim situation that faced the Byzantine emperor Constantine XI when he succeeded to the imperial throne in 1448: a shrivelled empire stripped of its wealth and assets, encircled by enemies, and dependent for its defence on the goodwill of its significantly estranged Christian neighbours in western Europe. A dedicated and courageous man who in other times would have made a fine ruler, he did everything in his power to shore up his crumbling domain. While looking to stabilize relations with the Ottoman sultan Mehmet II, newly enthroned in 1451, at the same time he actively courted the support of Christian magnates in the West. This policy culminated in December 1452 in the celebration of the official (re)union of the Roman and Orthodox Churches in Constantinople's magnificent St Sophia cathedral. Still, it remained unclear whether this act of reconciliation – or betrayal, as it seemed to many of the emperor's own people – would be rewarded, in time if at all, with the assistance that was so desperately needed.

In spite of his youth (he was just 21 years old at the time of the siege), Mehmet II was a formidable opponent. A highly talented but complex character – ruthlessly ambitious, clinical and calculating, dispassionate in displays of kindness and brutality alike – the new sultan made the capture of Constantinople (or liberation, as he would have called it) the first priority of his fledgling reign. Dream became obsession as he pored over plans, maps and designs for ever more ingenious weapons and siege engines. His first move in the campaign proper came in 1452, when he gave orders for the blockade of the Byzantine capital by sea. With the approach from the Aegean already under Ottoman control, Mehmet had an armed fortress built on the European side of the Bosphorus opposite the one built on the Asian shore by his grandfather Bayezid. He could now begin the process of strangling the life out of Constantinople, starving the city of the resources and commerce on which its survival depended.

THE SIEGE

In early April 1453 Mehmet arrived to take charge of the huge army that now formed a limitless sea of pennanted tents beneath the walls of Constantinople. The four miles (6.4 km) of triple land walls – the massive Walls of Theodosius – had repelled all comers for a thousand years, but now they would be tested by a new challenge: the ceaseless bombardment of Ottoman artillery (see Orban's Cannon, p.75). The size of Mehmet's forces is uncertain, though even conservative estimates put the number of fighting men in the region of 75,000, with

Portrait of Mehmet II, attributed to the Venetian painter Gentile Bellini (c.1429–1507).

probably at least as many again in support roles. In spite of Constantine's best efforts, it was a puny force indeed that he was able to muster in defence of the city. A headcount conducted by the one of the emperor's officials indicated that there were fewer than 5000 Greeks, plus around 3000 foreigners. Of the latter, the most important contingents were Venetian and Genoese, as both Italian states had important commercial interests in the city. The Genoese soldier Giovanni Giustiniani Longo, famed for his expertise in siegecraft, brought a body of 700 mercenaries and was given overall charge of the land walls, where the major Ottoman assault was expected.

The main artillery bombardment started on 12 April and continued with little respite for the duration of the siege. A pattern soon developed in which sections of wall that collapsed under cannonfire would be repaired under cover of night by parties from the city (including women and children). When Mehmet attempted full-scale assaults, they were usually repulsed with relative

In the early hours of 12 October 1492 three small sailing ships were scudding before a stiff breeze in the western Atlantic. Ten weeks at sea, the lookout on the leading boat gazed anxiously towards a horizon that appeared limitless and which he must have feared was actually so. Suddenly, clear beneath a bright moon in a cloudless sky, what he longed to see came into view. *'Land ahoy!'* he yelled, and his cry was swiftly followed by the boom of a cannon, alerting the other ships that land was ahead. Furling their sails, the sailors waited restlessly offshore until first light, when they would take their first steps onto a new world.

BAHAMAS

⊰ *12 October 1492* ⊱

The collision of two continents changes the course of history

The following morning the commander of the fleet, Christopher Columbus, ceremoniously decked out in the trappings of an admiral and with the royal standard of Spain in his hand, was rowed ashore, to be greeted warmly on the beach by the native people, naked and smiling. Marking the coming together of two continents and two worlds, this meeting in the surf of a Bahamian island was described 60 years later as *'the greatest event since the creation of the world'*. Few since have doubted the vast significance of the event, but many – especially in recent years – have questioned whether its colossal ramifications have been for good or evil.

GOD, GOLD AND GLORY

The radical revisionism that Columbus has been subjected to in recent years (see Civilization or Holocaust?, p.80) has been fuelled in part by a dark reading of his hopes and ambitions. In fact, though, he was remarkably consistent in his aims. These have been rather glibly summarized as 'God, gold and glory', which have struck some modern critics as being such unnatural bedfellows that their sincerity has been quickly dismissed. But they seem to have represented no contradiction to Columbus. His primary motive was always and explicitly religious. Increasingly he

This anonymous late 16th-century engraving depicts Columbus's first landing in the New World in 1492. Diseases against which the native Carib and other peoples had no immunity were soon to ravage the indigenous population.

'On the roads lie broken spears …/ Without roofs are the houses/ And red are their walls with blood./ Maggots swarm in the streets and squares/ And on the ramparts brains are spattered./ Crimson are the waters as if they were dyed/ And when we drink/ The water tastes bitter./ We struggled against the walls of adobe/ But our heritage was a net made of holes./ Our shields were our protection/ But not with shields could we fend off despair …/ jade, rich mantles,/ Plumage of the quetzal,/ All that has value/ Was then counted as nothing.'

ANONYMOUS AZTEC POET

TENOCHTITLÁN
⤙ *13 August 1521* ⤚

The Spanish empire rises from the ruins of the Aztec capital

A song of lament, written in the Nahuatl language by an unknown Aztec poet, expresses the suffering and despair at the fall of Tenochtitlán, the capital of the mighty Aztec empire, after a 75-day siege that reached its grisly conclusion on 13 August 1521. The city seemed like an *'enchanted vision'* to the astonished Spaniards when they first set eyes on it in November 1519: a second Venice rising from the waters of Lake Texcoco; a majestic mosaic of stone buildings and pyramids intercut by numerous canals and causeways. Little did they realize then that within just two years this wonder of the New World, one of the greatest and most populous cities on Earth, would be reduced by their hands to blood-spattered ruins; four out of five of its citizens would be dead, dying in the city's defence or from the smallpox plague brought in by the European invaders. And over the rubble the conquerors would build Mexico City, a teeming metropolis in a Spanish empire that would stretch from Cape Horn to California and would endure for more than three centuries.

THE AZTEC EMPIRE
In 1519, when the Spaniard Hernán Cortés and his band of adventurers landed on the southern coast of the Gulf of Mexico, the fortunes of the Aztec empire were at their peak. Less than a century earlier, in 1428, the dominant group within the

This undated and anonymous illustration shows the site of the Aztec capital Tenochtitlán on Lake Texcoco, with causeways linking it to the mainland.

TIMELINE

1502 Moctezuma II becomes ruler of the Aztec empire

10 Feb 1519 Cortés sails from Cuba

8 Nov 1519 Spaniards peacefully enter Tenochtitlán

June–July 1520 Death of Moctezuma; Spaniards flee on Night of Sorrows

26 May 1521 Siege of Tenochtitlán begins

13 Aug 1521 Tenochtitlán falls, marking the end of the Aztec empire

empire, the Mexica tribe, had joined up with two neighbouring states, Texcoco and Tlacopan, to form the Triple Alliance. Led by a series of forceful emperors and following an aggressive policy of military expansion, the alliance rapidly brought under its control several hundred minor tribute-paying states, containing some five to six million people. An extraordinary range of tribute, from gold and feather artefacts to luxury foods and textiles, flooded into the imperial metropolis, now established at the Mexica's capital Tenochtitlán, where the vast influx of wealth financed a magnificent programme of public works, including the massive flat-topped, double-stair pyramid temples.

The Mexica were one of a number of Nahuatl-speaking tribes, collectively known as Aztecs. From the 12th century, a succession of these tribes had migrated southwards into the elevated volcanic basin known as the Valley of Mexico, a fertile region which had been opened up by the recent collapse (for reasons unknown) of the Toltec civilization. Over the succeeding centuries the Aztecs, sharing a common culture but often in fierce and bloody competition with one another, created a prosperous and populous civilization that was based principally on a sophisticated system of agriculture, which involved intricate methods of irrigation and extensive reclamation of swampland.

It was against this background that the members of the Triple Alliance asserted themselves to gain control of an empire that at its greatest extent covered some 207,000 square kilometres (80,000 sq mi).

ARRIVAL OF THE SPANISH

Such was the young and dynamic empire, forged in war and still expanding and evolving, that faced Hernán Cortés when he landed on Mexican soil in February 1519. Well educated, articulate and ambitious, Cortés had grown restless as second-in-command of the recently established Spanish colony on Cuba. Investing his future in a fleet of just 11 ships, he set sail from Havana

Hernán Cortés and his men fight a desperate rearguard action in their hasty withdrawal from Tenochtitlán in 1520 (from an unsigned contemporary painting). Cortés later capitalized on discontent among the Aztecs' vassals to augment his meagre forces and overwhelm Moctezuma II.

THE NIGHT OF SORROWS

The first meeting of Moctezuma and Cortés in November 1519 was one of the most momentous in history. The Aztec emperor greeted the Spaniard with great honour, placing a garland around his neck and immediately signifying his own submission: '*You have come here to sit upon your throne ... which I have kept awhile for you.*' In reply Cortés expressed his esteem for the emperor, but his insincerity soon became apparent. The emperor, hopelessly compromised, was in effect put under house arrest and became a puppet through which Cortés exercised control. During their eight-month stay in the city, the Spaniards systematically despoiled the riches of the capital and began importing symbols of their own Catholic religion. Following a massacre of Mexica nobles and the deposition and death of Moctezuma (probably by a Spanish hand), Cortés was forced to flee the city under cover of dark on 30 June 1520, which came to be known as the 'Night of Sorrows'. In this desperate escape, he lost two-thirds of his men, demonstrating how vulnerable he would have been to a concerted Aztec attack. But such an attack never came and Cortés was allowed to regroup his forces and allies for the final onslaught.

with 450 men and 16 horses to explore the coast of Mexico. How such a tiny force managed to extinguish a vast and powerful empire in the space of just two years is, on the face of it, one of the most perplexing questions in history. There is little doubt that Moctezuma (or Montezuma, as he was known to the Spanish), ruler of the Aztec empire since 1502, could have wiped out Cortés' puny force with a wave of his hand. Yet he chose – or felt compelled – not to do so. The explanations for these puzzles are to be found both in Cortés' extraordinary skill and ruthlessness and in the advantage he gained from several improbably large slices of luck.

Much has been made of the Spaniards' technological superiority. The Aztec warrior's arms – obsidian-edged sword, wooden club, flint arrowheads – were no match for the Spaniards' steel weapons and full body armour. Gunpowder-powered cannons and harquebuses could do terrible damage, not least in an enemy's startled mind. And the sight of a heavily armed cavalryman on a steel-clad horse – an animal unknown in the New World at this date – must have had the shock value of a tank cresting a hill on a First World War battlefield. The massive advantage gained from this mismatch in weaponry was clear in the Spaniards' early encounters with native warriors and, crucially, with the Mexica's mortal enemies, the Tlaxcalans. The latter, moving from aggression to alliance in response to their bitter experience of Spanish arms and tactics, provided much of the manpower without which the Spaniards' ultimate victory would have been impossible. Indeed, throughout the conquest of Mexico, Cortés showed exceptional skill in understanding and then exploiting the deep hatreds and rivalries that existed between the various native groups. Yet he was enormously assisted in this by the rawness of Mexica domination and the readiness of disgruntled groups recently absorbed into the Aztec empire to line up behind him. And all Cortés' diplomatic guile would have counted for

HUMAN SACRIFICE

Soldiers of Christ bent on converting the benighted pagans of the New World, the Spaniards were particularly horrified at the Mexica's ritual of human sacrifice. The conquistador Bernal Diaz del Castillo gives the following gruesome account:

> 'The priests laid the victims on their backs on narrow stones of sacrifice and, cutting open their chests, drew out their palpitating hearts, which they offered to the idols before them. They then kicked the bodies down the pyramid steps, and the Indian butchers who were waiting below cut off their arms and legs and flayed their faces, which they afterwards prepared like glove leather, with beard still in place … Then they ate the flesh with a sauce of peppers and tomatoes.'

According to Aztec belief, the universe was created out of the blood of the gods, so a constant supply of blood – human blood – was required to keep the system in equilibrium. The skulls of the victims, mainly prisoners of war, were set out, row upon row, in the form of a theatre, and were reputed to number over 130,000. As a grim

Detail from an Aztec manuscript (the Codex Magliabicciano*) showing ritual human sacrifice on the steps of a temple.*

reminder of the relativity of custom, the Spanish practice of punishing enemies by burning them alive was no less repugnant to the Mexica.

nothing if he had not had the great good fortune to acquire in Malinche – an Amerindian woman who came to share his counsel and his bed – a translator capable of interpreting both the words and intentions of his opponents.

RETURN OF THE FEATHERED SERPENT

Perhaps Cortés' biggest stroke of luck was the timing of his landing in Mexico. In his 17 years on the Aztec throne Moctezuma had shown himself every bit as ambitious and bellicose as his predecessors, yet in the case of the Spanish he appears to have been almost totally paralysed by superstition and religious scruple. According to Mexica tradition, the hero-god Quetzalcoatl, the 'Feathered Serpent', had been driven off by the other gods and sailed away to the east, vowing to return in a 'One Reed' year, which on the Aztec cyclical calendar recurred (like any other year) once in every 52 years. By sheer chance, Cortés' arrival in Mexico in 1519 just happened to take place in such a year. Fearing that Quetzalcoatl had returned to take up his rightful position as ruler of the empire, Moctezuma embarked on a path of appeasement. The series of embassies sent out by the emperor were for the most part treated with contempt by the Spaniards, while the conciliatory gifts of gold and other precious items brought by the Aztec emissaries merely served to whet the greedy appetites of Cortés' followers.

Credit for Cortés' ultimate triumph over the Aztec empire must be given not only to his diplomatic skill in winning over allies and manipulating Moctezuma himself but also to his military genius and versatility. Again and again he showed his ability to learn and adapt to alien conditions, most importantly, perhaps, in his response to the near-catastrophe of the Night of Sorrows (see p.85), when it became clear that the Spaniards' technological superiority counted for little in the maze of canals and causeways around Tenochtitlán. Victory in the ensuing siege would never have been achieved without the small fleet of brigantines that Cortés had built. These sail-powered barges, capable of carrying several horses, cannon and a large body of soldiers, were carried in pieces and assembled close to Lake Texcoco. Suddenly the Mexica's most important asset – control of the waterways – was lost. Yet in the end the Spanish conquest of Mexico owed more to luck than to any human action or decision. In the interval between the Spaniards' bloody eviction from the Aztec capital at the end of June 1520 and their return in April 1521, it became horribly apparent that the Mexica's Spanish guests had introduced a visitor even more pestilential than themselves: the smallpox virus. A devastating plague ripped through the citizens of Tenochtitlán, who *'died in heaps, like bedbugs'*. More than half the population was dead even before the Spanish began their siege. The survivors, bereft and starving, held out with astonishing fortitude and courage, but in the end they succumbed to the twin blows of wretched fortune and a tireless enemy.

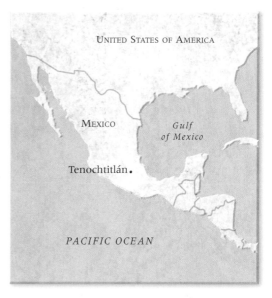

'When we saw all those towns and villages built in the water, and other great towns on dry land, and that straight and level causeway leading to Mexico, we were astounded. These great towns and pyramids and buildings rising from the water, all made of stone, seemed like an enchanted vision ... Indeed, some of our soldiers asked whether it was not all a dream ... It was all so wonderful that I do not know how to describe this first glimpse of things never heard of, seen, or dreamed of before.'

SPANISH CONQUISTADOR BERNAL DIAZ DEL CASTILLO (C.1570)

'There is time to finish the game and beat the Spaniards too.' Such was the nonchalant boast of Sir Francis Drake as the buccaneering hero's game of bowls was interrupted by news that the mighty Spanish Armada had been sighted off Lizard Point in Cornwall. In his own good time, the fiery dragon of the West Country – *'el Draque'* to the hapless Spaniards – led out the 'little boats of England', which, though greatly outnumbered, boldly confronted the 'huge sea-castles' of the enemy and drove them northwards to their doom on the rocky shores of Scotland and Ireland.

PLYMOUTH HOE
29 July 1588
A naval victory heralds the emergence of England as a world power

Deeply engrained though it is in English folklore, much of the tale of Drake and the destruction of the Armada is in fact pure fabrication. The story of his reluctance to break off his game, first told nearly 150 years after the event, probably derived from the awkward fact that the English fleet moored at Plymouth was prevented by wind and tide from sailing as soon as the sighting of the Armada was reported. And Drake's own role in the ensuing drama was far less dominant and arguably less heroic than legend would have it (see The Drake Cult, p.90). The fleet that finally sailed out of Plymouth was under the overall command of Lord Howard of Effingham, not Drake (he was Howard's vice-admiral), and was not outnumbered or outgunned by the Spanish ships. And in the end it was Spanish mistakes and the weather, not the English, that were the undoing of the Armada; as a campaign medal struck after the Armada proclaimed: *'God blew and they were scattered'*.

Yet the myth, or mythologizing, of the Armada is itself an essential part of the story. The propagandists quickly got to work, and before long the fortunate defeat of the Armada was represented, in contemporary writing and iconography, as the crowning triumph of the Elizabethan age. Elizabeth herself (whose role, like Drake's, was not unequivocally praiseworthy) skilfully insinuated herself into the heart of the action and drew much of the credit on herself. A paradigmatic case of how the

An anonymous contemporary painting of English ships attacking the Spanish Armada. In the foreground is one of the four large galleasses (ships powered by sails and oars) that sailed with the Spanish fleet. The painter satirizes it as a 'ship of fools' manned by, among others, a preaching monk and a skeleton in a jester's costume.

THE DRAKE CULT

Francis Drake was, literally, a legend in his lifetime. By the time of the Armada, he was already established as England's greatest sailor and buccaneer, lionized for his fearless attacks on the Spanish settlements in the New World and their treasure-laden ships. Between 1577 and 1580 he led the first expedition to circumnavigate the globe, accumulating in the process a vast amount of booty and cementing his place in the affections of the English people. Such was the awe in which Drake was held that supernatural powers were ascribed to him and he was credited with performing all manner of magical deeds. The cult that arose around him in succeeding centuries included the strange fable of 'Drake's drum' (still to be seen at his home in Buckland Abbey, Devon), which was said to beat when England was threatened with invasion from the sea. The heroic mariner would then rise to the call of the drum to save his country.

A Victorian engraving of the English hero Drake, from Sir Edmund Lodge's Portraits of Illustrious Personages of Great Britain *(1835).*

It is little surprise, then, that the Elizabethan public was quick to give Drake credit for seeing off the Armada in 1588 and to ignore the equal or greater claims of others such as Howard, Hawkins and Frobisher. Indeed, Drake's best-documented action in the Armada campaign – his capture of the Spanish ship *Rosario*, after it was accidentally disabled – appears to have been self-serving and in defiance of Howard's orders. His profile in the fighting itself was so low that he even drew accusations of 'cowardice or knavery' from his fellow commanders. Arguably Drake's greatest contribution came in April 1587, more than a year earlier, in his famous 'singeing of the King of Spain's beard'. His surprise raid on the shipyards of Cadiz, inflicting great damage on both ships and supplies, delayed the sailing of the Armada by a year and so gained England invaluable time to prepare for the inevitable attack.

significance of events lies as much in the mind as in the deed, the legend became, or at least nourished, reality. A country long regarded as a political backwater, under a sovereign whose rule many considered illegitimate, had humbled the most powerful nation in Europe; a troubled reign came to be seen as a golden age. Tales of English heroics at sea, much embellished, watered the seeds of real (though fledgling) naval power. And image became reality, as England flexed its new-found muscles and embarked on an adventure of empire that was to last three and a half centuries.

THE SLIDE TO WAR

'Invasion of the Spaniard is the meanes, advancing of Papistrie is the end,' declared William Lightfoot in 1587, writing in the fevered months prior to the expected Spanish onslaught. Two years earlier, in October 1585, Philip II, Catholic king of the richest and most powerful country in Europe, had finally made the decision to launch a massive assault on Protestant England and its heretic queen Elizabeth. In 1554 Philip, a devout Catholic, had married Elizabeth's half-sister Mary Tudor (Mary I), whose attempts to restore England to Catholicism had led to zealous persecution of dissenting Protestants and earned her the nickname 'Bloody Mary'. After she died childless in 1558, Philip supported Elizabeth's succession, since her main rival to the throne, Mary, Queen of Scots, though Catholic, was betrothed to the French dauphin and so seemed certain to bring England into the camp of Philip's French enemies.

Though divided by religion, England and Spain remained uneasy allies for the next two decades, as both sides had good reasons to avoid conflict. Naturally averse to foreign wars, Elizabeth feared above all the prospect of facing a Catholic triple alliance of France, Scotland and Spain, while Philip had plenty of other, more pressing business to attend to. As well as his ever-present difficulties over France, he was much preoccupied with the state of his American possessions and with a revolt (from 1568) of Dutch Protestants under Prince William of Orange against Spanish rule in the Low Countries. The project of forcibly bringing England back into the Roman fold – the so-called *Empresa de Inglaterra* (Enterprise of England) – was periodically pushed by the papacy (Elizabeth was excommunicated in 1570), but for many years Philip managed to postpone any decision.

It was not until the 1580s that events conspired to swing the balance towards conflict. Increasingly beset by Catholic plotting at home, Elizabeth finally felt compelled to increase her support for the Protestant rebels in the Netherlands and in 1585 signed a treaty promising them both military and financial aid. In a similar spirit, the long-standing policy of the English Crown – to refuse official sanction to the provocative ventures of privateers, who were crippling Spanish commercial interests – was abandoned and, in September 1585, Elizabeth gave Francis Drake free licence to *'impeach the provisions of Spain'*, whereupon he promptly sailed with a large fleet to plunder Spanish ports and shipping. Patience exhausted, Philip informed the pope of his intention to take up the *Empresa* and invade England.

'THE GREATEST AND STRONGEST COMBINATION'

The fleet that set sail from Lisbon on 20 May 1588 under the command of the seventh Duke of Medina Sidonia must have been an intimidating sight: *'the greatest and strongest combination that was ever gathered in all Christendom'*, in Sir John Hawkins's phrase, consisting of some 130 ships, nearly 2500 guns and 30,000 men. But the 'invincible' and 'most fortunate' (*felicissima*) Armada, as it was presumptuously called, was not quite what it seemed. Roughly half the vessels were fighting ships, while the rest were transports and supply vessels. Of the men on board, less than half were sailors; the rest were soldiers, there to

do service in the anticipated land campaign. In essence, the Armada was not a fighting force but a convoy, and the Spanish plan was, wisely in principle, to play to their strengths and to fight the war on land, not at sea. The primary function of the Armada was to hold the English navy at bay so that the main invasion force, which was based in the Spanish Netherlands under the command of the duke of Parma, could be ferried across to the Kent coast. Then, while Parma's forces were establishing a bridgehead, the Armada would disembark its additional forces, heavy artillery pieces and siege equipment. The combined force would then march on London, either to set up an interim government or at least to force Elizabeth to come to terms on Spain's grievances.

At its greatest extent, the English fleet was even bigger than the Armada, numbering some 200 vessels, but only 34 of these were 'royal ships' – purpose-built fighting vessels, swift and highly manoeuvrable with long, narrow 'race-built' hulls. With more and heavier guns and greater skill at repeat firing at distance, Howard's plan was to stand off the enemy ships and bombard them at long range. In the event, however, the Armada showed excellent discipline in holding its crescent formation against the English harrying tactics and reached the Strait of Dover on 6 August with just two ships lost, both to accident.

It was here that the Spaniards' real problems started. As Walter Raleigh shrewdly observed: '*To invade by sea upon a perilous coast, being neither in possession of any port, nor succoured by any party, may better fit a prince presuming on his fortune than enriched with understanding.*' Philip's strategy required the complex junction

GOOD(ISH) QUEEN BESS

Elizabeth's reign had been haunted for decades by the threat from Catholic Spain, and the queen was understandably jubilant at the victory in 1588. She was anxious to place herself at the centre of events, as is clear from her address to her troops at Tilbury on the Thames estuary, who were awaiting the arrival of the Spanish:

'I am come amongst you at this time, not as for my recreation or sport, but being resolved, in the midst and heat of the battle, to live or die amongst you all; to lay down, for my God, and for my kingdom, and for my people, my honour and my blood, even the dust. I know I have but the body of a weak and feeble woman; but I have the heart of a king, and of a king of England too; and think foul scorn that Parma or Spain, or any prince of Europe, should dare to invade the borders of my realms: to which, rather than any dishonour should grow by me, I myself will take up arms;

I myself will be your general, judge, and rewarder of every one of your virtues in the field.'

While the sincerity of these stirring and justly famous words has rarely been doubted, there is another, darker side to Elizabeth's presence at Tilbury. She goes on to note that the soldiers *'have deserved rewards and crowns'* and to assure them *'on the word of a prince, they shall be duly paid you'*. If the troops were nervous on this point, they were right to be so. In the aftermath of the victory, Elizabeth reverted to her habitual penny-pinching ways, wrangling over pay while the fighting men starved and succumbed to fatal illness. The kindly Howard was deeply concerned for his men and duly wrote to Parliament: *'before God, I would rather have never a penny in the world, than that they should lack'*. In desperation he finally had to use his own resources to pay off some of the more destitute sailors.

of two large forces on the coast near Calais, but the manner and timing of that junction appear to have been hazy at best. Parma had virtually no advance warning of Medina's arrival, and the latter, forced to drop anchor in an exposed position off Calais and unable to establish any control of the surrounding waters, was never in a position to protect the embarkation of Parma's troops. The decisive moment came on the night of 7 August, when the English sent eight fireships among the densely packed Spanish vessels, inducing panic and forcing them to cut their cables and lose formation.

At dawn the next day off Gravelines, the English attacked the enemy, which was already in disarray, inflicting severe damage and considerable loss of life. Saved by a sudden shift in the wind from total destruction in the shallows off the Dutch coast, the Armada was forced northwards into the North Sea. Abandoning any hope of effecting a union with Parma, Medina was obliged to attempt a return to Spain around northern Scotland and western Ireland. On the six-week voyage home appalling weather, including a violent storm fit *'to overwhelm and destroy the whole world,'* caused many ships to founder on the rocky shores. The battered remnant that limped into port towards the end of September had lost half its men to injury and disease and one-third of its ships were gone.

OPPOSITE: This engraving by John Pine (1690–1756), after a tapestry that once hung in the House of Lords, shows English ships harrying the Spanish fleet at the Battle of Gravelines on 8 August. Though they held their tight crescent formation up to this point, after the engagement Medina Sidonia's ships were scattered by storms.

In the course of the 16th century, Spanish and Portuguese ships plied their way across the Atlantic in ever greater numbers, laden with gold and other treasures stripped from their newly founded colonies in Central and South America. The activities of French and English privateers, including Hawkins, Drake and Raleigh, diverted a part of this flow of wealth into treasuries outside Iberia, but this did not long satisfy the appetite of rival European nations. Soon their envy turned to hope that they might mine their own share of the riches of the New World. North America, which had up to this point escaped the worst predations of the European colonists, rapidly became the focus of the most intense rivalry.

JAMESTOWN
❧ 14 May 1607 ❧

England's first foothold in the New World and the first step on the road to the United States

In the 1580s, in the reign of Elizabeth I, a series of attempts were made to establish an English settlement on the island of Roanoke, off the coast of what is now North Carolina, but on each occasion the settlers of the 'Lost Colony' disappeared in unexplained circumstances. Three years after the queen's death in 1603, her successor, James I, gave permission for a group of private investors to found a settlement on the east coast of North America. The resulting colony, named Jamestown in the king's honour, faced extinction on many occasions, and its struggle for survival would bring it into bloody conflict with native peoples and involve the import and exploitation of black Africans – bitter themes that would haunt subsequent American history. In the end, however, the small group of pioneers overcame appalling adversities to establish itself as a permanent and self-sufficient community. And in time this fragile, fledgling settlement grew to become one of the 13 British colonies that would join to form the United States of America.

FIRST LANDINGS

Anxious to emulate the successes of his continental rivals, on 10 April 1606 James I of England granted a charter to a group of private investors called the Virginia Company of London. The charter conferred the right *'to make Habitation, Plantation, and to deduce a colony of sundry of our People into that part of America commonly called Virginia'*. The colony had to be established between latitudes 34 and 45 degrees north; that is, approximately between present-day North Carolina and Maine. The venture had an ostensibly religious motive – it was hoped that it would spread

Christianity and *'bring the Infidels and Savages, living in those parts, to human Civility'* – but the profit motive was never far below the surface. Much of the charter was taken up with the terms and conditions under which the Virginia Company's agents would *'dig, mine, and search for all Manner of Mines of Gold, Silver, and Copper'*.

In the final days of 1606 the three ships financed and fitted out by the Virginia Company – the *Susan Constant*, the *Godspeed* and the *Discovery* – set sail from London. On board there were 105 colonists, all male – the first women did not join the colony until 1608. On 26 April 1607, after more than four months at sea, the tiny flotilla spotted the coast of Virginia and made the 'First Landing' at Cape Henry, on the southern edge of the entrance to Chesapeake Bay, where they set up a cross in gratitude for their safe passage. After spending the first two weeks of May in a frantic search for a suitable site, the colonists eventually chose a peninsula (now an island) on the north bank of the James river. There was deep anchorage nearby, and the location was

Alongside the dock at Jamestown lie replicas of the Discovery *(foreground) and the* Susan Constant, *two of the ships which, under the command of Sir Christopher Newport, brought the first successful English colonists to North America.*

readily defendable, as it was joined to the mainland by no more than a narrow sandbar. On the morning of 14 May the exhausted travellers began to unload and to throw up makeshift fortifications as fast as they could.

Defence against attack, either by rival Spanish newcomers or native Indian tribes, may have seemed the most pressing need, but it was by no means the only challenge facing the new colony. After an unusually long voyage, whatever provisions they had brought with them would have been long gone, and their late arrival, with summer almost upon them, meant that the seasons were already too far advanced for useful crops to be cultivated that year. So, while the colonists were inclined (with some justification) to regard the local peoples as hostile, they were yet largely dependent on them for food. And to make matters worse, malnourishment left the new settlers especially prone to disease. The near-island site was marshy and humid – ideal conditions for disease-bearing mosquitoes – and the water was brackish and scarcely fit for drinking. These problems, amongst others, were to take a terrible toll on the fledgling community, on several occasions bringing it close to annihilation.

A CLASH OF CIVILIZATIONS

A 19th-century artist's impression of the likely layout of the Jamestown settlement. The appalling winter of 1609–10 – which came to be known as the 'Starving Time' – was significantly worsened by Indian attempts to starve the newcomers out of Virginia by blockading Jamestown and attacking the English hunting and foraging parties.

For thousands of years before the arrival of the English, Powhatan Indians had occupied the forested high ground overlooking the many rivers and streams in the coastal, or 'Tidewater', region of eastern Virginia. The Indian way of life was marked by reverence and respect for the natural world. The Powhatans hunted, fished, gathered fruits and cultivated crops, always following the rhythm of the seasons and of the animals and plants that shared their world. By 1607 a chief named Wahunsenacah (known to the English as Powhatan) had gained supreme control of over 30 tribes along the James and York rivers.

From the outset, the dominant feeling of the local Indians towards the English settlers was suspicion, with an admixture of self-interested curiosity. This essential ambivalence would characterize the early interactions between the two groups. Deep-seated (and generally justified) distrust of English motives prompted sporadic displays of aggression. The first the new arrivals saw of the indigenous peoples of the Americas was when they were attacked

POCAHONTAS

The most famous of all the Powhatan Indians was Pocahontas, daughter of the supreme chief Wahunsenacah (Powhatan). Her fame initially rested largely on a story told by the Jamestown pioneer John Smith – an incident now thought to be apocryphal or based on a misunderstanding. Smith tells how he was captured by Powhatan's men in December 1607, and just as the chief was preparing *'to beate out his brains'*, Pocahontas, *'the King's dearest daughter, when no intreaty could prevaile, got his head in her armes, and laid her owne upon his to save him from death'*.

Whatever the truth here, Pocahontas apparently became a friend to the colony and an important influence in improving relations between the settlers and the local Indians. In a later episode, in 1613, she was taken hostage in the hope that she might be exchanged for some English prisoners and various tools and weapons held by Powhatan. When her father did not fully comply, the English held on to Pocahontas, who soon afterwards was baptized and in 1614 married John Rolfe, pioneer of the tobacco economy in Jamestown. In 1616 she travelled with Rolfe and their son to England, where she was treated as

Copperplate engraving showing a council of Wahunsenacah and other elders above a depiction of the Powhatans' camp.

something of a celebrity, but in the following year she became ill and died in Gravesend.

as they set foot on Cape Henry. The grave food shortages and bouts of mass starvation that scarred the early years of the Jamestown colony were significantly aggravated by the hostile attentions of the Powhatans.

In stark contrast, at other times the local Indians could be friendly, co-operative and generous. There is little doubt that the European settlers would have been annihilated during the first terrible winter of 1607–8 but for the willingness of the Indians to barter for food, and sometimes they even brought provisions as gifts to the colony. Throughout the early period distrust by the local tribes existed alongside a willingness to exchange food for metal tools, woollen cloth and other goods. A shared desire to trade, however, could not in the end obscure deep-seated and irreconcilable differences. At the heart of Anglo-Indian relations there was a profound problem of communication, both

'A WEED THAT GROWS ON EVERY SOIL'

Tobacco may have been the salvation of Jamestown, but it spawned another weed – a weed (in Edmund Burke's phrase) *'that grows on every soil'*: slavery. In August 1619 a Dutch privateering ship, the *White Lion*, arrived in Virginia. On board were a group of Africans, men, women and children, who had been captured from a Portuguese slaver sailing from Angola; 20 or more of these captives were sold to Jamestown colonists – the first known African arrivals in English America. Initially these workers probably had the status of indentured servants, and some were able to win their freedom and work for themselves. But as the 17th century wore on, the demand for labour – first for the tobacco plantations, then for cotton – steadily increased, and a number of harsh and discriminatory laws were passed that effectively institutionalized the use of slaves in the American colonies.

In this undated painting, African slaves are offloaded from a Dutch merchant ship at Jamestown in the late 1610s.

literal and psychological, and attempts to interpret and understand one another were often tragically misconceived. If the Indians had an opportunity to eradicate the Jamestown colony, it vanished for good as the settlement began to establish itself and expand. Such expansion set off an ever-growing demand for land, and in time the Indians found themselves pushed off their ancestral grounds and into poorer areas and reservations. Such iniquities eventually became enshrined in discriminatory laws, and the wretched fate of the Native Americans was sealed.

GOLD AND TOBACCO

The early years of Jamestown were blighted by a conflict between the commercial motives that had justified the colony in the first place and the basic needs required to keep bodies and souls together. Many of the early settlers were probably

VIRGINIA

In the early 17th century the name 'Virginia' was applied with little precision to the whole of the North American eastern seaboard between northern Florida and Maine. The area was named, possibly by Walter Raleigh, after the 'Virgin Queen' Elizabeth, who never married.

not so much interested in making their home in the New World as their fortune; like the Virginia Company itself, their primary motivation was profit. It is little surprise, then, that much of the first colonists' energy, which would have been better spent on more practical activities for the good of the community, was given to searching for gold. '*There was no talke, no hope, no worke, but dig gold, wash gold, refine gold, loade gold,*' one colonist complained.

Such futile effort did nothing to reduce the settlers' dependence on bartering with the local Indians for food and on supplies from England. This left them desperately exposed when these sources failed. With little preparation made for the first Virginia winter of 1607–8, the Jamestown population was devastated by starvation and disease, leaving just 38 survivors by January 1608. Worse was to follow in the winter of 1609–10 – the 'Starving Time' – when the colonists were first forced to eat their horses, dogs and cats, and then reduced to feeding on rats and shoe leather. By autumn of 1609 new arrivals had raised the Jamestown population to around 500; by spring of the following year, when a party of new settlers arrived, the inhabitants of the colony numbered just 60, and these were wretched, skeletal creatures, '*famished at the point of death*'.

The extent to which these horrors were self-inflicted and due to mismanagement is clear from the presidency of John Smith, one of the few Jamestown leaders who anticipated the catastrophe that threatened them if they became dazzled by the lure of gold. As president of Jamestown's governing council from September 1608, Smith sought to introduce some order and discipline, including a new regulation aimed at reforming the workshy culture of the colony: '*He that will not worke shall not eate (except by sicknesse he be disabled)*'. During the year of Smith's administration, there were no deaths from starvation and some real progress was made in the settlement: 12 to 16 hectares (30–40 acres) of land were cleared and planted; a well was dug; and some 20 houses and a new fort were built. But it was not to last. In September 1609 Smith was injured and forced to return to England, and within months starvation had engulfed the community.

The spectre of extermination would continue to hover over the colony while its fate remained in the hands of others, be they Indians or Virginia Company officials in London. In the end salvation lay in a '*noisome weed*' (to use King James's phrase): tobacco. John Rolfe, who had arrived in 1610, began experimenting with a West Indian variety of tobacco which gave a less harsh, sweeter-tasting product than the native Virginian plant. In 1614 he shipped his first barrels of tobacco to England, where it soon became popular. Other growers quickly followed Rolfe's example and within a few years tobacco had become the economic mainstay of the colony. The future of Jamestown now looked far more secure, but security came at a terrible price. Tobacco cultivation was highly labour-intensive, and from 1619 onwards an ever larger part of that labour was provided, against their will, by black Africans. Inadvertently Rolfe had fostered the growth of slavery in North America.

TIMELINE

1585–90 Failure of the English settlement at Roanoke

10 Apr 1606 James I grants charter to Virginia Company of London

Dec 1606 Colonists' three ships sail from London

26 April 1607 'First Landing' made at Cape Henry, Virginia

14 May 1607 Colonists start building Jamestown settlement

Winter 1607–8 Starvation and disease devastates the colony

Sept 1608 John Smith made president of governing council

Winter 1609–10 The Starving Time nearly wipes out the colony

1614 John Rolfe sends first shipment of tobacco to England

Aug 1619 Arrival of first black Africans at Jamestown

1699 Williamsburg replaces Jamestown as capital of Virginia

'Notwithstanding that the three files of the front line of English poured forth their incessant fire of musketry – notwithstanding that the cannon, now loaded with grape-shot, swept the field as with a hailstorm – notwithstanding the flank-fire of Wolfe's regiment – onward, onward, went the headlong Highlanders, flinging themselves into, rather than rushing upon, the lines of the enemy, which indeed they did not see for smoke, till involved amid their weapons. All that courage, all that despair, could do was done … Nevertheless, almost every man in their front rank, chief and gentleman, fell before the deadly weapons which they had braved; and although the enemy gave way, it was not till every bayonet was bent and bloody with the strife.'

ROBERT CHAMBERS – *JACOBITE MEMOIRS OF THE REBELLION* (1834)

CULLODEN
16 April 1746

A crushing defeat ends the dream of a Stuart returning to the throne of England

Spring was still bitter winter on Drummossie Moor, near Culloden House, on 16 April 1746. It was cold and stormy, with icy rain blowing into their faces, as the Highlanders made their brave but forlorn charge into the teeth of the enemy's devastating artillery. The engagement on the Hanoverian left wing, the bloodiest of the battle on both sides, swiftly decided the issue. Scottish author and publisher Robert Chambers takes up the story once more:

> *'...the assailants continued their impetuous advance till they came near the second [line], when, being almost annihilated by a profuse and well-directed fire, the shattered remains of what had been, but an hour before, a numerous and confident force, began to give way.'*

Outnumbered and outgunned, the Jacobite army of 'Bonnie Prince Charlie' was swept aside, and retreat soon turned to bloody rout. In the space of an hour, the Young Pretender's dreams of reclaiming his grandfather's throne were shattered, and with them the flames of the Jacobite cause, which had blazed for more than half a century, were all but extinguished.

The failure of Jacobitism, marked by the collapse of the 'Forty-five' rebellion at Culloden, snuffed out any lingering hopes that a Stuart king might be restored to the throne of England. What such a restoration would have meant will of course never be known. The Glorious Revolution of 1688, which had seen the Stuart king

James II ousted by his daughter Mary and her husband William of Orange, had heralded a further, progressive revolution in the political and constitutional arrangements of the kingdom. A country being steered towards Catholicism had suddenly become stridently Protestant; absolute monarchy upheld by the divine right of kings had been replaced by a monarchy that was constitutionally constrained by a bill of rights and subject to the will of parliament; Scotland and Ireland had been largely integrated, willy-nilly, into the United Kingdom; Britain had set itself against Bourbon France, further establishing itself as master of the seas and an imperial giant. None of this (and much else

A contemporary, unsigned engraving of the duke of Cumberland directing operations at the Battle of Culloden. On unfavourable terrain and faced with deadly artillery, the Jacobite forces were crushed within an hour.

besides) would have happened, at all or in the same way, but for the events of 1688; and much of it would have been reversed or altered if Jacobitism had prevailed and a Stuart monarchy had been restored at any time over the succeeding half-century. As such, the defeat at Culloden that ensured that 'the king over the water' would never return stands as a defining moment in both British and European history.

THE JACOBITE CAUSE

The original motivation behind Jacobitism was simple enough: to place a Stuart monarch of the direct male line on the English throne and to reverse the results of the Glorious Revolution. However, picked up by different interest groups and mangled by contemporary propagandists, it quickly acquired a highly variegated complexion.

The notion that Jacobitism was essentially an issue between Scots and English, though firmly entrenched, was transparently false. In fact, the Jacobite cause was deeply divisive even within Scotland, where many and varied factors were in play. Religion was a significant issue, but the imagined Catholic–Protestant divide was not (as it was in Ireland) the principal point of difference. While most Scottish Catholics doubtless favoured a Stuart restoration, they were always a minor constituency. Much more important was the rift within Protestantism, between Presbyterians and Episcopalians. The power and position of the Episcopal Church, disestablished as the Church

of Scotland in the wake of the Glorious Revolution, had been seriously eroded, and its followers always formed a clear majority of those mobilized to fight for the Stuarts. By contrast, the Presbyterians of the central Lowlands, whose standing had been correspondingly enhanced after 1688, tended to take the British side. The Presbyterian–Episcopalian split broadly defined the geographical range of Jacobitism within Scotland, where the Highlands and the northeast remained the dominant rebel recruiting grounds. For most Highlanders, dynastic propriety appears to have consistently trumped religious affiliation. Imbued with the feudal notion of clan chief as protector of the clan, they naturally extended this to the idea of a Stuart king as divinely appointed protector of the nation.

Still other Jacobite constituencies were formed by opposition to the Act of Union of 1707, in which the Scottish parliament was dissolved and Scotland was joined with England to form Great Britain; and by hostility towards the Hanoverian succession, which had brought the German king George I to the throne in 1714. One of the great unknowns in all Jacobite planning was the level and strength of

MORE BONNIE THAN BRIGHT

In spite of his undoubted charisma and a degree of personal courage, Charles Edward Stuart was clearly limited in military skill and apparently in general intellect, as the British conservative periodical the *Anti-Jacobin Review* rather cuttingly suggested: *'Humanity and gentleness were surely rather the prominent qualities of this amiable Prince than any real vigour of mind, or any extraordinary perspicuity... Although justice must class him among the* men not greatly fitted to recover a crown, yet he might have worn it had it descended to him without reproach.' After the defeat at Culloden, the prince managed to escape to the Continent, assisted by Jacobite sympathizer Flora MacDonald (amongst others), who disguised him as her spinning maid. There he passed his remaining years enveloped in disappointment and pickled in drink. He died in Rome on 31 January 1788, the centenary of the Glorious Revolution.

English support for the Stuarts, since in England sympathy for the cause was mainly clandestine and driven principally by political disaffection and disappointment with the Whig monopoly of power in the first half of the 18th century. The final crucial variable in Jacobite support was the international dimension. Catholic Spain and, most significantly, Louis XIV's France were strong but sporadic backers of a Stuart restoration. Opposed to the new European order created by the 1688 revolution and 'Dutch Billy' (William III), the self-appointed champion of Protestant Europe, France generally supported the Jacobites as a useful tool to destabilize its enemy and imperial rival Britain, but was inclined to be fickle if strategic considerations suggested other priorities.

JACOBITES

The name Jacobitism is derived from *Jacobus*, the Latin word for James, the name of the Stuart king (James II) who was deposed in the Glorious Revolution of 1688 and whose restoration was the original aim of his Jacobite supporters.

THE FORTY-FIVE

As with earlier Jacobite risings, the great rebellion of 1745–6 was to some extent opportunistic. Not only was Britain in a state of great political instability following the fall in 1742 of Robert Walpole , the dominant British statesman over the previous quarter century, but most of its armies were deployed in Flanders and Germany fighting the French, leaving an inadequate force of some 4000 to defend Scotland. A French invasion of England planned for 1744 had gone awry, but there were realistic hopes that – if only Scottish and English support for a rebellion could be seen to be gathering – France would launch another attack and so split the government forces in Britain. And in Charles Edward Stuart – Bonnie Prince Charlie – the Jacobites at last had a leader of some charisma and flair. Indeed, in promoting the claim of his father James Francis Edward, son of James II, Charles became the first Stuart to lead his forces in person (his father, the 'Old Pretender', had arrived in Scotland for the 1715 rebellion so late that his sole contribution was to lead the flight back to France).

So it was that the Bonnie Prince landed on the island of Eriskay in the Outer Hebrides on 23 July 1745. And at first it appeared that the hopes stirred

OPPOSITE: This engraving, from historian Theophilus Camden's Imperial History of England *(1832), shows Bonnie Prince Charlie landing on the Hebridean island of Eriskay to begin the Forty-five rebellion.*

'BUTCHER' CUMBERLAND

The Battle of Culloden is most notorious today for its bloody aftermath, which earned the duke of Cumberland the nickname 'Butcher'. Roughly half of the 2000 Jacobite casualties in the battle were inflicted when the army was already in full retreat. The scenes of carnage were vividly captured in the *Scots Magazine* of 1746:

> *'Immediately after the conclusion of the battle, the men, under the command of their officers, traversed the field, stabbing with their bayonets, or cutting down with their swords, such of the wounded of the defeated party as came under their notice. This was done as much in sport as in rage; and, as the work went on, the men at length began to amuse themselves by splashing and dabbling each other with blood! They at length looked, as one of themselves has reported, more like so many butchers than an army of Christian soldiers.'*

Much more serious in the long term were the subsequent reprisals against the Scots, including thousands of deportations to the Caribbean plantations and a legislative onslaught aimed at eradicating clanship and the Highland ways of life: the clansmen were disarmed, their Gaelic language proscribed, the wearing of kilts and tartan banned.

An engraving from a painting by 19th-century artist William Hole depicts the bedraggled remnants of the Jacobite army retreating from Culloden.

by his arrival were not altogether misplaced. Charles had come with just a handful of companions (the so-called 'seven men of Moidart' beloved of later Jacobite folklore), but within weeks of his raising his father's standard at Glenfinnan, his forces had been boosted by the clan levies to such an extent that he was able to make a grand show of entering and occupying Edinburgh. Then, on 21 September, he smashed Sir John Cope's government army (the only Hanoverian army in Scotland) at Prestonpans. Buoyed by these successes, the prince persuaded the Jacobite leaders to carry the campaign over the border and south into England. This proved, however, to be the high-water mark of the Forty-five, for although the Highland army had reached Derby – just 130 miles (208 km) from London – by 4 December, it was clear by this time that enthusiasm in England for a Stuart restoration was tepid at best. The English support that might have galvanized the rebellion and prompted a French invasion did not materialize, so on 5 December, 'Black Friday', at Exeter House in Derby, Charles was reluctantly persuaded by Lord George Murray and other Jacobite leaders to withdraw northwards. The retreat in the face of clearly superior government armies was well managed (by Murray) and included a rearguard victory at Falkirk in January 1746, but all momentum had been lost and parts of the Jacobite army began to splinter off and return home. Relentlessly pursued by William Augustus, duke of Cumberland and third son of George II, Charles was driven into the northeast, towards Inverness and the fateful encounter at Culloden.

SLAUGHTER AT CULLODEN

Rejecting advice from Murray to make for the hills and regroup to fight a guerrilla campaign against the British, Charles quickly showed his military naiveté. First he attempted an abortive night attack on Cumberland's camp at Nairn; then, on the very next day, he chose to send his men, now exhausted and hungry, against fresher, larger and better-armed forces on flat, sodden ground that was quite unsuited to the Jacobites' most effective tactic – the fearsome Highland charge that had won the day at Prestonpans. Indeed, the encounter at Culloden was one of the briefest and most one-sided in British military history. Outnumbered nearly two to one, the Jacobite army of 5000, mainly Highlanders with some French troops, was armed for the most part with broadsword and shield; confronting them, Cumberland's force of around 9000, consisting of many Scots as well as English, was mainly equipped with musket and bayonet. The most telling difference, though, was in artillery strength, and it was here that the battle was quickly decided. As Cumberland himself reported, the enemy *'began firing their Cannon, which was extremely ill served, and ill pointed; Ours immediately answer'd them, which began their Confusion. They then came running on in their wild manner.'* All to no avail; hampered by Charles's delay in ordering the charge, the Highlanders, *'all plaided and plumed in their tartan array'*, were either torn to shreds by the Hanoverian cannonade or impaled on the points of the enemy bayonets.

TIMELINE

1688 The last Stuart king, James II, is ousted in the Glorious Revolution

1707 Act of Union in which Scotland becomes part of Great Britain

1714 Hanoverian George I becomes king

1715 Failure of the great 'Fifteen' rebellion

23 July 1745 Bonnie Prince Charlie lands in Scotland

21 Sept 1745 Jacobite victory at Prestonpans

6 Dec 1745 Jacobites begin retreat from Derby

17 Jan 1746 Final Jacobite success at Falkirk

16 April 1746 Jacobite army crushed at Culloden

'We stood into the bay and anchored under the South shore about 2 miles within the Entrance … Saw, as we came in, on both points of the bay, several of the Natives and a few hutts; Men, Women, and Children on the South Shore abreast of the Ship, to which place I went in the Boats in hopes of speaking with them … As we approached the Shore they all made off, except two Men, who seem'd resolved to oppose our landing … We then threw them some nails, beads, etc., ashore, which they took up, and seem'd not ill pleased with, in so much that I thought that they beckon'd to us to come ashore; but in this we were mistaken, for as soon as we put the boat in they again came to oppose us …'

FROM THE DIARY OF LIEUTENANT JAMES COOK

BOTANY BAY
❧ 29 April 1770 ❧

Cook's landing in Botany Bay marks the beginning of modern Australian history

In the journal entry above – for Sunday 29 April 1770 – Lieutenant James Cook describes one of the defining moments in the recent history of Britain and Australia: his first landfall on the Australian mainland, at Botany Bay. Cook was not the first European to set foot there: in the 17th century the Spanish explorer Luis Váez de Torres and, most notably, the Dutch navigators Dirk Hartog and Abel Tasman had made several landings (sometimes unwittingly) on the northern and western coast of the landmass named by the Dutch 'New Holland'. Indeed, Cook was not even the first Englishman, as the buccaneer William Dampier had reached the northwestern coast of Australia (and formed a strong dislike of the local people and their customs) in 1688. But Cook is the first European known to have landed on Australia's eastern seaboard. After sailing the entire length of the east coast to its northernmost point at Cape York, on 22 August 1770 he landed on an island (subsequently called Possession Island) and *'hoisted English Colours, and in the Name of His Majesty King George the Third took possession of the whole Eastern coast'*, which he called New South Wales. Within two decades, the first British settlement (a penal colony) had been established at Port Jackson, now Sydney Harbour, and the modern era of Australian history had begun.

The Landing of Captain Cook at Botany Bay in 1770 (1902; detail) by the Australian naturalist painter Emanuel Phillips Fox (1865–1915) epitomizes the long-cherished view of Cook as an empire builder. His 'discovery' of Australia is now seen in a more equivocal light.

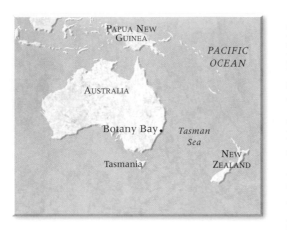

Although European knowledge of the southern Pacific had made some progress through the efforts of Spanish and Dutch explorers, European ignorance was still more impressive by far. Innumerable islands and island groups had yet to be discovered, let alone charted; the dimensions of New Zealand were unknown; it was even unclear whether New Guinea, Australia and Tasmania were separate or joined as a single landmass. The most fiercely debated issue of all, which (in Cook's words) had *'ingrossed the attention of some of the Maritime Powers for near two Centuries past and the Geographers of all ages'*, was the supposed existence of a *Terra Australis Incognita* – an 'unknown southern land', which had long been shown on medieval maps as a vast continent centred on the South Pole.

COOK'S FIRST VOYAGE TO THE SOUTH SEAS

In the middle of the 18th century, in Britain as elsewhere, ignorance of the South Seas was matched by a growing concern to remedy it. It was against this background and following several largely unsuccessful missions that, in 1768, the 39-year-old James Cook, recently promoted to the rank of lieutenant, was appointed to lead the first of three expeditions he made to the Pacific. Though relatively obscure, Cook had already demonstrated in a 13-year-long Royal Navy career remarkable talent in navigation, cartography and other skills required for command at sea. Organized by the Royal Society in association with the Navy Board, the expedition's first task was to transport various gentlemen of the Society to Tahiti, where they were to observe a transit of the planet Venus across the Sun. Then, in accordance with secret instructions issued by the navy, Cook was to sail south in order to determine the existence or otherwise of *'a Continent or Land of great extent'*; a mission that would *'redound greatly to the Honour of this Nation as a Maritime Power, as well as to the Dignity of the Crown of Great Britain'*.

Before enlisting in the Royal Navy, Cook had had nine years' invaluable experience of hauling coal in the treacherous waters of the North Sea, plying between the Tyne and London, so he naturally chose as his boat for the expedition a compact and sturdy Whitby-built collier, a 336-ton vessel that was renamed His Majesty's Bark *Endeavour*. On 26 August 1768 Cook put to sea from Plymouth, *'having on board 94 persons including Officers Seamen Gentlemen and their Servants, near 18 months provisions, 10 Carriage guns, 12 Swivels with good store of Ammunition and stores of all kinds'*. Stopping off at Madeira and Rio de Janeiro, the *Endeavour* rounded Cape Horn and dropped anchor in Tahiti on 13 April 1769 and, after the transit had been duly observed in early June, headed south in July. After reaching latitude 40°S without sighting land, Cook steered west to investigate 'Staten Landt', the country (New Zealand) that Tasman had encountered in 1642. A six-month survey of the North and South Islands proved that they were not connected to the imagined southern continent. It was at this point that Cook made his fateful decision not to plot a northerly course home as all his predecessors had done, but to head *'westward until we fall in with the East coast of New Holland'*.

LIEUTENANT COOK

Although he is usually referred to as 'Captain Cook', Cook was not in fact promoted to that rank until August 1775. At the time of his first great voyage he was still a lieutenant.

COOK ON NATIVE PEOPLES

Cook arose from very humble origins (his father was a day labourer) and had little formal education, yet the man that emerges from his writings is remarkably free from prejudice and sensitive to the customs and cultures of the various peoples he meets. Such open-mindedness is particularly unusual in an age where European superiority over other 'races' was generally taken for granted. In an extraordinary passage in his journals, Cook paints a sympathetic picture of the native Australians that is reminiscent of Jean-Jacques Rousseau's 'noble savage':

'In reality they are far more happier than we Europeans, being wholly unacquainted not only with the Superfluous, but with the necessary Conveniences so much sought after in Europe; they are happy in not knowing the use of them.

They live in a Tranquility which is not disturbed by the Inequality of Condition. The Earth and Sea of their own accord furnishes them with all things necessary for Life. They covet not Magnificient Houses, Household-stuff, etc.; they live in a Warm and fine Climate, and enjoy every wholesome Air, so that they have very little need of Cloathing; and this they seem to be fully sencible of, for many to whom we gave Cloth, etc., left it carelessly upon the Sea beach and in the Woods, as a thing they had no manner of use for.'

Engraving of Cook's first contact with Hawaiians, after a sketch by John Webber, a draughtsman on Cook's third voyage.

TIMELINE

27 Oct 1728 Birth of James Cook in Yorkshire, England

1768–71 Cook's first Pacific voyage (voyage of the *Endeavour*)

29 April 1770 Cook makes first landing at Botany Bay

22 Aug 1770 Cook claims 'New South Wales' for British Crown

1772–5 Cook's second Pacific voyage (first voyage of the *Resolution*) finally dispels myth of an unknown southern continent

1776–9 Second voyage of the *Resolution*

14 Feb 1779 Death of Cook at Kealakekua Bay on Hawaii

1788 First penal colony established in New South Wales

LANDING AT BOTANY BAY

After a three-week crossing of the Tasman Sea from New Zealand, on 19 April 1770 Cook's second-in-command Lieutenant Zachary Hickes made the first sighting of the Australian coast at the headland named Point Hicks (Cook's spelling) in his honour. Over the next ten days Cook skirted the coast northwards, awaiting a favourable wind and a suitable landing place. Then, after two earlier aborted attempts, the *Endeavour* finally dropped anchor in Australian waters on 29 April and the first momentous steps were taken on the shore of Botany Bay.

Cook's subsequent voyage up the eastern coast of Australia to Cape York, covering some 2000 miles (3200 km) in four months, is itself one of the great navigational feats in maritime history. Sailing through some of the world's most treacherous coastal waters, the *Endeavour* was nearly wrecked on 11 June when it *'struck and stuck fast'* on the Great Barrier Reef (near the settlement in northern Queensland that now bears his name – Cooktown), suffering grave damage to the hull. Disaster was narrowly avoided again in mid-August, when the ship was suddenly becalmed and began drifting helplessly with the current towards the breakers on the reef: *'between us and destruction was only a dismal valley, the breadth of one wave …'* Extraordinary tenacity and courage, however, on the part of Cook and his crew eventually saw them to Possession Island, where the declaration was made that would shape the future of the continent.

PIONEER OR INVADER?

It is hard to exaggerate the extent of Cook's achievements. Not only did he set new standards in every aspect of seamanship but he transformed the map of the world probably more than any other single man in history. Through his own tireless efforts and those of his scientific colleagues, important strides were made in a range of disciplines, including botany, zoology, astronomy, anthropology and oceanography. Cook's fame, already great in his lifetime, grew colossal following his exotic death, bludgeoned by natives on a Hawaiian beach. His death was deeply mourned by King George III and the empress of Russia, while Benjamin Franklin regarded him as a *'common friend to mankind'*. His global standing is testified by the innumerable places, landmarks and institutions that bear his name. Most tellingly, Cook was held in the highest esteem by those who followed him to the limits of the known world. The French explorer Jules Dumont

This lithograph of 1832 shows Captain Cook being set upon and killed by islanders at Kealakekua Bay on Hawaii on 14 February 1779.

NAMING BOTANY BAY

Cook's choice of the name 'Botany Bay' for his first landing place in Australia is apt in that scientific research remained an important part of the voyage. The team of scientists and artists on board the *Endeavour*, led by Joseph Banks, a wealthy young naturalist, made many valuable observations and collected a mass of samples that ensured that Cook's first voyage would set the standard for later British scientific expeditions. '*The great quantity of plants Mr. Banks and Dr. Solander found in this place occasioned my giving it the Name of Botany Bay*,' Cook wrote in his journal entry for 6 May 1770. In fact, he initially christened the place 'Stingray Harbour', after two large rays that were caught in the bay, but later changed his mind when the richness of the botanists' haul became apparent. It was originally intended that the first convict settlement would be established at Botany Bay, which Cook had described as '*capacious, safe, and commodious*,' but when Captain Arthur Phillip, commander of the First Fleet, arrived in the bay in January 1788, he found the area unsuitable and moved the colony a little further north to Port Jackson (Sydney). Despite the geographical discrepancy, during the period of penal transportation in the century after 1788 the name 'Botany Bay' was often used to refer to penal colonies, especially the one in New South Wales.

d'Urville, for instance, writing in the early 19th century, judges him '*the most illustrious navigator of both the past and future ages whose name will for ever remain at the head of the list of sailors of all nations*'.

'*Well may Englishmen be proud that this greatest of navigators was their countryman*,' exclaimed Cook's Victorian editor, Captain William Wharton, in 1893. '*Such was the man whose name will ever stand in the very first ranks of the British Empire Builders*,' concludes his Edwardian biographer, Arthur Kitson, in 1907. Yet the jingoistic tone of such utterances only serves to remind us that there is another side to the story of British imperialism. Less than two and a half centuries of white settlement in Australia has been a catastrophe for over 50,000 years of Aboriginal occupation. Cook's failure to make any meaningful contact with the indigenous peoples of Australia is a poignant counter-theme that recurs again and again in his journal: '*We could know but very little of their Customs, as we never were able to form any Connections with them.*'

Cook himself was generally held to be a man of considerable compassion and humanity, but many of the white settlers who followed him to Australia – most of them, initially, anything but willing – made little or no effort to understand the cultures and ways of life of the Aboriginal inhabitants. Without necessarily seeking to diminish the magnitude of Cook's achievement in the context of his own time, many now prefer to characterize the advent of Europeans not as settlement but as invasion.

FIRST WORDS

According to a tradition passed down through the Cook family, Cook's first words on reaching the shore of Botany Bay were '*Now then, Isaac, you go first*,' whereupon his young midshipman Isaac Smith (a cousin of Cook's wife and later an admiral) leaped ashore, so becoming the first Englishman to set foot on the soil of eastern Australia.

On 4 July 1776 the Second Continental Congress, made up of delegates from the 'thirteen united States of America', convened in the Assembly Room of the Pennsylvania State House (later Independence Hall) in Philadelphia. There they formally adopted the text of what is, arguably, the most important document in American history: the Declaration of Independence. A masterpiece of political argument and rhetoric, Thomas Jefferson's handiwork is an impassioned yet dignified exposition to a 'candid world' of the American colonies' reasons for breaking their ties with Britain and establishing themselves as an independent nation.

PHILADELPHIA

4 July 1776

Congress approves the document that gave birth to the United States of America

Dignified solemnity, clear logic, graceful prose, brilliant rhetoric, perfect balance of form and content: the many qualities that distinguish the declaration helped to galvanize 13 separate and often divided states to unite against their overbearing parent and to persevere through years of bitter fighting to victory. Such is the resonance and power of the declaration that it has continued to inspire not only the country whose birth it assisted but other nations that have fought against oppression in the struggle for democracy and freedom.

RELUCTANT REVOLUTIONARIES

The American Revolution which severed the links between Britain and its transatlantic colonies may have been the most momentous in history; it was also one of the oddest. Nowhere else can revolutionaries have been so reluctant to revolt. Never before can rebels have been so reactionary, determined only to resist the British government's attempts to upset the comfortable status quo.

For a century and a half, in matters of government, the English settlers in North America had been for the most part left to their own devices. The principal area of engagement with the mother country was commercial. A body of statutes known collectively as the Navigation Acts regulated the management of trade between metropolis and colonies, but while these measures controlled shipping and access to ports, the privileged position that the colonists enjoyed with the most powerful maritime economy on Earth also brought them great benefits. The consequence was that by the middle of the 18th century Britain's American

provinces had grown prosperous while exercising a substantial degree of autonomy over their own affairs.

In parallel with this tale of growing American prosperity, the British had toiled through the 18th century in a series of wars against their perennial imperial rivals, the French. On his accession to the throne in 1760 George III described the latest of these, the Seven Years' War, as *'expensive but just and necessary,'* and whatever view one takes of the justice of the case, he was clearly correct in his assessment of the costs involved. The war ended in 1763 with a major British victory in which France ceded its claims to Canada and all American territory east of the Mississippi, but it also saddled victor and vanquished alike

Declaration of Independence, *a painting by American artist John Trumbull. A large reproduction by the artist hangs in the rotunda of the United States Capitol.*

113

TIMELINE

1760 George III accedes to the British throne

1763 British victory in the Seven Years' War crushes the French in North America

1765–6 The Stamp Act is introduced and repealed amid furious protests

1770 The Boston Massacre leaves five protesters dead

1773 The Boston Tea Party

1774 Britain imposes the Coercive Acts on Massachusetts

Sept 1774 The First Continental Congress meets in Philadelphia

April 1775 Battles of Lexington and Concord

May 1775 First meeting of Second Continental Congress

Jan 1776 Thomas Paine's *Common Sense* published

7 June 1776 Richard Henry Lee makes independence resolution

11 June 1776 Committee of Five appointed to draft Declaration of Independence

2 July 1776 Lee Resolution adopted

4 July 1776 Declaration adopted by Congress

2 Aug 1776 Signing of Declaration

1778 American colonies form alliance with France

1781 British under Cornwallis surrender at Yorktown

1783 The Treaty of Paris sees the recognition of the USA

with massive debts. Faced with greatly extended territories to garrison and administer, the British government took the view that it was reasonable for their American colonies, who stood to gain as much as anyone from the removal of the French threat, to make some contribution to the cost of the war and of their continuing defence.

At its core the dispute between Britain and its colonies was driven not by the fact of taxation *per se* but by the notion that taxes might be imposed by a legislative body on which the Americans themselves were not represented: hence the slogan '*No taxation without representation*'. As there was never any possibility of such representation at Westminster, the colonists were in effect insisting that the power of the British parliament was limited. At issue, then, was the nature of British sovereignty – was it absolute or was it qualified? This proved to be a matter over which the two sides refused to back down and were prepared to go to war.

STAMPS AND TEA

So it was that Britain's somewhat laissez-faire attitude towards its American colonies was replaced by a determination to implement a more clearly defined and more interventionist policy. The most significant early move in the attempted implementation of this policy was the passing of the Stamp Act of 1765, a taxation measure which required that legal and commercial documents should bear a revenue stamp. The fury of the protests that greeted this measure, orchestrated in part by a pressure group who styled themselves the Sons of Liberty, led to its rapid repeal in 1766 and set the tone for a decade of confrontation and deteriorating relations.

Throughout the 1760s each successive attempt by the British parliament to levy taxes in the American colonies was met with a range of countermeasures, including riots, petitions and boycotts of imports to and from Britain. Much of the fiercest resistance was centred in Massachusetts, and it was here that matters came to a head in the early 1770s. In March 1770 clashes between protesters and troops sent to restore order led to the 'Boston

The Bostonians Paying the Excise-Man, *a British engraving from 1774 showing the tarring and feathering of John Malcolm, a loyalist who worked for the British customs service.*

Massacre', in which five townspeople were shot. Then, at the end of 1773, tragedy mingled with farce as a protest against the unpopular duty on tea culminated in the notorious Boston Tea Party, in which a group of some 50 men dressed as 'Mohawks or Indians' boarded three British ships in Boston harbour and emptied the contents of 340 tea chests into the water. The British government then retaliated in the following year by introducing a series of punitive measures which were scathingly referred to by the colonials as the 'Coercive' or 'Intolerable Acts'. One of these required the closure of the port of Boston until such time as the cost of the destroyed tea had been repaid; another effectively rewrote Boston's constitution and brought its government under British control.

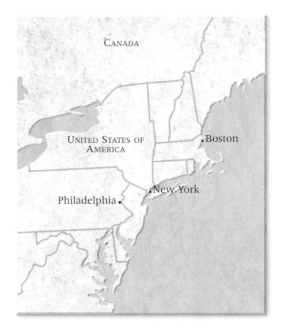

TOWARDS A DECLARATION

The crisis in Massachusetts was the catalyst for the calling of the First Continental Congress, a body of 55 representatives from the colonies which met for the first time in Philadelphia in September 1774. While expressing their outrage at the draconian measures introduced by the British government, most delegates at this point still favoured some form of negotiated settlement within the empire. However, by the time the Second Continental Congress met in May of the following year, the mood had begun to shift. The *'shot heard around the world'* had already been fired in the previous month, when a small force of Massachusetts minutemen (militiamen who undertook to be ready 'at a minute's notice') had clashed with British troops in minor engagements at Lexington and Concord, some 20 miles (32 km) northwest of Boston. Momentum was gathering behind radicals such as Thomas Jefferson and John Adams, who advocated a complete break from the motherland, and in June the Congress voted to raise a Continental army (in effect a federal force) under the command of George Washington. A royal proclamation in August 1775, declaring that His Majesty's American subjects were *'engaged in open and avowed rebellion'*, was followed by an escalation of activities on both sides, legal and military, which served only to widen the gulf between colonies and motherland.

At the start of 1776 the separatist movement was given intellectual weight with the publication of Thomas Paine's *Common Sense*. This pamphlet, filled with rousing rhetoric, poured scorn on the supposedly balanced nature of the British constitution and on the notion of reconciliation with *'the royal brute of*

'Is life so dear, or peace so sweet, as to be purchased at the price of chains and slavery? Forbid it, Almighty God! I know not what course others may take; but as for me, give me liberty or give me death!'

CONCLUSION OF PATRICK HENRY'S FAMOUS SPEECH OF MARCH 1775 IN SUPPORT OF HIS RESOLUTION THAT THE STATE SHOULD TAKE UP ARMS AGAINST THE BRITISH.

The Pennsylvania State Hall in Philadelphia, now known as Independence Hall, where Congress officially adopted the Declaration of Independence in 1776.

THE GLORIOUS SECOND

'The Second Day of July 1776, will be the most memorable Epoche in the History of America. I am apt to believe that it will be celebrated, by succeeding Generations, as the great anniversary Festival.'

So wrote John Adams, great revolutionary and future president, to his wife Abigail on 3 July 1776. History decided otherwise, but many have agreed with Adams that the adoption of the Lee Resolution on 2 July was the decisive step and that the USA's great birthday is celebrated on the wrong day!

Britain'. Perfectly in accord with the emerging mood, within weeks it had sold tens of thousands of copies. By spring 1776 most of the Congress had come to the view that independence was the only way forward, and on 7 June the Virginia representative Richard Henry Lee proposed his momentous resolution:

> *'That these United Colonies are, and of right ought to be, free and independent States, that they are absolved from all allegiance to the British Crown, and that all political connection between them and the State of Great Britain is, and ought to be, totally dissolved.'*

A MASTERLY PEN

On 11 June a 'Committee of Five', including Jefferson, Adams and Benjamin Franklin, was appointed to draft the Declaration of Independence, which embraced Lee's proposal and set out in detail the colonies' case for independence. Most of the drafting fell to the Virginian Thomas Jefferson, the future third president

LIFE, LIBERTY AND THE PURSUIT OF HAPPINESS

'We hold these truths to be self-evident, that all men are created equal, that they are endowed by their Creator with certain unalienable Rights, that among these are Life, Liberty and the pursuit of Happiness. –That to secure these rights, Governments are instituted among Men, deriving their just powers from the consent of the governed, –That whenever any Form of Government becomes destructive of these ends, it is the Right of the People to alter or to abolish it, and to institute new Government, laying its foundation on such principles and organizing its powers in such form, as to them shall seem most likely to effect their Safety and Happiness.'

The best-known part of the Declaration of Independence is the so-called preamble, which sets out the philosophical justification for the colonists' decision to claim their independence from Britain. According to the natural rights theory of government, derived from John Locke and others, humans enjoy certain inalienable rights, including life, liberty and the pursuit of happiness, and it is the duty of government to protect these rights. If the government fails in this duty – if it breaks the contract between ruler and those who have consented to be ruled – it is the right and duty of the latter to overthrow their governors. The long, central part of the document then gives a devastating 27-part indictment of George III, detailing *'the history of repeated injuries and usurpations'* which render him a *'Tyrant ... unfit to be the ruler of a free people'*.

The final section of the declaration recapitulates Lee's momentous resolution of 7 June and then adds that the United Colonies *'have full Power to levy War, conclude Peace, contract Alliances, establish Commerce, and to do all other Acts and Things which Independent States may of right do'*. As the Boston radical Samuel Adams had pointed out, *'no foreign Power can consistently yield Comfort to Rebels, or enter into any kind of Treaty with these Colonies till they declare themselves free and independent'*. An immediate and practical consequence of the declaration was the freedom to form foreign alliances; the colonists' alliance with France, concluded in 1778, was a crucial factor in their eventual victory in the Revolutionary War.

of the USA. According to his committee colleague John Adams (the future second president), Jefferson was chosen for the work as he had a reputation for *'a masterly pen'* and *'a happy talent of composition'*. Jefferson's final draft, amended by Adams and Franklin, was then put before the full Congress on 28 June.

Congress proceeded to cut 630 words and add 146, leaving a text of 1322 words. This final process of amendment left it *'mangled'* and *'much for the worse'*, according to Jefferson himself, but posterity has taken a more favourable view. On 2 July Congress took the historic step of formally adopting the Lee Resolution, and within two further days the amended text of the declaration had been approved. The ideological leap, final and irreversible, had been taken and the future trajectory of the United States of America had been set.

'The people rushed against the place, and almost in an instant were in possession of a fortification, defended by 100 men, of infinite strength, which in other times had stood several regular sieges & had never been taken. How they got in has as yet been impossible to discover. Those who pretend to have been of the party tell so many different stories as to destroy the credit of them all. They took all the arms, discharged the prisoners & such of the garrison as were not killed in the first moment of fury, carried the Governor and Lieutenant Governor to the Greve (the place of public execution), cut off their heads, & sent them through the city in triumph to the Palais Royal.'

LETTER OF THOMAS JEFFERSON, US MINISTER TO FRANCE 1785–9

THE BASTILLE
⊰ *14 July 1789* ⊱

The storming of a medieval fortress becomes the symbol of the French Revolution

Hero of the American Revolution Thomas Jefferson, recounted the historic, iconic moment when a Parisian mob stormed the Bastille, the medieval fortress-turned-prison that loomed over the centre of the capital. A mob of townspeople, many of them women, had gathered in front of the Bastille, demanding that weapons be handed over and prisoners released. After some half-hearted resistance by the garrison, the fortress fell. A hated symbol of the *ancien régime*, the building was then razed to the ground within months. Although few arms and fewer prisoners were liberated, the day's symbolic power remained undiminished: tyranny was dead and liberty triumphant.

BEGINNINGS

The common perception of the French Revolution is of a popular rising against a reactionary monarchy, but this is almost the reverse of the truth, initially at least. It was actually sparked by an aristocratic revolt against Louis XVI's attempts at reform. By the end of the 18th century, long-standing economic problems had brought France to the point of bankruptcy. In particular, a ruinous foreign policy, funding first the Seven Years' War and then the American revolutionaries, had left the

The painting The Storming of the Bastille *(1789; detail) by French artist Jean-Pierre Houël (1735–1813) portrays the assault as a fierce battle between attackers and defenders. In reality, the fall of the fortress was far less dramatic.*

French state with vast debts, unserviceable through existing taxation. In the archaic French system, the upper classes – nobles and clergy – enjoyed extensive privileges and immunity from taxation. Instead, most of the burden fell on the common people. Louis' aim was to shift much of the tax burden onto his more privileged subjects, and to this end he called an assembly of 'Notables' in February 1787. They proved, however, quite unwilling to bear any extra burden or to sacrifice any of their rights. Faced with continuing resistance to reform, especially from the *parlements* (judicial assemblies that had long been bastions of entrenched privilege), and growing popular unrest, Louis finally agreed to the widespread demand to call a meeting of the Estates-General.

The Estates-General was an ancient, largely obsolete body (it had not been convened since 1614), whose members represented the three 'estates', or classes, into which France was traditionally divided – the nobles, the clergy and the 'third estate' – peasants, tradesmen, craftsmen and other urban workers. No sooner had the Estates-General met at Versailles on 5 May 1789 than they fell to wrangling over what system of voting to adopt. The stalemate was finally broken on 17 June, when the third estate announced their intention to form a National Assembly (renamed the Constituent Assembly soon afterwards) and to proceed on their own if need be. Three days later, they swore the 'Tennis Court Oath' (named after the place where they gathered after being locked out of their usual meeting hall), pledging not to disperse until France had a new constitution. The king reluctantly gave in and ordered the other orders to join the new assembly.

In this French caricature from the late 1780s, three members of the 'third estate' – a peasant, a poor clergyman and a soldier – struggle under the huge weight of the national debt and local taxation. The cartoon's title ironically cites a royal edict: 'Present circumstances demand that we all shoulder the great burden'.

THE LIBERAL PHASE OF THE REVOLUTION

From July 1789, fears (not unfounded) that the king was planning to dissolve the new assembly by force caused widespread alarm in town and country. In Paris bands of ordinary people formed impromptu militias that forced the king's soldiers to change sides or stand down. This popular show of strength culminated in the siege of the Bastille, which set an example of armed resistance that rapidly spread to most of France's main cities. At the same time, discontent in the provinces grew among peasant tenants and smallholders, whose habitual grievances over taxation and seigneurial dues, tariffs and tithes were exacerbated by food shortages caused by the previous year's dire harvest. This highly charged atmosphere, which became known as the 'Great Fear', erupted in widespread violence against nobles and their property.

In an attempt to quell the unrest, on 4 August the Constituent Assembly issued a decree abolishing feudal dues and

Le temps present veut que chacun supporte le Grand Fardeau &c.

LIBERTY, EQUALITY, FRATERNITY

The great rallying cry of the French revolutionaries, as it had been for the Americans a few years earlier, was 'liberty'. Initially this meant liberty from the absolute monarchy exercised for centuries by the Bourbon kings. Richard Price, a Welsh minister and keen supporter of the Revolution, caught the mood of the times when he spoke of *'the love for liberty catching and spreading, a general amendment beginning in human affairs; the dominion of kings changed for the dominion of laws'*. The crucial point of the early, liberal phase of the Revolution was the promotion of the sovereignty of the people and the subordination of the king to the constitutional framework of the laws. Power formerly exercised by virtue of birth and blood was transferred to the 'people'.

With a written constitution in place and the principles of political conduct codified by the Declaration of the Rights of Man and of the Citizen, dynasty was replaced by nationhood; subject by citizen. Or so it appeared in principle, at least. The devil, as ever, was in the detail, especially in deciding whose liberty and which citizens really mattered. With the introduction of a property requirement and the notion of 'active' and 'passive' citizens, it soon turned out that liberty and its usual stable-mate, equality, would make uneasy bedfellows.

The most significant legacy of the third part of the revolutionary triptych – fraternity – was the concept of nation that emerged most strongly after France went to war in 1792. Before the Revolution, loyalty had been principally owed to the king and to one's immediate locality; now, with people united in common cause against foreign enemies without and counter-revolutionaries within, the idea of a community of like-minded citizens, bonded by shared ideals and interests, came to the fore. And with this heightened awareness of nationhood came deeper-seated nationalism – a more exclusive sense of national identity whose necessary corollary was xenophobia. It is questionable whether the greatest ideological horror of the 20th century – the rise of Nazi Germany – would have occurred in the way it did had it not been for the extreme sense of nationalism and 'otherness' that was first engendered by the radical phase of the French Revolution.

privileges, thus sounding the death knell of the *ancien régime*. Later that same month, the Assembly promulgated the Declaration of the Rights of Man and of the Citizen, an epochal statement that proclaimed both the inalienable rights and liberties of the individual and the prerogatives of the state and its sovereignty in terms of representative government.

Another crucial step of the early Revolution was the secularization of both politics and society, a move that saw reason elevated over traditional authority, received opinion and superstition. In November 1789 legislation was enacted nationalizing the property of the Catholic Church. At a stroke this paid off the public debt and allowed a redistribution of land, thus easing one of the peasants' most persistent grievances. Stripped of its traditional resources, the church was then forced (in July 1790) to adopt a new administrative and financial framework known as the Civil Constitution, which caused a serious rift with Rome and a deep schism within the French clergy. The resulting

separation of church and state, combined with toleration of different beliefs, was one of the central legacies of the Revolution.

In the first two years of the Revolution, the Assembly laid down many of the basic principles of a modern constitution. The legal system was completely reorganized, while local government reform divided France into *départements* and a hierarchy of smaller units governed by elected assemblies. Following a failed attempt to flee the country in June 1791 (the 'Flight to Varennes'), Louis was forced to assent to the new constitution, and in October the Constituent was replaced by a new body, the Legislative Assembly. By the end of that year, the transformation of France's absolute monarchy into a constitutionally based one was complete.

THE RADICAL PHASE

This relatively peaceful transition might have lasted had it not been for external pressure. Many opponents of the Revolution who had fled the country (the *émigrés*) were busy fomenting fears that popular revolt might be exported beyond France's borders. Acting pre-emptively in April 1792, France went to war against Austria and then Prussia, who were soon joined by other European nations in a broad anti-revolutionary coalition. In Paris rumours of 'enemies within' soon stoked an atmosphere of frenzied suspicion. The king's position became untenable when he was found to have been scheming with France's enemies abroad. In August 1792 Louis was deposed, and in the following month the monarchy was formally abolished by a new body called the National Convention, set up in place of the Legislative Assembly to provide a republican constitution. The following year Louis and his wife Marie Antoinette were tried for treason and executed. The turmoil in Paris reached a climax in the bloody 'September Massacres', when over a thousand supposed counter-revolutionaries were murdered in the city's prisons.

Many of France's more radical voices now began to call for revolutionary dictatorship. In the summer of 1793, following French military reverses, the moderate delegates in the Convention (the Girondins) were expelled by the radical Jacobins, who enjoyed the support of the revolutionary mob known as the *sansculottes* – working men who wore trousers and so were '*without* (aristocratic) *breeches*'. The Convention then conferred almost dictatorial powers on a body called the Committee of Public Safety, which was dominated first by Georges Danton and then by the more radical Maximilien Robespierre. With no regard for rights or due process, the Committee unleashed a 'Reign of Terror' throughout France to push through its radical programme of social and economic reform; about a third of a million suspected counter-revolutionaries were arrested and some 17,000 guillotined. A huge citizen army of over one million men helped lift France's fortunes in the war from the spring of 1794; with the supposed justification for the Terror thus removed, Robespierre was toppled and executed at the end of July.

In October 1795 the Convention dispersed and a new regime – a body of five members known as the Directory – was set up. Presiding over what was essentially a bourgeois republic, this body was prevented from achieving any kind of stability by the ongoing war and was finally abolished in a coup d'état led by the most powerful soldier of the day: a young general from Corsica named Napoleon Bonaparte.

SIGNIFICANCE

It is hard to overstate the importance of the French Revolution. In a quarter of a century, from the start of the Revolution to Napoleon's defeat at Waterloo, the French overturned the age-old conventions of European society. The origins of modern Europe are often traced to the Revolution, and European history since 1789 can be seen as a series of attempts – for good or ill – to accommodate or challenge ideas and ideals that were first brought to the fore during the Revolution. The paradox of the French Revolution was that France itself in many ways failed to live up to the ideals that it had promoted. Liberty, equality and fraternity were never fully or permanently realized in revolutionary France, and within a decade the universal idealism of the revolutionaries had turned into the military dictatorship of Napoleon. The end result of ten years of radical experimentation, turmoil, bloodshed and war was merely to have replaced one absolute ruler by another.

Liberty Leading the People (1830) by the Romantic artist Eugène Delacroix is an iconic painting that has come to epitomize French revolutionary zeal. It personifies the abstract concept of Liberty, one of the main battle cries of the Revolution; here, she is shown wearing a Liberty (or Phrygian) Cap, the chosen headgear of the sansculottes.

123

'Not a man present who survived could have forgotten in after life the awful grandeur of that charge. You discovered at a distance what appeared to be an overwhelming, long moving line, which, ever advancing, glittered like a stormy wave of the sea when it catches the sunlight. On they came until they got near enough, whilst the very earth seemed to vibrate beneath the thundering tramp of the mounted host. One might suppose that nothing could have resisted the shock of this terrible moving mass. They were the famous cuirassiers, almost all old soldiers, who had distinguished themselves on most of the battlefields of Europe. In an almost incredibly short period they were within twenty yards of us, shouting "Vive l'Empereur!" The word of command, "Prepare to receive cavalry," had been given, every man in the front ranks knelt, and a wall bristling with steel, held together by steady hands, presented itself to the infuriated cuirassiers.'

ENSIGN REES HOWELL GRONOW

WATERLOO
18 June 1815

The defeat that eclipsed France as the superpower of Europe

The subject of many a subsequent painting, Marshal Ney's mid-afternoon madness, recounted above by Ensign R.H. Gronow of the British army's First Regiment of Foot Guards, has become an iconic image of the Battle of Waterloo. Misreading minor shufflings as signs of an incipient disintegration, Ney called up a force of some 5000 cavalry to launch an assault – decisive, as he supposed – on the enemy drawn up on the opposing ridge. Lining up shoulder to shoulder in 'squares' to receive the cavalry, the Allied infantry presented a bristling hedge of bayonets, impenetrable to cavalry lacking infantry and artillery support. The Allied gunners, meanwhile, stayed outside the squares till the last possible moment, delivering salvoes of canister and grapeshot that tore through the oncoming mass of horses and men, then scurried from their cannon to take cover

Allied Prussian and British troops defeat Napoleon Bonaparte at the Battle of Waterloo on 18 June 1815, in this unidentified painting.

Napoleon I is shown leading his men into battle in this 1803 painting by Antoine-Jean Gros.

in the midst of the infantry. Wave after wave of French cavalry came on, sweeping in frustration between the immovable squares. A signature moment in the Napoleonic Wars: courageous and bloody; magnificent and magnificently pointless.

'The nearest run thing you ever saw in your life,' Wellington famously conceded in the aftermath of Waterloo. Ney's error in sending unsupported cavalry against infantry was but one of many on the day; if any of those poor decisions – or any of the countless strokes of ill fortune – had turned out differently, the issue could easily have gone the other way. But the defeat, finally, was total and meant the end for Napoleon, arguably the greatest military genius the world has seen. Nearly a quarter of a century of almost unbroken fighting in Europe and beyond came to a close in 1815. The greatest empire in Europe since Roman times was quickly broken up, and the star of France, the European superpower for centuries, had finally been eclipsed. Other nations, Britain first amongst them, would now enjoy a century of unprecedented ascendancy.

THE RISE AND FALL OF NAPOLEON

Napoleon Bonaparte, a Corsican of relatively obscure origins, had first come to prominence amid the 'whiff of grapeshot' during the French Revolutionary wars. Armed with unlimited talent, charisma and ambition, he quickly transformed military prestige won at the head of the victorious Army of Italy to political power, becoming First Consul of France in 1799 and proclaiming himself emperor in 1804. By then he had already embarked on one of history's most comprehensive and ruthless adventures of conquest. His crushing defeat of a Russo-Austrian army at Austerlitz in December 1805 – arguably the greatest and most distinctive feat of Napoleonic blitzkrieg – left the British prime minister William Pitt under no illusions: *'Roll up the map of Europe,'* he ordered, *'We shall not need it these seven years.'* He might just as well have thrown his map away, for within a couple of years, after inflicting crippling defeats on Russia and Prussia, the 'God of War' (Clausewitz's accolade) had all but redrawn the map of Europe.

It was at this time, at the pinnacle of his success, that the tide began to turn against Napoleon. After Nelson's victory at Trafalgar in October 1805, the prospect of invading Britain by sea evaporated, so the emperor of the French determined to *'conquer the sea by the power of the land,'* by bringing *'the nation of shopkeepers'* to its knees through economic strangulation. However, putting into force his so-called Continental System – closing all French-controlled ports and coastlines to British trade – proved a long and tricky business, and over the coming years, in a forlorn attempt to perfect the system, Napoleon found himself embroiled in disastrous engagements in the Iberian Peninsula and Russia. The Peninsular War (1807–14) – the 'Spanish Ulcer', as Napoleon called it – and the catastrophic retreat from Moscow (1812) devastated French manpower and crushed French morale. With support at home waning and

THE NAPOLEONIC WAY OF WAR

Napoleon revolutionized military tactics and strategy, sweeping aside the assumptions of the 18th century and developing methods that looked forward to the total war and blitzkrieg of the 20th. Exploiting to the full the mass conscript army of the French Revolution, Napoleon always sought swift and decisive action – a knockout blow that would crush an enemy and force it to come to terms. The ingredients of military success were strict security, to maintain the element of surprise; excellent intelligence; good communications; precise staff work; and great mobility.

The last of these called for astonishing feats of marching that saw Napoleon's armies cover in days distances that earlier armies would have covered in weeks. A master of rapid manoeuvre, Napoleon developed a fluid organization of self-contained corps and divisions and a flexible system of logistical support, including the practice of living off the land. The final aspect of Napoleon's genius was the loyalty and devotion that he was able to generate in his officers and men. His nickname *Petit Caporal* ('Little Corporal') indicated not only the affection in which he was held but the fact that his soldiers always considered him to be one of their own.

The Imperial Guard engage in military manoeuvres in front of Napoleon Bonaparte, in this undated hand-coloured print.

allies deserting him, Napoleon was at last cornered and broken in the 'Battle of the Nations' at Leipzig in October 1813. Before long all Germany was lost, Paris had fallen and his marshals were close to mutiny, finally forcing the emperor to abdicate on 6 April 1814.

RETURN FROM EXILE

Over two decades of fighting were at an end and it was all up for Napoleon. Or so it appeared to all but Napoleon himself. Retaining his title of emperor, he was set up in comfortable exile on the Mediterranean island of Elba by victors who felt they could afford to be generous. But any comfort was cold comfort for the thwarted 45-year-old emperor. He kept a careful watch on the growing embarrassment of the restored Bourbon king Louis XVIII, whom many considered to have been brought back *'in the baggage train of the foreigners'* and who made a singularly poor fist of dealing with France's innumerable problems. Seizing his opportunity, Napoleon escaped from Elba and landed at Cannes on 1 March 1815. Cautious at first, his welcome became ever warmer, as his entourage was swollen by those who were sent to stop him. *'The mad enterprise of this man will no longer trouble the repose of Europe nor my own,'* Louis had boasted, but his bravado soon evaporated, and by the time Napoleon reached Paris on 20 March the king had fled and the emperor had been restored in a bloodless coup.

In spite of his triumphant reception, however, Napoleon's fate was hanging by a thread. His foreign enemies – principally Britain, Austria, Russia and Prussia – rapidly formed the Seventh Coalition and began mobilizing forces to mount a multi-pronged attack on Paris that was certain to overwhelm him utterly. Napoleon quickly grasped that his only hope was to launch a lightning strike against the two enemy armies that were already deployed in Belgium, in the hope that the shockwaves of defeat would urge the other Coalition powers, who were still making their preparations, to sue for peace.

THE WATERLOO CAMPAIGN

'The art of war is simple; everything is a matter of execution.' It is hard to suppose that Napoleon could have written these words, at the end of his life, in exile on St Helena, without casting a rueful glance back to his final defeat at Waterloo. For it is generally agreed that his plan was brilliant in conception but ruined by shoddy execution. In early June 1815 the duke of Wellington, with a combined Anglo-Dutch-German army of 107,000, was holding the western half of Belgium, while a Prussian army of nearly 150,000, under Field Marshal Gebhard von Blücher, was occupying the eastern portion. In devising a plan to destroy the two armies that together held a two-to-one superiority over his own force of around 123,000, Napoleon fell back on one of his favourite ploys: taking the so-called 'central position'. Relying principally on speed and stealth, he would drive his own Armée du Nord as a wedge between Wellington's and Blücher's armies and then destroy them in detail before they could concentrate.

The principal reason why the French were defeated at Waterloo was that they failed to keep Wellington and Blücher apart, and this failure was in large part due to botched execution in the military engagements that took place two days earlier, on 16 June. The crossroads at Quatre Bras, the key 'hinge' between the two Coalition forces, had been left exposed by Wellington, who had been completely wrongfooted (or '*humbugged*', as he said himself) by Nalopeon's swift movement north through Charleroi. But Ney, in charge of the French left wing, fatally delayed his attack on Quatre Bras until Wellington had time to remedy his error. In the end, not only was the crossroads held by Wellington's men, but Ney himself was unable to support the rest of the French army, under Grouchy and Napoleon, in its simultaneous engagement with the Prussians at Ligny.

The upshot was that the French victory at Ligny (Napoleon's last) failed to deliver the knockout blow that would have taken Blücher out of the contest. As it was, and in spite of a heavy mauling, the Prussians were able to retreat north and regroup at Wavre. Wellington, meanwhile, falling back from Quatre Bras to a position about three miles (5 km) south of the village of Waterloo, blocked the road to Brussels. The stage was set for one of recent history's most momentous engagements.

THE BATTLE

Neither Wellington nor Napoleon fielded his full force at Waterloo. Grouchy had been sent in pursuit of Blücher with over 30,000 men, leaving a force of 72,000 men and 246 guns to face Wellington's 68,000 and 156 guns. Plagued by prolapsed piles and cystitis, Napoleon played only a sporadic part in the battle, delegating command to Ney, in spite of his lacklustre performance just two days earlier.

Wellington had taken up a strong defensive position on a narrow three-mile (5-km) front along the Mont St Jean ridge. This virtually obliged the French to launch a full-frontal offensive, and the issue of the battle crucially depended on the ability of Wellington's centre to hold out against successive onslaughts. The start of the battle was marked by the first of these: the *grande batterie* of 84 guns, drawn up on the ridge facing Mont St Jean, which may have succeeded in '*astonishing the enemy and shaking his morale*', but did little physical damage, as the Iron Duke had deployed his troops on the far,

SOME CAKE

Napoleon professed to have a low opinion of Wellington, referring to him as the 'Sepoy general' – a contemptuous reference to his military service in India. At breakfast on the morning of Waterloo, he scornfully dismissed Marshal Soult's suggestion that Grouchy's substantial contingent should be recalled: '*Because you have been beaten by Wellington, you consider him a great general. And now I tell you that Wellington is a bad general, that the English are bad troops, and ce sera l'affaire d'un déjeuner – this will be a piece of cake.*'

The French storm the farmhouse at La Haye Sainte, as shown in a watercolour by Richard Knötel. Napoleon's failure to follow up Ney's breach at this point in Wellington's line was a crucial moment in the battle.

reverse slope. His centre's magnificent resistance to Ney's unsupported cavalry charges elicited his famous declaration that he '*never saw the British infantry behave so well!*' The poor judgement of his on-field commander must have shaken Napoleon's confidence and doubtless contributed to his fatal hesitation when Ney did finally achieve a breach at La Haye Sainte, a farmhouse in the centre of Wellington's line. To Ney's request for reinforcements to push home the advantage he had won, Napoleon replied in exasperation: '*Troops! Where does he expect me to get them from? Make them?*' By the time Napoleon complied, the opportunity was lost.

'*In all my life I have not experienced such anxiety, for I must confess that I have never been so close before to defeat.*' Wellington's anxiety was well founded, for there is no doubt that – for all the stubborn resistance shown by his troops – he would have lost had it not been for the arrival of the Prussians from mid-afternoon. Entrusted with a third of all Napoleon's forces, Marshal Grouchy failed twice over – either to prevent some 50,000 Prussians (eventually) from supporting Wellington's beleaguered army or to '*march to the sound of the guns*' (as a subordinate advised) and bring his own forces to relieve the French right. Instead, he got bogged down with the Prussian rearguard at Wavre and played no significant part in the battle. In the evening, when the game was already up, Napoleon made one final, desperate gesture, throwing his élite Imperial Guard against the enemy centre. '*With high, hairy caps and long red feathers nodding to the beat of the drum*', Napoleon's magnificent band of veterans marched to the top of the ridge, only to be greeted by a withering fusillade of short-range musket fire and grapeshot. As they staggered back in their tracks, the horrified cry spread through the French ranks: 'La Garde recule!' – '*The Guard retreats!*' The unthinkable had happened and panic began to set in. Sensing the moment had come, Wellington raised his hat and ordered the general advance: '*No cheering, my lads, but forward, and complete our victory!*'

Scotland Forever! (1881) by Elizabeth Butler depicts the heroic charge of the Royal Scots Greys at the Battle of Waterloo.

WHO WON THE BATTLE OF WATERLOO?

The British habit of claiming the Battle of Waterloo as a quintessentially British victory has recently been subject to fierce criticism, not least because the majority of Wellington's forces were not British. Napoleon himself, mouldering in exile on St Helena, was quite clear about where credit was due:

'*Ah! Wellington ought to light a fine candle to old Blücher. Without him, I don't know where His Grace, as they call him, would be; but as for me, I certainly wouldn't be here.*'

'It is to be doubted whether any spot on Earth can, in desolateness, furnish a parallel to this group... On most of the isles where vegetation is found at all, it is more ungrateful than the blankness of Atacama; tangled thickets of wiry bushes, without fruit and without a name... a parched growth of distorted cactus trees. In many places the coast is rock-bound, or, more properly, clinker-bound; tumbled masses of blackish or greenish stuff like the dross of an iron furnace, forming dark clefts and caves here and there, into which a ceaseless sea pours a fury of foam, overhanging them with a swirl of gray, haggard mist ...'

AMERICAN WRITER HERMAN MELVILLE

GALAPAGOS ISLANDS
⁓ *16 September 1835* ⁓

A visit that forced a reappraisal of man's position in the world

The awful desolation of the Galapagos Islands made a lasting impression on Herman Melville, author of *Moby Dick*, who landed on them in 1841, during his time as a merchant seaman. Straddling the equator and now belonging to Ecuador, these isolated volcanic islands lie in the Pacific Ocean around 620 miles (1000 km) west of the South American mainland. The group consists of 13 major islands and six smaller ones, together with countless rocks and islets. They cover some 8000 square kilometres (3088 sq mi) of land altogether, but they are scattered over an area of ocean roughly eight times that size.

Six years before Melville's visit, on 16 September, 1835, HMS *Beagle* reached the Galapagos, carrying a 26-year-old English naturalist named Charles Darwin. The two men's view of the islands could scarcely have been more different: Melville took as dim a view of their fauna as he did of their topography: *'Little but reptile life is here found: tortoises, lizards, immense spiders, snakes, and that strangest anomaly of outlandish nature, the iguana. No voice, no low, no howl is heard; the chief sound of life here is a hiss.'* The young Darwin, by contrast, was deeply impressed by what he saw: ground finches and mockingbirds, seaweed-eating iguanas, giant tortoises – animals that were not only peculiar to the island group but even, in some cases, to particular islands. The inspiration he took from these extraordinary encounters contributed in due course to the formulation of his theory of evolution by natural selection. This theory, which provided a compelling explanation of the *'mystery of mysteries'*, the origin and extinction of species, has not only revolutionized the biological sciences but has profoundly altered the way that humans regard themselves and their place in the world.

THE VOYAGE OF THE *BEAGLE*

Showing little enthusiasm for the careers marked out for him – first physician, then clergyman – Darwin developed an early and abiding passion for natural history. His great opportunity, and the experience that was to define his subsequent life and work, came in 1831, when his botany professor at Cambridge procured for him a position on the survey ship HMS *Beagle*, where he would serve as naturalist and gentleman companion to the captain, Robert Fitzroy. So it was that, on 27 December 1831, he set sail from Devonport on a gruelling yet exhilarating five-year adventure that would take him around the world and change him and his ideas forever.

Darwin turned out to be a poor sailor – he was constantly plagued by seasickness – but fortunately he was able to spend far more time on land than at sea and to indulge his passion for exploring, observing and collecting specimens. His mind was almost overwhelmed by exposure to a staggering variety of life and land forms. Terrestrial rocks on Cape Verde teeming with oyster shells; stunning panoramas of time-sculpted landscapes viewed from the foothills of the Chilean Andes; a devastating earthquake in Chile that destroyed the city of Concepción: all helped to reinforce his sense (already prompted by his simultaneous reading of the pioneering work of the geologist Charles Lyell) of the impermanence of the environment and of the vast time-scales over which mountains had risen and fallen and other seemingly immutable features had come and gone. The luxuriance of the Brazilian rainforest filled his head with a *'chaos of delight'*, while the massive fossil bones of long-extinct mammals in Argentina set his mind racing on the reasons for the disappearance of the great animals of the past. He was confronted with the wondrous beauty and the dreadful brutality of nature – not least of human nature. He observed and occasionally became

The rocky shore of Bartolomeo Island, one of the Galapagos Islands. The sheer diversity and peculiarity of the flora and fauna of the Galapagos provided Darwin with the seeds of his revolutionary ideas on evolution.

TIMELINE

1809 Darwin born in Shrewsbury, England

Dec 1831–Oct 1836 The voyage of the *Beagle*

16 Sept 1835 The *Beagle* reaches the Galapagos Islands

1841 Herman Melville visits the Galapagos Islands

1859 First edition of the *Origin of Species* published

1882 Darwin dies in Downe, Kent

Despite the many years Darwin spent 'patiently accumulating and reflecting on all sorts of facts' before publishing his theory of evolution, the Origin of Species *was still savagely satirized, as in this cartoon of 1874.*

embroiled in local politics; in South America he was distressed to see the European settlers bent on the destruction of the indigenous peoples.

In this kaleidoscope of wonders and horrors, human and animal, history has given special prominence to Darwin's five-week visit to the Galapagos Islands in September and October 1835. While he was clearly impressed by the unusual plants and animals that he saw there, he did not, as is often said, have a 'eureka' moment in which the idea of evolution by natural selection suddenly came to him. Like much else on his momentous voyage, however, the unique geology, flora and fauna of the islands fired his imagination and sent him searching for explanations for the extraordinary phenomena he observed.

The *Origin of Species*

When the *Beagle* entered Falmouth harbour on 2 October 1836, the young naturalist on board, weighed down by thousands of specimens and reams of notes, was beset by riddles inspired by his journey. Yet within a year of his return Darwin had begun to formulate the ideas that would eventually define his theory of evolution. It was more than two decades, however, before he published (in 1859) the classic statement of the theory: the momentous *On the Origin of Species by Means of Natural Selection, or the Preservation of Favoured Races in the Struggle for Life*. Many commentators have suggested that this long delay was due to fear for his reputation and of the public reception that would greet his ideas. It is true that the orthodox scientific view in Darwin's day was that each species was immutable and the product of an independent act of divine creation. But the idea of evolution – or '*descent with modification*', as Darwin called it – was not new. Many, including the naturalist's own grandfather, Erasmus Darwin, had speculated on the notion that the various kinds of plants and animals might be derived from earlier forms and share common ancestors. Such thinking was widely condemned on theological grounds, as it appeared to displace God from his central role in creation, but without any explanation of how such modification might occur, it remained mere speculation. Indeed, the ideas of natural theology – in particular, the so-called 'argument from design', which inferred the existence of a creator from the wonderful complexity and order of the natural world – were generally held to be decisive in favour of the orthodox view.

Darwin's genius was to undermine the argument from design by providing an alternative mechanism that could account for the '*perfection of structure and coadaptation*' of living things. He went to extraordinary pains to gather evidence to support his theory and to anticipate likely objections and criticisms. Most notably, in his own view, he made '*a careful study of domesticated animals and cultivated plants*', where he saw a process (artificial selection) closely analogous to the natural mechanism he proposed. In the end, though, the attraction of his theory was its simplicity and its capacity to reconcile otherwise-baffling facts, such as the existence of fossils and the geographical distribution of plants and animals. In the *Origin*, he encapsulates natural selection as follows:

ISLANDS OF INSPIRATION

The Galapagos may not have provided the 'eureka' moment of legend, but their central role in inspiring Darwin's thoughts on descent with modification and natural selection is clear on many occasions in the *Origin of Species*. One justly famous example appears in the discussion of biogeography:

> 'Why should the species which are supposed to have been created in the Galapagos Archipelago, and nowhere else, bear so plain a stamp of affinity to those created in America? There is nothing in the conditions of life, in the geological nature of the islands, in their height or climate ... which resembles closely the conditions of the South American coast: in fact there is a considerable dissimilarity in all these respects. On the other hand, there is a considerable degree of resemblance in the volcanic nature of the soil, in climate, height, and size of the islands, between the Galapagos and Cape de Verde Archipelagos: but what an entire and absolute difference in their inhabitants! The inhabitants of the Cape de Verde Islands are related to those of Africa, like those of the Galapagos to America. I believe this grand fact can receive no sort of explanation on the ordinary view of independent creation; whereas on the view here maintained, it is obvious that the Galapagos Islands would be likely to receive colonists ... from America; and the Cape de Verde Islands from Africa.'

'As many more individuals of each species are born than can possibly survive; and as, consequently, there is a frequently recurring struggle for existence, it follows that any being, if it vary however slightly in any manner profitable to itself, under the complex and sometimes varying conditions of life, will have a better chance of surviving, and thus be naturally selected. From the strong principle of inheritance, any selected variety will tend to propagate its new and modified form.'

In the first edition of the *Origin*, Darwin offers no more than hints of the implications of his theory in its application to humans. He was acutely conscious of the uproar that would follow the suggestion that the difference between humans and (other) animals was one of degree only, not kind, and hence that man was not the special and favoured object of divine creation. The public furore came anyway and has blazed away ever since. Indeed, as the target of Creationists and Intelligent Design theorists, the theory of evolution, or 'Darwinism', is today as contentious in some quarters as it has ever been. Among the vast majority of scientists, however, the theory is unquestioned and recognized as the cornerstone and unifying principle of the biological sciences. And its significance extends far beyond the confines of science. No other scientific theory has forced humans to make so radical a reappraisal of their own position in the world and their relationship to other living things.

NOT DARWIN

The phrase most commonly associated with Darwin's theory of natural selection, *'survival of the fittest'*, was not in fact used by him at all. It was coined by his follower and supporter, Herbert Spencer.

'Nothing in biology makes sense except in the light of evolution.'

THEODOSIUS DOBZHANSKY (EVOLUTIONARY BIOLOGIST)

Over three days in the summer of 1863, at a small crossroads town in southern Pennsylvania, a battle raged that proved to be the defining moment in the American Civil War, arguably the most important event in the history of the USA. It also turned out to be the bloodiest battle ever fought on American soil. The wounds, physical and psychological, inflicted at Gettysburg were destined to remain festering and unforgiven for many generations.

GETTYSBURG

1–3 July 1863

A bloody battle that changed the course of American history

The retreat from Gettysburg of Confederate general Robert E. Lee and the simultaneous fall of Vicksburg represented a double blow from which the secessionist southern states never recovered. Although some 20 months of bitter fighting lay ahead before the final surrender, in truth the war was already lost. The South's dreams of freedom to pursue its own destiny – a freedom, however, that depended on enslaving others – lay shattered in the blood and dust of Gettysburg.

PRELUDE TO THE BATTLE

Much romanticizing of the 'noble South' had taken place in the decades leading up to the outbreak of war in April 1861, but at core the conflict was about slavery. The way of life of the rural southern states, whose wealth was founded mainly on cotton plantations worked by black African slaves, was increasingly challenged by abolitionists in the North, where the economy was based on manufacturing and commerce underpinned by free labour. Matters came to a head with the election to the presidency of the pro-abolition Republican Abraham Lincoln in 1860. Within months 11 southern states had seceded from the Union and set up their own government. On the face of it, the odds were heavily stacked against the South, which was dwarfed by the North in terms of industrial might and manpower. Yet while outright military victory was probably never within its reach, it could realistically hope to foment enough political instability to bring about a change to a more accommodating government.

Fortunes fluctuated in the early years of the war, but in northern Virginia – the most sensitive and critical theatre – things had generally gone badly for the North. Following a crushing victory at Chancellorsville in May 1863, Lee, the most respected general on either side, decided to cross the Potomac river, fully aware that a major Confederate victory on Union soil might do untold political damage. Blocking Lee's

A scene from the Gettysburg Cyclorama, a huge, circular painting of the decisive battle created in 1882–3 by the French artist Paul Philippoteaux. The 109-m (359-ft) long canvas, which depicts all the phases of the engagement, is displayed in a purpose-built facility at Gettysburg National Military Park.

path north to Washington was the Union commander General George G. Meade. Untested in the highest command, Meade realized that if he buckled now, there was a real risk that the whole Union effort might collapse. It was at this critical juncture, with a measure of desperation on each side, that the two great armies met at Gettysburg.

'THE LAST FULL MEASURE OF DEVOTION'

Although everyone knew the clash had to come, the precise time and place were more accident than design. It all started off as little more than skirmishing following chance encounters to the west of Gettysburg. It was only by morning on the second day that Lee's Army of Northern Virginia (75,000 strong) and Meade's Army of the Potomac (88,000) had arrived in full force.

On the first day the flow of battle clearly favoured the Confederates. By late afternoon the Union columns had been forced to beat a retreat southwards through the town and to take up defensive positions (in the now-famous 'fish-hook' formation) on elevated ground known as Cemetery Ridge and Culp's Hill. Numerous blunders and missed

137

opportunities on both sides on the second day left things little advanced, leaving the stage set for a dramatic climax on the third day.

Having failed to take their flanks on the previous day, Lee determined to soften up the Union centre with a sustained artillery bombardment and then to launch a frontal assault with his infantry. In the event the advance of some 12,000 infantry under Major General George Pickett was exemplary. At first their march up the hill proceeded in eerie silence, but hopes that the Union gunners had been knocked out were dashed with a deafening boom as devastating volley after volley cut through the Confederate ranks. As those still standing neared the enemy line, they roared the rebel yell, then chaos engulfed all: '*There are bayonet-thrusts, sabre-strokes, pistol shots; men spinning around like tops, throwing out their arms, gulping up blood, falling, legless, armless, headless ... ghastly heaps of dead men.*' The bloody repulse of Pickett's charge spelt the end for the Confederates and soon they were in full retreat.

The Civil War is often said to be the forerunner of modern warfare – the first of a kind that paved the way for the great wars of the 20th century. In truth, though, the tactics employed at Gettysburg were little changed from those used in the Napoleonic Wars half a century earlier. Infantry typically moved in close formation and most of the fighting was at relatively close quarters. The advent of rifled muskets and cannon, however, dramatically increased casualty rates in the Civil War and at Gettysburg above all, where combined casualties (approximately equal on each side) stood at over 50,000.

AFTERMATH OF DEFEAT

Lee's Invasion of the North – probably his best and last shot at victory – had been thwarted; the initiative had been lost, never to be regained. The day after the calamitous defeat at Gettysburg the Confederate stronghold on the Mississippi at Vicksburg fell to Ulysses S. Grant, cutting the Confederacy in two. It was now only a matter of time before the South was crushed and reeled back

'*Up and down the line men reeling and falling; splinters flying from wheels and axles where bullets hit; in rear, horses tearing and plunging, mad with wounds or terror; drivers yelling, shells bursting, shot shrieking overhead, howling about our ears or throwing up great clouds of dust where they struck; the musketry crashing on three sides of us; bullets hissing, humming and whistling everywhere; cannon roaring; all crash on crash and peal on peal, smoke, dust, splinters, blood, wreck and carnage indescribable.*'

PRIVATE AUGUSTUS BUELL, A TEENAGE UNION CANNONEER AT GETTYSBURG

THE GETTYSBURG ADDRESS

Four months after the battle, on 19 November 1863, Abraham Lincoln delivered a short speech at Gettysburg at a ceremony in commemoration of fallen Union soldiers. At the time, he thought the speech had missed its mark – '*That speech won't scour. It is a flat failure*', he remarked to a friend as he sat down – but it has since come to be recognized as one of the most noble expressions of the democratic ideal. Within a further five months Lincoln himself was dead, killed by an assassin's bullet, so ensuring that his brief 272-word speech has remained one of the defining statements of the American nation.

President Abraham Lincoln, pictured in the same year as he gave his famous address.

'*Four score and seven years ago our fathers brought forth on this continent a new nation, conceived in Liberty, and dedicated to the proposition that all men are created equal.*

Now we are engaged in a great civil war, testing whether that nation or any nation so conceived and so dedicated, can long endure. We are met on a great battlefield of that war. We have come to dedicate a portion of that field, as a final resting place for those who here gave their lives that that nation might live. It is altogether fitting and proper that we should do this.

But, in a larger sense, we can not dedicate – we can not consecrate – we can not hallow – this ground. The brave men, living and dead, who struggled here, have consecrated it, far above our poor power to add or detract. The world will little note, nor long remember what we say here, but it can never forget what they did here. It is for us the living, rather, to be dedicated here to the unfinished work which they who fought here have thus far so nobly advanced. It is rather for us to be here dedicated to the great task remaining before us – that from these honored dead we take increased devotion to that cause for which they gave the last full measure of devotion – that we here highly resolve that these dead shall not have died in vain – that this nation, under God, shall have a new birth of freedom – and that government of the people, by the people, for the people, shall not perish from the Earth.'

into the Union. The myth of the Lost Cause of the South – the vision famously captured in Margaret Mitchell's 1936 novel *Gone with the Wind* – soon began to take root: a romanticized view of a noble southern culture destroyed by a combination of northern treachery and bad luck. Yet the reality, social and political, was stark enough. The South had been mauled and humiliated, its economic and social structure shattered. All talk of secession and independence was done for good; slavery was finished. The federal power of the USA – soon to become the mightiest country on Earth – was massively enhanced, hard won on the bloodied fields and hills around Gettysburg.

'What is this? This is the wrong way! We're supposed to take the Appel Quay!' shouted General Oskar Potiorek, the Austrian provincial governor in Sarajevo, as the driver unexpectedly turned off the river road north into the Franz Josef Strasse. The luxurious black Gräf & Stift Double Phaeton, its soft top pulled down and Habsburg pennant flying, drew to a halt and the driver began to back up. Just as the car came alongside Schiller's food store, a pale, meagre-looking youth, who had just emerged from the shop, stepped forward to within a few feet of the royal couple, drew a pistol from his coat, and fired several shots at the passengers. The archduke was fatally wounded in the neck, his wife in the stomach.

SARAJEVO
⋖ 28 June 1914 ⋗

The assassination that sparked the First World War

Such was the moment of climax, on 28 June 1914, a sunny Sunday in the Bosnian capital of Sarajevo, when Archduke Franz Ferdinand, heir to the Austro-Hungarian empire, and his wife were assassinated by a young Serb nationalist named Gavrilo Princip. The murder sparked a crisis that rapidly spread from Austria and Serbia, which was blamed for the crime by the government in Vienna, and by the end of August had engulfed Germany, Russia, France, Britain and Japan. No one knew it at the time, but a war had started that would turn into the first global conflict, engaging some 65 million combatants, of whom around a third would be wounded and a sixth killed. By the end of the war, four great imperial dynasties – German, Austro-Hungarian, Turkish and Russian – had been snuffed out, while the British and French empires had been dealt crushing blows from which they would never fully recover. The bloody eclipse of European hegemony was matched by the simultaneous rise of the USA as a global superpower. And – bitterest irony of all – the Great War, supposedly the 'war to end all wars', would sow the seeds of an even greater, bloodier and more appalling conflict.

THE WRONG TURN

In the end, the plot to assassinate the nephew of the Austro-Hungarian emperor Franz Josef and heir to the Habsburg throne only succeeded through sheer luck. Indeed, before the fatal and fateful shots were fired, Princip and his fellow plotters feared that it had already failed.

In his capacity as inspector-general of the imperial army, Franz Ferdinand had been invited by Bosnia's governor, General Potiorek, to review military manoeuvres

taking place outside Sarajevo. After the inspection, the archduke and his wife were due to attend an official reception hosted by Sarajevo's mayor at the city hall. The route chosen for the imperial motorcade lay along the Appel Quay, a broad avenue that followed the north bank of the Miljacka river. Mingled among the large crowd that had gathered to enjoy the occasion and the warm morning sunshine were seven would-be assassins, who were spread out along the route. The plan was that each should attack the imperial visitors as they passed, if a clear opportunity presented itself. The first of the conspirators apparently lost his nerve, but the second, Nedjelko Cabrinovic threw his bomb

A vivid portrayal of the moment the assassin Gavrilo Princip struck, by the contemporary American illustrator Isaac Brewster Hazelton.

141

at the archduke's car, the second vehicle in the six-car motorcade, only to see it bounce off the intended target and explode near the car behind, injuring some of its passengers and a number of spectators. Aware of the danger, the archduke's driver sped off towards the city hall, giving the remaining plotters no chance to act.

A comedy of chaos and recrimination was then played out at the city hall. The outraged archduke protested that he had visited the city, only to be welcomed by bombs, while Potiorek bridled (in a manner he must have later regretted) at the suggestion that the town was *'full of assassins'*. Most bizarrely of all, the mayor, clearly not a man adept at thinking on his feet, went on to deliver his pre-scripted speech: *'All the citizens of the capital city of Sarajevo find that their souls are filled with happiness, and they most enthusiastically greet Your Highnesses' most illustrious visit with the most cordial of welcomes …'* After the official reception, Franz Ferdinand insisted on altering his schedule to include a visit to the hospital to look in on those injured in the earlier explosion, but in an extraordinary oversight the change in route that this visit required was not passed on to the drivers. So it was that the fatal wrong turn was taken and chance brought the imperial party face-to-face with young Princip.

In this 1908 cartoon from the French periodical Le Petit Journal, *the Austrian and Russian emperors are shown grabbing pieces of the moribund Ottoman empire, while a dejected Turkish sultan looks on.*

THE EASTERN QUESTION

The waning of Turkish (Ottoman) influence, highlighted in a series of costly wars with Russia in the second half of the 19th century, had threatened to create a power vacuum in southeastern Europe. In this volatile climate, a number of South Slavic groups, including Bulgarians, Serbians, Croatians and Macedonians, began to clamour for national recognition. Britain, France and the newly unified Germany were fearful that realization of Slavic ambitions would upset the balance of power by strengthening Russia (which was regarded as the Slavic motherland) and undermining Austria-Hungary (whose southern territories included substantial Slavic contingents). So in 1878 the Congress of Berlin was convened to resolve the so-called 'Eastern Question': the independence of Serbia, Montenegro and Romania was recognized, but the 'Big Bulgaria' coveted by Russia was denied and Bosnia-Herzegovina, though remaining under Turkish suzerainty, was occupied and administered by Austria. The main thrust of these arrangements was to prop up the remnants of Turkish power, but in the event they failed to satisfy anyone and did little to douse nationalist aspirations. When, in 1908, the Bulgarians declared their independence, Austria-Hungary immediately responded by formally annexing Bosnia-Herzegovina, which only served to confirm fears of Austrian expansionism among the Slavic peoples. The two Balkan Wars of 1912–13 saw Serbia, Bulgaria, Montenegro and Greece, with Russian backing, cast off the last vestiges of Turkish control in Europe, so further intensifying the tension between Austria and Russia.

'STAY ALIVE FOR OUR CHILDREN!'

Count Franz von Harrach, who was serving as the archduke's bodyguard, owned the Gräf & Stift Double Phaeton and was riding in it at the time of the shooting. Here, in his later memoir of the event, he takes up the story immediately after Princip's attack.

'As the car quickly reversed, a thin stream of blood spurted from His Highness's mouth onto my right cheek. As I was pulling out my handkerchief to wipe away the blood from the Archduke's lips, Her Highness cried out: "For God's sake! What has happened to you?" Then she sank down from her seat with her face between the Archduke's knees. I had no idea that she had been hit too and thought that she had fainted from shock. Then the Archduke pleaded: "Sopherl! Sopherl! Sterbe nicht! Bleibe am Leben für unsere Kinder!" ("Sophie dear, Sophie dear, don't die! Stay alive for our children!") I seized the Archduke by the coat collar to prevent his head from sinking forward and asked him: "Is Your Highness in great pain?" To this he distinctly replied: "It is nothing." His expression was slightly contorted, and he repeated the same thing six or seven times, each time more faintly as he gradually lost consciousness: "It is nothing." Then came a brief pause, followed by a convulsive rattle in his throat. This stopped as we arrived at the governor's residence. The two unconscious bodies were carried into the building, where their death was soon established.'

The royal party, pictured driving through Sarajevo earlier on the fateful day of 28 June 1914.

Plagued by incessant nationalist unrest, the creaking, multi-ethnic Austro-Hungarian empire had never looked more vulnerable than it did in June 1914. Its politicians felt that any weakness shown in its response to the events in Sarajevo would seriously undermine its status as one of the great European powers. So even before the facts of the case had been looked into, many of the decision-makers in Vienna were already determined to take a tough stance. Wide-ranging police investigations were quickly set in train, and hundreds of people were rounded up and questioned. All but one of the seven conspirators

THE BLACK HAND

Commenting on the Sarajevo assassination in his memoirs, the German Field-Marshal Karl von Bülow declared that '*many details prove that the Serbian government had neither instigated or desired it*' and that '*the horrible murder was the work of a Serbian society with branches all over the country*'. As later became clear, the idealistic and naïve conspirators at Sarajevo had in fact been recruited, trained and equipped by a powerful Belgrade-based secret society called Union or Death, or the Black Hand. Intoxicated by the prospect of realizing the

Gavrilo Princip is arrested immediately after the assassination. He and his co-conspirators were supplied with weapons by the Black Hand.

ideals of Pan-Slavism and forming a 'Greater Serbia', the society's members set as their primary goal the liberation of Serbs everywhere from Habsburg and Ottoman control. The leader and co-founder of the Black Hand, Dragutin Dimitrijevic (whose codename was *Apis*, 'the bee'), was a Serbian intelligence officer, and the group had strong roots in the army, but there is no evidence of a formal connection with the Serbian government. Indeed, when Pasic's government got wind of the Sarajevo plot, it tried (rather obliquely and half-heartedly) to stop it, but sadly the warning was not acted upon.

had been arrested, and it was quickly established not only that all those in custody were Serbian but that the weapons used had been supplied by Serbian sources. Connections between the plotters and various secret societies dedicated to Serbian nationalism were suggested (though not, apparently, the Black Hand, the one that was later implicated), but no serious effort was made to distinguish between these unofficial and clandestine organizations and the Serbian government. Indeed, an Austrian official sent to Sarajevo reported on 13 July that there was '*nothing to show the complicity of the Serbian government in the direction of the assassination or its preparations or in supplying of weapons*'. No matter. Whatever the justice of the case, political expediency demanded that the Austrian authorities take swift and severe measures against the Serbian government.

THE JULY CRISIS

Intent on fomenting a crisis rather than reaching a compromise, the Habsburg leaders decided to issue an ultimatum that was couched in such extreme terms that the government in Belgrade would be certain to reject it. And sure enough, the ultimatum delivered on 23 July – in particular, the demands that

Austrian officials be allowed to intervene in Serbia's domestic judicial and police activities – was duly rejected by the Serbian prime minister, Nikola Pasic. When the 48-hour deadline expired, on 25 July, Vienna broke off diplomatic relations, and three days later Austria-Hungary declared war on Serbia.

The aim of the Austrian government's high-risk strategy was probably to provoke a limited and localized confrontation that would allow them to crush Slav nationalist ambitions and then cool things down through diplomacy. To this end, before issuing the ultimatum, officials in Vienna had already gained the infamous 'blank cheque' from their German allies, guaranteeing military support in the event of the conflict spreading. But if the Austrian government hoped that Berlin's promise would deter Russia from intervening on behalf of its Serbian ally, it was quickly disabused. Refusing to lose face by backing down and to compromise its own interests in the Balkans, the leadership in St Petersburg resolved to support its ally and ordered a full mobilization of its armed forces on 30 July.

At this point the intricate system of European alliances whose purpose was to maintain a balance of power and so avoid major confrontations suddenly cut in to escalate the crisis. German military thinking had long been dominated by the fear of fighting a war on two fronts. To avoid being caught simultaneously between Russia in the east and its ally France in the west, the German chief of staff Alfred von Schlieffen had devised his eponymous plan of 1905. Responding to Russian mobilization in accordance with the Schlieffen Plan, Germany declared war on Russia on 1 August and immediately prepared to launch an offensive against France, with the aim of knocking out the French before the Russian army had time to move into position.

Unfortunately, the strength of the French border defences meant that the German pre-emptive strike against France had to be routed through Belgium, and it was the violation of Belgian neutrality that convinced the British, already alarmed at the growth of German power, to come in on the side of France. In little over a month *some damn foolish thing in the Balkans* (as the far-sighted German chancellor Otto von Bismarck had predicted in the 1890s) had mushroomed into a European, soon-to-be-global, conflict.

TIMELINE

June–July 1878 Congress of Berlin attempts to resolve the Eastern Question

5 Oct 1908 Bulgarians declare independence

6 Oct 1908 Bosnia-Herzegovina is annexed by Austria-Hungary

1912–13 Two Balkan Wars all but wipe out Ottoman presence in Europe

28 June 1914 Archduke Franz Ferdinand is assassinated at Sarajevo

23 July 1914 Austrian ultimatum is delivered to Serbia

25 July 1914 Vienna breaks off diplomatic relations with Belgrade

28 July 1914 Austria declares war on Serbia

30 July 1914 Russia orders full mobilization in support of Serbia

1 Aug 1914 Germany declares war on Russia

3 Aug 1914 Germany declares war on France

4 Aug 1914 Britain declares war on Germany

23 Aug 1914 Japan declares war on Germany

NO STUFFED SHIRT

In spite of his stiff appearance, Franz Ferdinand was touchingly devoted to his children and wife Sophie: 'She is everything to me: my wife, my adviser, my doctor … in a word: my entire happiness.' Politically, the archduke was a curious mixture: a reforming conservative. One of his planned schemes was to preserve the empire by granting greater rights to the South Slavs; it was fear of such a policy, which would have diminished the prospects of a Greater Serbia, that made him an obvious target for the Black Hand.

'IRISHMEN AND IRISHWOMEN: In the name of God and of the dead generations from which she receives her old tradition of nationhood, Ireland, through us, summons her children to her flag and strikes for her freedom ... We declare the right of the people of Ireland to the ownership of Ireland, and to the unfettered control of Irish destinies, to be sovereign and indefeasible. The long usurpation of that right by a foreign people and government has not extinguished the right, nor can it ever be extinguished ... In this supreme hour the Irish nation must, by its valour and discipline and by the readiness of its children to sacrifice themselves for the common good, prove itself worthy of the august destiny to which it is called.'

PROCLAMATION OF THE IRISH REPUBLIC

DUBLIN
24 April 1916

The failed rising that ensured the emergence of the modern Irish state

At 12.45 on 24 April, 1916 – Easter Monday – republican rebel leader Patrick Pearse took up his position beneath the magnificent Georgian portico of Dublin's General Post Office (GPO) in Sackville Street, the city's main thoroughfare. Standing in the shadow of Nelson's Pillar, Pearse then proceeded to read out, in his capacity as acting president of the Provisional Government, the Proclamation of the Irish Republic. Within a week, all but the facade of the famous post office, most of Sackville Street and much of the centre of Dublin had been reduced to rubble beneath a hail of British artillery fire. Within three weeks Pearse himself and 14 of his fellow rebels, including his six co-signatories of the Proclamation, had been tried and executed by firing squad in Kilmainham Jail.

Only a small crowd was present on Easter Monday 1916 to hear Pearse's words, and most of those there apparently derived more amusement from the occasion than enlightenment. But the rebels' brave resistance to the military onslaught over the coming days and the heavy-handed measures taken by the British authorities in Dublin Castle following their surrender soon turned the

The devastation on Sackville Street in Dublin in the immediate aftermath of the Easter Rising of 1916. After Ireland won its independence, this thoroughfare was renamed O'Connell Street in honour of the early 19th-century Irish nationalist leader Daniel O'Connell ('the Liberator').

revolutionaries into martyrs and heroes. As underlying resentment against British rule quickly turned to outright hostility, the 'Sovereign Independent State' that was proclaimed by Pearse became a reality in the minds and hearts of Irish people half a decade before it became a (partial) reality in law. The ruined interior of the post office was gradually rebuilt behind the old facade, and when it was formally reopened in 1929, it was the postal headquarters of the Irish Free State and it stood not on Sackville Street but on O'Connell Street, which had aptly been renamed in honour of one of Ireland's greatest nationalist heroes. Within a further decade, in 1937, the central hope of the Easter rebels had been fully realized as the Irish Free State – still formally a dominion within the British empire – became a sovereign and independent republic.

THE HOME RULE CRISIS

For the half-century before the Easter Rising of 1916, nationalist passions in Ireland had mainly flowed within constitutional channels. Under the charismatic leadership of Charles Stewart Parnell and then John Redmond, the Irish Parliamentary Party (IPP) had dedicated itself to the cause of winning 'home rule' – a constitutional arrangement in which an Irish parliament would exercise control over domestic affairs while Ireland itself remained part of the United Kingdom. In 1914, after decades of frustration, it appeared that the IPP had finally won the day, when on 28 September the third Home Rule bill, which allowed for a parliament in Dublin with jurisdiction over all 32 Irish counties, was passed into law. The outbreak of war in Europe changed everything, however. Implementation of the new law was suspended until the end of the conflict, but the very fact that Westminster had finally granted assent to such a law confirmed the worst fears of those who were opposed to it.

Militiamen of the Irish Citizen Army stand guard during the Rising on top of Liberty Hall, the headquarters of James Connolly, commandant of the Dublin Brigade of the Irish Volunteers.

Since the 1880s the most resolute opposition to home rule had come from the unionists of protestant Ulster (the six counties in the northeast of Ireland), who were single-mindedly committed to preserving the Union between Britain and Ireland. To give vent to the outrage felt throughout Ulster when the new Home Rule bill was first brought before Parliament in 1912, the unionist leadership organized a series of public protests, at the climax of which, on 28 September 1912, nearly half a million people signed a 'Solemn League and Covenant', pledging *'to stand by one another in*

A BLOOD SACRIFICE?

Republican romantics before and after the Easter Rising were drawn to the idea of the 'blood sacrifice'. Patrick Pearse, in particular, could write mystically of bloodshed as 'a cleansing and sanctifying thing' and of the 'old heart of the earth' being 'warmed by the red wine of the battlefield'.

The signatories of the Proclamation all agreed that Ireland must prove its mettle by 'the readiness of its children to sacrifice themselves', and it is clear that none of them thought that the outcome of the Easter Rising could be judged purely in terms of

Patrick Pearse, renowned for his passionate oratory, coined the famous phrase 'Ireland unfree shall never be at peace'.

military success. They felt, rightly as it turned out, that a grand gesture – one that might bring on their own deaths – could prevent the Irish people from drifting along the path to home rule and revitalize the spirit of revolutionary nationalism among them.

In the end the rebels were prepared to go ahead with an insurrection that was virtually doomed to military failure because of the promise it held out for the future. But there is little reason to suppose that they set out to achieve such a triumphant failure. Simple triumph would have been enough.

defending … our cherished position of equal citizenship in the United Kingdom'. This impressive show of solidarity was followed, more sinisterly, in December 1912 by the setting-up of the Ulster Volunteer Force (UVF), a citizen militia whose function was to oppose a Dublin-based government by all means, including physical force. Fearful of the UVF's impact in influencing British policy, nationalists of all hues came together in November 1913 to form a rival militia known as the Irish Volunteers, but almost at once this fledgling organization was torn apart when Redmond, at the outset of the European war, urged all nationalists, including the Volunteers, to enlist in the British army and to support Britain's war effort. The great majority of the Volunteers – some 170,000 – backed Redmond, but a small rump of around 10,000 viscerally opposed the idea of assisting Britain and split from the main body.

PRELUDE TO INSURRECTION

Like the unionists, the leaders of the 1916 Rising were alarmed at Redmond's apparent success in delivering home rule, but their concern was that the reality of Irish self-government within the British empire would forever kill off the dream of winning full independence. Pearse and his comrades belonged to a different, more radical nationalist tradition that over the previous 100 years and more had sporadically flared up in open rebellion. They had grown up at a time when there was a great resurgence of interest in Ireland's past – in its language, its literature, its culture, its folklore and mythology, even its sporting traditions. The influence of societies such as the Gaelic League, which was set up to promote Irish as a spoken and literary language, created an intense sense of an Irish national identity and a distinct national culture. This potent blend of cultural and political awareness reinforced the case for full independence and nationhood and stoked up a passion for activism and revolution. One of the most significant upshots of this process of radicalization was the rejuvenation of the Irish Republican Brotherhood (IRB), a small and clandestine organization, largely overshadowed during the Parnellite ascendancy, that had originally sprung from Fenian roots and was dedicated to achieving Irish independence by revolutionary means, at any time that a suitable opportunity arose.

In August 1915 Pearse and five of the other six activists who were later to sign the Proclamation of the Irish Republic – Thomas Clarke, Sean MacDermott, Eamonn Ceannt, Joseph Plunkett and Thomas MacDonagh – formed a small, covert faction within the IRB known as the 'military council'. Operating (like other Irish republicans before them) on the principle that '*England's difficulty is Ireland's opportunity*', they recognized that the outbreak of war in 1914 presented an ideal opportunity and at once set about planning an armed insurrection. The members of the military council were all key figures in the Irish Volunteers,

British soldiers armed with rifles and a Lewis gun (an early form of machine-gun) man a makeshift barricade in a Dublin street on 11 May 1916.

ROGER CASEMENT AND THE 'GALLANT ALLIES'

In their Proclamation the rebel leaders declare that Ireland, in her moment of crisis, enjoys the support of her 'gallant allies in Europe'. In the event, assistance from Germany was blocked by the Royal Navy, but the failure was certainly not due to any lack of effort by the rebels' chief intermediary – celebrated British diplomat and Irish patriot Sir Roger Casement. After making little headway in recruiting an Irish Brigade from Irish prisoners taken on the Western Front, his next move was to squeeze a promise of munitions from the German government, who in February 1916 agreed to send 25,000 captured Russian rifles and a million rounds to assist the insurrection. Poor planning and execution prevented the shipment reaching Ireland, and Casement himself, convinced that the German pledge was inadequate and that the uprising was doomed, landed on the Kerry coast on board a German submarine, only to be arrested by the British.

Notoriously, the British government tried to smear Casement before his execution by releasing extracts from his diaries detailing homosexual activities, though the diaries' authenticity is still disputed. Casement was hanged in London in August 1916. Forty-nine years later his remains were returned to Ireland, where he was given a state funeral.

which now comprised only the group that had opposed and broken away from Redmond. It was the council's intention to use the Volunteers as their main strike force in the rising. In January 1916 the six original members of the military council were joined by James Connolly, a revolutionary socialist who had done more than anyone to mobilize the desperately impoverished and exploited working people of Dublin. He brought with him a small but well-drilled militia group called the Irish Citizen Army (ICA). Originally established to protect protesting workers during the great Dublin Lockout of 1913, it was founded on the principle that *'the ownership of Ireland, moral and material, is vested by right in the people of Ireland'*.

THE EASTER RISING

By January 1916 the rebel leaders had agreed that the insurrection should be country-wide, both in Dublin and in the provinces, where the action would be supported by a shipment of German arms and (it was hoped) German troops. The time was set for Easter Sunday, 23 April, on which date supposedly routine Volunteer manoeuvres would be advertised as cover for the rising. Things began to go wrong shortly before the agreed date, when news of the planned rising reached the ears of the chief-of-staff of the Volunteers, Eoin MacNeill, whose opposition to armed rebellion was well known and who had therefore been kept in the dark by the military council. After initially acquiescing in the planned rising, MacNeill changed his mind and countermanded the rebels' mobilization orders by publishing a newspaper notice in which he cancelled all Volunteer movements on Easter Sunday. General confusion caused by conflicting commands, exacerbated by news that the landing of German

THE UNSUNG HEROES

The least appreciated contribution to the Easter Rising was the very considerable one made by women. Most famously, Countess Markievicz was the second-in-command in the rebel unit that occupied St Stephen's Green and was the only woman to be sentenced to death: *'I do wish you lot had the decency to shoot me,'* she rebuked the officer at Kilmainham Jail who informed her that her sentence had been commuted to life imprisonment on account of her sex. But the countess was one of many. Members of the *Cumann na mBan* (Women's League) and female members of Connolly's Citizen Army not only served as auxiliaries but were in the thick of the fighting in all the rebel garrisons except de Valera's at Boland's Mill: their role, as one female rebel put it, was *'to knit and darn, march and shoot'*.

This celebratory poster produced after the Easter Rising shows Countess Markievicz on the far right of the third row. Éamon de Valera is pictured second from left on the bottom row.

munitions on the west coast had failed, meant that most of the Volunteers outside Dublin stayed at home. Meeting in emergency session on the Sunday morning, the military council decided to postpone the start of the rising to the following day and to proceed with whatever forces they could muster.

In late morning on Easter Monday some 1200 Volunteers and 200 of Connolly's Citizen Army gathered at agreed meeting points. Facing little resistance, they then proceeded to occupy a number of strategically placed public buildings in the centre of the city, including the GPO, which served as the rebels' HQ and seat of the provisional government, the Four Courts, Jacob's biscuit factory, Boland's Mill, the South Dublin Union and St Stephen's Green. Crucially, however, they failed to take Dublin Castle and were unable to stop the flow of reinforcements into the city over the coming days. By the end of the week the British commander, General Sir John Maxwell, had some 20,000 troops at his disposal. The GPO, which by Thursday had been totally isolated from the other rebel positions, was then heavily shelled. Forced to evacuate the building, on Saturday 29 April the rebel leaders chose to surrender rather than see their men wiped out. Fighting with discipline from well-defended positions, only 64 rebels were killed (less than half the number of British soldiers and police). The use of artillery in densely populated areas led to high civilian casualties, with over 250 killed and many more injured.

AFTERMATH

In the midst of an appalling war, the outcome of which was still far from certain, the British reaction to the Easter Rising was predictable if hardly well judged. The rebels never sought to hide their links with Germany – the Proclamation even refers to *'our gallant allies in Europe'* – and the decision by the British authorities to execute the ringleaders may even have been what they desired. Certainly they would have welcomed the consequences of that decision. In the event only 15 of the 90 tried and sentenced to death by firing squad were actually executed, but an unpopular state of martial law was maintained until November 1916 and thousands were arrested by the security forces, nearly 2000 of whom were deported to England and interned. During the Rising the popular reaction had generally been tepid – a mixture of incomprehension and indifference – but a sense that the British response had been harsh and disproportionate quickly spread. Men who had been widely denounced as traitors only days earlier began to acquire the aura of heroes.

Politically, growing sympathy for the rebels was rapidly translated into ever-deepening alienation from Britain and renewed energy in the cause of Irish independence. To make matters worse, at the very time when all Irish affairs demanded the utmost sensitivity, the question of introducing conscription in Ireland was being vigorously debated in Westminster. Redmond, home rule and the whole cause of moderate nationalism were damaged beyond repair at this time. The biggest beneficiary, unexpectedly, was Sinn Féin, a hitherto somewhat peripheral organization that was wrongly credited with playing a major role in the rising and went on to crush the IPP in the 1918 general election. And it was two of the most prominent survivors of the Rising who would do more than anyone else to set the future direction of the Irish nation: Michael Collins, mastermind of the guerrilla campaign against the British in the War of Independence; and Éamon de Valera, rebel commander at Boland's Mill, who as Sinn Féin president, founder (in 1926) of Fianna Fáil and first *taoiseach* (prime minister) of the Irish Republic, was to dominate the politics of Ireland for half a century.

TIMELINE

Dec 1912 Ulster Volunteer Force formed to oppose home rule

Nov 1913 Irish Volunteers formed

4 Aug 1914 Britain declares war on Germany

28 Sept 1914 Third Home Rule bill becomes law

Aug 1915 IRB military council formed

24 April 1916 Start of Easter Rising; reading of Proclamation of Irish Republic

29 April 1916 Rebel leaders at GPO surrender unconditionally

3–12 May 1916 Execution of rebel leaders

1919–21 War of Independence (Anglo-Irish War)

ANNIVERSARY

In the 50th anniversary year of the Easter Rising, on 8 March 1966, Nelson's Pillar – a monument celebrating one of Britain's greatest heroes and an unloved reminder of British rule – was brought crashing down by an IRA bomb. The surviving plinth, briefly rechristened 'the Stump', was destroyed two days later by the Irish Army.

153

'The terrain was rather like the Sussex downland, with gentle swelling hills, folds and valleys, making it difficult at first to pinpoint all the enemy trenches as they curled and twisted on the slopes… Immediately in front, and spreading left and right until hidden from view, was clear evidence that the attack had been brutally repulsed. Hundreds of dead … were strung out like wreckage washed up to a high-water mark. Quite as many died on the enemy wire as on the ground, like fish caught in the net. They hung there in grotesque postures. Some looked as though they were praying; they had died on their knees and the wire had prevented their fall… How did our planners imagine that Tommies, having survived all other hazards – and there were plenty in crossing No Man's Land – would get through the German wire?'

CORPORAL GEORGE COPPARD

THE SOMME

❧ 1 July 1916 ❧

The bloodbath that finally buried the lie of the romance of war

George Coppard, a machine-gunner in the Royal West Surrey Regiment who survived the Somme offensive, here describes the appalling carnage that met his eyes on 2 July 1916, the day after the battle began. When the platoon officers' whistles had blown along the line of Allied trenches at Zero Hour (7.30 a.m.) on 1 July, wave after wave of troops from Britain and its empire – some 120,000 men in all – climbed the ladders and clambered 'over the top' and into No Man's Land. Their hopes that the German guns had been knocked out and the barbed wire cut by days of artillery bombardment were soon blown away, as they found themselves advancing into the teeth of pitiless machine-gun and mortar fire. *'You didn't have to aim,'* one German gunner recalled, *'We just fired into them'*. Whole battalions were decimated, *'mown down like grass'*. In a single day the British lost 57,470 men, 19,240 of them killed, the rest missing or wounded. Around 60 percent of the officers in attacking units were killed. These catastrophic casualties were rewarded by the

The remains of a wooded hillside near the River Somme, turned into a barren, blasted landscape by incessant artillery barrages.

The Western Front
1914–18

German troops reading, writing and smoking in a trench during a lull in hostilities. In wet and cold weather, conditions in the trenches became appalling, as rats fed on corpses and soldiers developed 'trench foot', which could lead to amputation.

paltriest of gains – less than 8 square kilometres (3 sq mi) of territory.

The first day of Britain's first major offensive on the Western Front had turned into the single most calamitous day in the history of the British army. The response of the British commanders was not, however, to withdraw and reconsider. The offensive lasted for 141 days in all, leading finally to combined casualties of over one million. Historians continue to dispute the impact that the Somme campaign had on the final defeat of Germany two years later, but in the popular imagination it quickly established itself as a symbol of futility – of wasted heroism and crass leadership, of 'lions led by donkeys'. The psychological scars left by the loss of a generation – the flower of European youth trampled in the mud and squalor of the trenches – ran even deeper than the physical ones. Wilfred Owen's *'old Lie'* – that it was glorious to die for one's country – had been exposed once and for all, the scales had fallen from people's eyes; it would never again be possible to blithely extol the romance of war.

STALEMATE ON THE WESTERN FRONT

In early August 1914 Kaiser Wilhelm II sent off his soldiers with the promise that they would be *'home before the leaves fall'*. The Schlieffen Plan, on which German hopes were pinned, indeed depended on rapid victory in the west, and in the early weeks of the war German forces made stunning progress, taking great swathes of Belgian territory and sweeping into northern France. But in early September, just as they seemed certain to take Paris, they were stopped bloodily in their tracks by an Anglo-French rearguard at the River Marne.

By November, as both sides were digging in along a front that would soon extend over 450 miles (720 km) from the Channel to the Swiss border, the deluded optimism of those who boasted the war would be 'over by Christmas' had become evident.

The static trench warfare that characterized the next four years of gruesome fighting on the Western Front was due in large part to blinkered military thinking that failed to meet the challenges posed by recent technological advances. Both infantry and horses were desperately vulnerable to the devastating firepower of machine guns and artillery, and at a time when the internal-combustion engine was still in its infancy, mobility on the battlefield virtually disappeared. At the same time, the field communication on which movement of troops and coordination of operations depended was massively cumbersome: it has been estimated that for every mile of front there were some 500 miles (800 km) of telephone cable, every inch of which was prone to failure and exposed to enemy action. In an age when attacking troops on the move were at so

LIONS AND DONKEYS

The Somme offensive has often been denounced as the paradigmatic case of 'lions being led by donkeys': a tragic tale of brave young men being needlessly sacrificed by the heartless stupidity of those in high command. In this view, Field Marshal Douglas Haig himself is held up as the arch bungler: failing to learn from his mistakes; stubbornly persisting with worn-out methods; refusing to abandon attacks even when it was clear to all that they could not succeed; utterly unrealistic in setting objectives that accorded with experience and available resources. The next push, for Haig, was always the one that would finally cause the enemy to buckle, so it was always a push worth making – whatever the human cost.

While there is some truth in this picture (as with any caricature), there is also hyperbole, and since the 1960s a number of

Field Marshal Douglas Haig commanded the British Expeditionary Force from 1915 to 1918.

revisionist historians have attempted to restore the battered reputations of Haig and his fellow commanders.

In a similar vein it is argued that the Somme, far from being a military failure, was in fact a significant victory and an important step towards Germany's defeat two years later. Certainly a degree of correction is due – it is unfair to blame Haig for failing to find answers to problems that others found insoluble; commanders schooled in the efficacy of the cavalry charge struggled to evolve tactics suited to attritional trench warfare. Even so, the case for complete absolution is hard to make.

Even if a link between the paltry gains won at the Somme and eventual victory in 1918 could be established, it would still be difficult not to conclude that the price paid – over a million young lives bloodily snuffed out – was far too high.

great a disadvantage when faced with well-dug-in defenders, it was almost inevitable that paralysis would quickly set in. In time, elaborate defensive systems developed, in which miles of trenchwork were linked by saps and communication trenches, reinforced by concrete dug-outs, and protected by machine-gun posts and belts of impenetrable barbed wire.

THE 'BIG PUSH'

Confronted with this stalemate, the Allied high command that met at Chantilly in December 1915 resorted to a plan for the 1916 campaign similar to those that had been tried and largely found wanting over the previous 15 months of fighting. As the Germans were in occupation of most of Belgium and a large tract of northern France, it was politically incumbent on the French and British commanders to remain on the offensive. The 'Race to the Sea' – the rapid extension of Allied and German lines to the Channel in late 1914 – had left the entire combat frontage filled and hence there was no exposed flank. The only option, it seemed, was to use the infantry to punch a hole through the German lines, having first softened up their defences with a sustained artillery bombardment, and then (in age-old military tradition) to drive the cavalry through the breach. The point chosen for the famous 'big push' was a 20-mile (32-km) length of front in the region of the Somme – a choice based not on any great strategic value but merely on the fact that it happened to be the junction of the British and French lines. The push, as later described in a British army statement, was to be 'slow, continuous, and methodical', continuing 'until the day when the enemy's resistance, incessantly hammered at, will crumple up'. The plan was originally championed by the French commander-in-chief, Marshal Joseph Joffre – his British counterpart, Douglas Haig, favoured an offensive further north. But following a massive German assault on critical French fortified positions around Verdun from February 1916, execution of the Somme offensive fell largely on Haig, and relief of the

Each battle would commence with an artillery bombardment, intended to destroy the front line of enemy defences before the infantry crossed No Man's Land on foot.

beleaguered French defenders further south at Verdun became a significant part of its purpose.

The preliminary artillery bombardment that was supposed to cut paths through the German defences was one of the heaviest ever staged. Over a period of eight days from 24 June 1916, over 1.6 million shells were fired into enemy positions. The most intense barrage of all, combined with the simultaneous explosion of 17 huge mines under key German strong points, served as a prelude to the first day of the battle. At dawn on 1 July, there was, according to an eyewitness report, *'a rolling thunder of shell fire, and the earth vomited flame, and the sky was alight with bursting shells. It seemed as though nothing could live, not an ant, under that stupendous artillery storm.'* But something could, and did, survive. Perhaps as many as a third of the British shells failed to explode, and many of those that did were not powerful enough either to penetrate the deep, concrete-shrouded German bunkers and dug-outs or to destroy the dense barbed-wire entanglements.

Far from eradicating their defences, the prolonged bombardment alerted the German commanders to the forthcoming assault and allowed them to bring forward reinforcements. Many of the German gunners and mortar-men escaped unscathed and were waiting for the Allied infantry as they emerged from their trenches at Zero Hour. In these chaotic early stages the chances of war remained unclear: *'flashes of hope, half-lights of expectation, hints of calamity only penetrated the smoke and dust and bullets that smothered the trenches'*, one journalist later recorded. Within a few days the scale of the horrors and meagreness of the gains began to emerge. In spite of the dreadful loss of life, few of the first-day objectives had been achieved. On the Allied right, in the southern section of the line, the French in particular had made significant progress, but the British on the left and in the centre had been almost entirely thwarted.

TIMELINE

4 Aug 1914 German forces invade Belgium

5–12 Sept 1914 German army repulsed at the Marne

Sept–Oct 1914 Race to the Sea extends opposing lines to the Channel

Dec 1915 Allies meet at Chantilly to determine 1916 campaign

Feb–Dec 1916 Germans assault French defences at Verdun

1 July–18 Nov 1916 The Somme offensive

11 Nov 1918 Ceasefire comes into effect on the Western Front

THE APOGEE OF BLOODY ATTRITION

The appalling casualties on the first day notwithstanding, the Somme campaign persisted for a further 140 days. The fighting was almost continuous, but periods of intense fighting across a broad front alternated with more focused engagements against enemy strong points. The battle is noteworthy for the first appearance of the tank, although it was more a marker for the future – the tank's impact at the Somme was slight. There were sporadic Allied successes, but all too often the Germans were able to plug breaches made in their line before they could be fully exploited. In the final three weeks of the offensive, from the end of September, heavy rain fell, turning No Man's Land, already churned up by incessant artillery fire, into an ocean of mud. Poor visibility made artillery aiming almost impossible, so futile attacks were launched against virtually untouched defences; casualties became heavier as men were sucked into the mud, to die choking in the filth. Determined to bring a less-than-totally-ignominious end to the campaign, Haig waited for something like a

THE COMING OF THE TANK

During the Somme offensive, the tank made its first appearance on the battlefield, supporting the British attack at Flers-Courcelette on 15 September 1916. *'Sinister, formidable, and industrious,'* the *Manchester Guardian* solemnly intoned, *'these novel machines pushed boldly into "No Man's Land", astonishing our soldiers no less than they frightened the enemy.'*

Initially known as the 'landship', the tank was developed under a cloak of great secrecy. When curious parties asked about the huge steel boxes that were being built, they were told they were water tanks for India. From then on, the name 'tank' became associated with the weapons we know today.

Early tanks were little more than armoured bulldozers designed to crush barbed wire and overcome trenches. Too slow and unreliable to make much impact at the Somme, by the final months of the war they had begun to demonstrate the potential that would make them such dominant weapons in later 20th-century conflicts.

The advent of the tank heralded the end of trench warfare, as the armoured vehicles were able to attack and destroy enemy trenches with little resistance.

victory, which at last came when Beaumont Hamel and Thiepval Ridge were finally captured. The fact that the capture of these had been set as a first-day objective must have been silently passed over. The scale of losses of the opening day was never repeated, but by the time the campaign ended on 18 November, after four and a half months of fighting, the total casualties exceeded one million. The British had lost nearly 420,000, including 125,000 dead, the French nearly 200,000, and the Germans around half a million.

By the end of the Somme offensive, the Allied forces had advanced on average about six miles (10 km) across the battlefront, to occupy a position that was strategically almost identical to the one that they had held 20 weeks earlier. For every two inches of ground gained, three Allied soldiers had been killed or wounded. Writing after the war, the Chief of the Imperial General Staff, Sir William Robertson, opined that the second objective of the Somme offensive (relief of the French at Verdun being the first) was to 'inflict as heavy losses as possible upon the German armies'. In the war of attrition which fighting on the Western Front had become, it is true (in a grisly sense) that the Allies' greater resources of manpower meant that they could probably afford their vast casualties at the Somme somewhat better than Germany could afford its not-quite-so-vast casualties. It is within the rules of this nasty numbers game that a German officer would describe the Somme as 'the muddy grave of the German field army'. And it is only in this attenuated sense that the Battle of the Somme can be seen as anything but a ghastly human tragedy.

To the bitter end

The fighting along the Western Front carried on for over two more years, without either side making any great advances. It was not until 1918 that the German army, using new weapons and tactics that were to prove successful 20 years later, broke the stalemate and advanced quickly through the French and British lines. But the war had taken its toll behind the lines. Without the materials and supplies needed for the advance, it faltered against the Allied counter-offensive, now bolstered by the arrival of American troops in 1917. At the eleventh hour of the eleventh day of the eleventh month the guns finally fell silent to mark the end of the war to end all wars.

The monumental arch commemorating the Somme in the Commonwealth cemetery at Thiepval. The names of more than 72,000 soldiers, 90 percent of whom fell in the First Battle of the Somme, are inscribed on the Portland stone plaques around its base.

'We had neither time nor space for burials, and the wounded could not be got away. They stayed with us and died, pitifully, with us, and then they rotted. The stench of the battlefield spread for miles around. And the sight of the limbs, the mangled bodies, and stray heads.'

John Raws, an Australian soldier, in a letter to his brother shortly before his death in August 1916

'The time for words is over.' As the cruiser *Aurora* opens fire, shaking the magnificent crystal chandeliers of the Winter Palace, a Bolshevik sailor places a rough boot on the menacing bronze Romanov double eagle that adorns the massive iron gates of the palace. The gates have been barred in a vain attempt to protect Russia's provisional government, but the sailor flings them wide open. Amid a crash of artillery and machine-gun fire, into the splendid interior floods a tide of Red Guards, screaming *'For peace! For bread! For land!'* Some workers and peasant soldiers rush into the tsarina's former apartments. First stupefied, then angered by the opulence within, they drive their bayonets through the thick, plush mattresses: the last vestiges of the Romanov dynasty are blown away in a blizzard of feathers. The bedraggled women soldiers and young cadets defending the palace swiftly surrender and the ministers of the provisional government, cowering in their council chamber, are arrested. Meanwhile, at the Congress of Soviets, Lenin takes the podium and announces: *'The workers' and peasants' revolution has triumphed!'*

PETROGRAD
7 November 1917

The storming of the Winter Palace marks the defining moment of the Russian Revolution

Such were the dramatic scenes in Petrograd in 1917 as Bolshevik revolutionaries stormed the Winter Palace, former residence of the last Romanov tsar, Nicholas II, and seat of the ineffectual provisional government that succeeded him. Or, more precisely – such was the course of events as portrayed at the climax of *October: Ten Days that Shook the World*, the film made by the great Soviet director Sergei Eisenstein to celebrate the tenth anniversary of the revolution. The 'Great October Socialist Revolution' (as it came to be officially designated) that swept Lenin and his revolutionary comrades to power needed a great climax, and Eisenstein, with his newsreel-style scenes of hobnailed boots on imperial eagles, provided it. The

In common with Sergei Eisenstein's famous portrayal of the event on film, this undated Soviet illustration depicts the storming of the Winter Palace as a heroic massed assault against a strongly defended position. In fact, the Winter Palace fell virtually without a shot being fired.

problem, for Soviet propagandists in need of a good story, was that the actual 'storming' was something of an anticlimax.

A GENTLE STORM

In most respects, the October Revolution (which actually took place in November, according to the Gregorian calendar now in use) was a well-staged coup d'état. The decision to overthrow the provisional government had been taken two weeks earlier and the date was carefully chosen so that power could be transferred to the All-Russian Congress of Soviets (elected regional councils), which was due to meet in Petrograd on 7–8 November. Starting early on 6 November, small units of Red Guards (essentially armed factory workers) began to occupy stations, bridges, telegraph agencies and other key installations in the capital. The almost bloodless rising was likened in one contemporary account to a *'changing of the guard'*, in which the *'weaker defence force, of cadets, retired; and a strengthened defence force, of Red Guards, took its place'*.

By the evening of 7 November, with most of Petrograd already in Bolshevik hands, the capture of the Winter Palace, the last refuge of the provisional government, was of largely symbolic importance. As in Eisenstein's version, the signal to move on the palace was given by a salvo fired by the cruiser *Aurora* on the Neva river at around 9.40 in the evening, but the salvo itself was blank. Another 30 or so shells were then fired at the palace from the Peter and Paul Fortress, only two of which actually found their mark. This was still enough, however, to convince most of those defending the palace – some Cossacks, young army cadets and a few hundred of the so-called Women's Death Battalion – to run away or surrender. When Red Guards and Bolshevik sailors finally moved in, they found most of the many doors open and undefended.

Leon Trotsky, co-architect of the Russian Revolution, perceptively analysed its anticlimactic conclusion:

> *'The final act seems … too brief, too dry, too businesslike – somehow out of correspondence with the historic scope of the events. The reader experiences a kind of disappointment. He is like a mountain climber, who, thinking the main difficulties are still ahead, suddenly discovers that he is already on the summit.'*

As usual, propaganda was called upon to remedy the shortcomings of history.

UNDERLYING TENSIONS

The provisional government that was unseated in the October Revolution had only been in place itself for a few months, from the time that Tsar Nicholas II had been forced to abdicate in March 1917 in the wake of the February Revolution. The immediate reason why matters came to a head in that year was the disastrous conduct of the war, but the underlying causes, though exacerbated by the war, had a longer history.

THE NEW CALENDAR

The Gregorian (New Style) calendar in use today was introduced by Pope Gregory XIII in 1582 to replace the Julian (Old Style) calendar, which by that date was out of step with the seasons by ten days. The change was not accepted in most Orthodox Churches till much later and was not introduced in Russia till February 1918. For this reason, according to the New Style calendar, the October Revolution occurred between 6 and 8 November.

THE MAD MONK

A decisive factor in breaking the age-old bond of loyalty between the Russian people and the Romanov dynasty was the baleful influence on the tsar's wife of the 'mad monk' Grigori Yefimovich Rasputin. The son of a peasant, the sinister but charming Rasputin worked his way into the affection and trust of the tsarina by using the mystical healing powers he claimed to possess to treat the haemophilia of the imperial couple's only son, Alexis.

Alexandra's unquestioning devotion to Rasputin became especially damaging after 1915, when the tsar took command of the army in person and left his wife to attend to matters at home. Mismanagement of affairs, aggravated by rumours of financial corruption, sexual liaisons and even collusion with the enemy, became so severe that a group of nobles, led by Prince Felix Yusupov, the tsar's nephew by marriage, hatched a plot to assassinate Rasputin in order to *save Russia and the dynasty from ruin and dishonour*. The manner of Rasputin's death, as recounted by Yusopov himself, did nothing to dispel the mystique surrounding the mad monk. Shot through the heart and pronounced dead, Rasputin nevertheless *leapt to his feet, foaming at the mouth. A wild roar echoed through the vaulted rooms, and his hands convulsively thrashed the air. He rushed at me, trying to get at my throat, and sank his fingers into my shoulder like steel claws. His eyes were bursting from their sockets.* After poisoned

Grigori Rasputin, pictured in 1914 seated between two of the tsar's advisers, Colonel Loma (left) and Prince Putianin.

food and drink had initially failed, it took five bullets before Rasputin slumped dead in the snow.

When Russia went to war against Germany and the other Central Powers in August 1914, it was an ailing giant, desperately ill prepared for a protracted conflict and deeply riven by long-standing social and political tensions. On the eve of war over three-quarters of some 150 million subjects of the vast Russian empire lived on the land, eking out a life of poverty on small plots of land. Things were little better in the towns and cities, where factory workers worked long hours in filthy conditions for paltry wages. Neither peasant nor worker

TIMELINE

1904–5 Russian army and navy humiliated in war with Japan

1905 First Russian Revolution leads to limited political reform

Aug–Sept 1914 Russian army heavily defeated at Tannenberg

Autumn 1915 Tsar takes personal control of battlefield operations

Dec 1916 Assassination of Rasputin

March–Nov 1917 Provisional government under Lvov and then Kerensky

March 1917 February Revolution ends the Romanov imperial dynasty; creation of Petrograd Soviet

15 March 1917 Nicholas II abdicates

July 1917 Final Russian offensive (Kerensky offensive) in First World War fails

Aug–Sept 1917 Kornilov Affair (coup) fails to re-establish order

6–8 Nov 1917 October Revolution overthrows Russian provisional government

7–8 Nov 1917 The Winter Palace is captured by Bolshevik revolutionaries

March 1918 Treaty of Brest-Litovsk marks Russia's formal exit from First World War

1918–21 Russian Civil War between anti-communist White Army and Red Army

1927 Eisenstein's film *October* commissioned by Soviet government

had any significant say in the decisions that affected their lives, as all power resided ultimately in the tsar, 'emperor and autocrat of all Russia', who was buttressed by a large land-owning aristocracy and who sat at the top of a huge bureaucracy of civil servants, whom he could appoint, dismiss or disregard at will. Frustrated peasants and workers, denied any real political expression, were naturally responsive to the calls of both liberal reformers and radical revolutionaries, who were variously clamouring for changes in government and society.

These tensions boiled over in early 1905, when a procession of over 150,000 marched on the Winter Palace in St Petersburg to present a petition to the tsar, demanding political representation, better working conditions and an end to the war with Japan, which since the previous year had brought one humiliating defeat after another. Losing control, Cossacks and police fired on the crowd, killing over 100 and causing public outrage that led to nationwide strikes, demonstrations and mutiny. Although the tsar

No Problem

Grand Duke Nikolai, the tsar's cousin and commander-in-chief of the Russian armies in the first year of the war, responded to the losses at Tannenberg (140,000 dead, wounded or captured) with typical aristo-cratic hauteur: *'It is an honour to make such a sacrifice for our allies.'*

himself was deeply opposed to any reform, the gravity of these events (which came to be known as the 1905 Revolution) forced him to make concessions, allowing various civil rights and the formation of a parliament (*duma*). This compromise did little to satisfy those who were now set on radical reform or revolution, and their suspicions were confirmed over the coming years, as Nicholas did everything he could to claw back the powers he had ceded and to prevent the *duma* taking a path of radical reform.

STUPIDITY OR TREASON?

Nicholas and his advisers embarked on war against Germany and its allies to honour Russia's treaty with France, but they also had ambitions of extending their own territory. There would have been hope, too, that military success would restore pride at home and help to heal the wounds in Russian society. Any such hopes must have been seriously dented in the early weeks of the war. At the Battle of Tannenberg, the first major engagement on the Eastern Front, the Russian Second Army was virtually wiped out, with the loss of 50,000 dead or wounded and another 90,000 taken prisoner. Ill-conceived strategy, dismal leadership, poor communications and intelligence, defective logistics and staff work, inferior equipment – all played a part in the Russian defeat and set the dominant tone for the following three years. By the middle of 1915 the Russian army had yielded in the 'Great Retreat' most of Russian Poland, Lithuania and Latvia to the German advance. Reacting to the catalogue of disaster, in autumn 1915 the tsar decided to take personal charge of operations in the field. It was an unwise decision that meant that subsequent military failures would be blamed on him. By 1917 Russian casualties had rocketed to 5.5 million dead and wounded, with a further 2.5 million captured.

Sure enough, the stream of bad news from the front was mirrored by a steady decline in the tsar's popularity. The demands of fighting a modern war had cruelly exposed the limitations of his senior officers (appointed from among his own courtiers) and the gross incompetence and corruption of his government. At the same time, Nicholas's own absence on campaign obliged him to leave management of affairs at home in the far-from-safe hands of his German wife, Alexandra, and her sinister mentor Rasputin (see The Mad

OPPOSITE Peasants from the countryside around St Petersburg, photographed in the 1890s, enjoy a rare moment of leisure. Although serfdom was abolished in 1861, the fact that most people in tsarist Russia continued to live in grinding poverty created a fertile seed-bed for revolution.

Tsar Nicholas II (centre) and his army commanders inspect a regiment during the First World War. Tsarist military leadership in this conflict was woefully inadequate, and after heavy defeats by Germany, Russian forces on the Eastern Front were effectively neutralized by the spring of 1915.

Monk, p.165). Damaging rumours spread that they were somehow in league with the German government and that the country's problems were due as much to treason as to stupidity.

PEACE, BREAD, LAND

The strains caused by feeding and equipping an army (however inadequately) were more than Russia's creaking economy could bear. By the beginning of 1917 food was in such short supply in the capital Petrograd that women had to wait on average 40 hours a week in bread queues. In a more or less spontaneous popular uprising against the tsar's government, food shortages and the war, Petrograd women workers decided in early March to go on strike, thereby starting a series of 'bread riots'. Over the following days around half the capital's industrial workforce – some 200,000 people – joined the protests. Tensions rose to boiling point as soldiers were ordered to fire into the unarmed crowds, but many of those sent in to break up the riots chose instead to side with the protesters. It soon became clear that, after more than three centuries in power, time for the Romanov dynasty had run out, and on 15 March 1917, realizing at last that his position was hopeless, Nicholas abdicated.

In an attempt to prevent insurrection from developing into outright revolution – and hence to protect their own positions and privileges – leading members of the imperial *duma* stepped forward to form a provisional government. From the outset, however, this ill-starred mixture of liberals and moderate socialists was hobbled by the presence alongside it of the Soviet of Soldiers' and Workers' Deputies – the so-called Petrograd Soviet, which was created just days before the tsar's abdication. As the government's first leader, Prince Lvov, noted, his administration was always '*an authority without power*', while the Soviet was '*a power without authority*'. In the end, coming off a very poor second in the division of 'dual power', the provisional government proved itself utterly incapable of establishing any sort of constitutional order and failed to satisfy any of the constituencies that were crying out for change. Industrial workers became ever more aggrieved as the economy lurched into deeper crisis, while reluctance to introduce much-needed land reform angered the peasants. Finally, and terminally, in spite of the growing clamour for peace, the government's policy of continuing the war came to grief in a disastrous summer offensive in which the Russian army lost amid the carnage any lingering will to fight and

NAME GAME

The city now known as St Petersburg was renamed Petrograd in 1914 and Leningrad in 1924. It reverted to its original name in 1991, following the break-up of the Soviet Union. It was the Russian capital from 1712 to 1918, when the Soviet authorities moved the centre of government to the Kremlin in Moscow.

began to disintegrate. A military coup led by General Lavr Kornilov to take control of the deteriorating situation failed, but the government itself and its new leader, Alexander Kerensky, were totally discredited in the process, ensuring that no military support was forthcoming when the Bolshevik coup was staged in November.

A radical socialist group with minority support at the start of the year, the Bolsheviks shrewdly distanced themselves from the provisional government, thus allowing them to present themselves at an opportune moment, under the banner 'Peace, Bread and Land', as the champions of the people's frustrated demands. The new Soviet government under Lenin was quick to encourage peasants to seize land, so eliminating the power of the old nobility, and wasted no time in suing for peace. The peace settlement they agreed to, however, was so humiliating that the country was quickly plunged into three years of bitter civil war. Tragically for the Russian people, the communist government that emerged at the end of that bloody ordeal was every bit as autocratic, bureaucratic and oppressive as the 300-year-old dynasty that it had replaced.

A painting in the Soviet 'socialist realist' style by Vladimir Serov showing Lenin addressing the Second All-Russian Soviet Congress in the Smolny Institute in Petrograd on 7 November 1917.

'Guernica, the most ancient town of the Basques and the centre of their cultural tradition, was completely destroyed yesterday afternoon by insurgent air raiders. The bombardment of this open town far behind the lines occupied precisely three hours and a quarter, during which a powerful fleet of aeroplanes consisting of three German types, Junkers and Heinkel bombers and Heinkel fighters, did not cease unloading on the town bombs weighing from 1,000 lbs downwards and, it is calculated, more than 3000 two-pounder aluminium incendiary projectiles. The fighters, meanwhile, plunged low from above the centre of the town to machine-gun those of the civilian population who had taken refuge in the fields.'

EYEWITNESS AND *TIMES* CORRESPONDENT GEORGE STEER

GUERNICA

❧ 26 April 1937 ❧

The aerial bombardment of a Basque town creates a symbol of the barbarism of war

Visiting the Basque town of Guernica just hours after it had been mercilessly bombarded by German and Italian aircraft, George Steer, the *Times* special correspondent on the Spanish Civil War, wired to London one of the most influential wartime reports ever filed. Soon to be syndicated around the world, Steer's cool and measured account immediately stirred up a storm of public indignation and outrage and, just as significantly, inspired the Spanish artist Pablo Picasso, working in Paris at the time, to produce what would prove to be, arguably, the most powerful anti-war statement ever made.

The most portentous aspects of the horrors visited on Guernica were highlighted by Steer later in his report:

'In the form of its execution and the scale of the destruction it wrought, no less than in the selection of its objective, the raid on Guernica is unparalleled in military history. Guernica was not a military objective ... The town lay far behind the lines. The object of the bombardment was seemingly the demoralization of the civil population and the destruction of the cradle of the Basque race.'

The town selected for attack was of great symbolic and cultural significance to the Basque people but had limited military value. The time and date chosen – 4.30 in the afternoon on a market day – were planned to maximize civilian casualties. The implication was clear: the objective was to achieve a military outcome (defeat of the Basque forces fighting for the Republic) by targeting non-combatants and so breaking the spirit of resistance among the population at large. And just as important as the tactic itself was the clear evidence of Axis involvement in its execution. Suddenly a small bombed-out Basque town had been elevated into a symbol of resistance to fascist aggression.

THE SPANISH CIVIL WAR AND THE BASQUES

Since the creation of the Second Republic in 1931, there had been a steady polarization of left and right in Spanish politics. In the general elections of February 1936 an uneasy alliance of left-wing factions, mainly communists and socialists, united as the Popular Front in a successful bid to keep the reactionary right out of power. As the new government instituted social and economic reforms, conservative politicians of the right began to conspire with the army to 'restore order' (as they saw it) and to protect the interests of the land-owning middle classes and of the (reactionary) Catholic Church. Over the following months there was a steady increase in politically inspired violence, which

The destruction wrought by German bombers on the Basque town of Guernica was a foretaste of the widespread carpet-bombing of European cities that took place during the Second World War.

finally erupted on 17 July in a military coup against the Republic. The success of the ensuing rebellion was patchy, however. While large areas came under rebel control, Madrid, Barcelona and most of the large cities remained in Republican hands. While the Nationalists were generally united under General Francisco Franco and well supplied with men and equipment by the fascist governments in Berlin and Rome, the Republicans remained a motley and ill-disciplined assemblage of different factions that often appeared keener on fighting each other than their opponents. They received considerable Soviet aid from Stalin but were blocked from obtaining arms legally from Britain, France and other nations that had signed and adhered to a non-intervention agreement (openly flouted by the Axis powers and the Soviet Union). The stage was set for a bitter period of civil conflict.

An important contingent in the Republican ranks were the Basques. Their aspirations towards regional self-government were openly scorned by the Nationalists, while the Madrid government had repaid their support by allowing them to form, in October 1936, an autonomous Basque republic (known by the Basque name 'Euskadi'). During the early months of fighting Euskadi became a virtual enclave, blockaded at sea and cut off by land from other loyalist areas, and at the end of March 1937 Franco launched a major assault on it. On the eve of the campaign Franco's general, Emilio Mola, issued a chilling proclamation, declaring that *'if submission is not instant, I will eradicate Vizcaya* [the Basque province], *beginning with the industries of war. I have more than sufficient means to do so'*. Mola proved himself as good as his word, and within a month news of the desperate Basque resistance – and of the attack on Guernica in particular – was being widely reported abroad.

THE WAR OF WORDS

International abhorrence aroused by the reports of Steer and others quickly ensured that the Guernica bombing achieved a level of notoriety that was scarcely warranted by its severity or, sadly, its uniqueness. Steer himself had witnessed Mussolini's bombings of civilians in Abyssinia. Indeed, the Guernica raid was not even the first such case in the Basque campaign of the Spanish Civil War, as similar methods had been used to similar effect just days earlier against the civilian population of the town of Durango. But thanks to Steer in particular, it was Guernica that gripped public attention.

The propaganda machines on both sides immediately whirred into action. In what Steer justly characterized as *'the most horrible and inconsistent lying'*, the Nationalists wavered between playing up the significance of Guernica as a military target, playing down the seriousness of the incident, and outright denial. This led, bizarrely, to their issuing a logic-mangling statement which, attempting to do all three at the same time, referred to a *'comparatively minor event such as the*

SEAT OF BASQUE CULTURE

Twenty miles (32 km) northeast of Bilbao, capital of the Vizcaya province, Guernica (Gernika in Basque) was the seat of the ancient Basque parliament and was described by José Antonio Aguirre, the Basque president in 1937, as the *'sanctuary which records the centuries of our liberty and our democracy'*. In the shade of the famous 'Tree of Guernica' (an ancient oak), the kings of Spain traditionally swore an oath to respect the democratic rights of Vizcaya in return for a pledge of allegiance. Despite its symbolic importance, in 1937 the town was small, with a population of less than 7000. It was not without strategic value, however, as Basque propagandists claimed; at the time of the raid there were several thousand retreating Republican soldiers and refugees in the town.

AN OCEAN OF PAIN AND DEATH

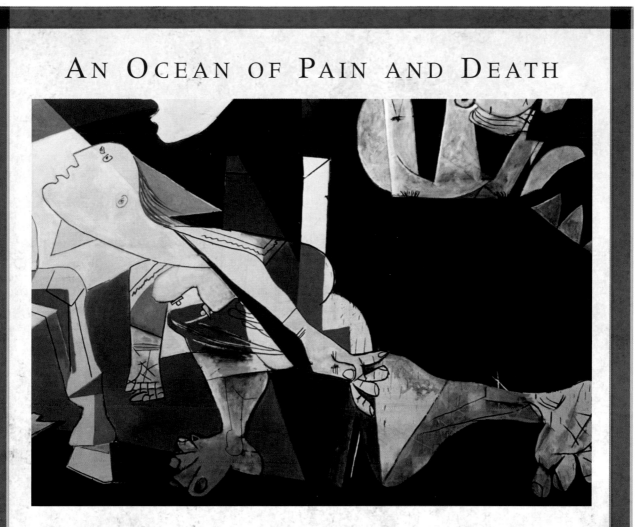

At the time of the Guernica raid, Pablo Picasso was working on a commission by the Spanish Republican government to produce a mural for the Spanish pavilion at the Exposition Universelle in Paris, which was due to open in June 1937. He had worked up a few preliminary sketches on the theme of the artist's studio, but on 1 May, two days after reading Steer's report in a French newspaper, he switched track and began work on what would become his most famous painting, *Guernica*. Over the following weeks, amid a frantic flurry of studies and revisions, he produced the vast canvas, nearly 8 metres (26 ft) long, in which he expressed his *'abhorrence of the military caste which has sunk Spain in an ocean of pain and death'*. Working in oil, he

Detail from Picasso's iconic painting Guernica. Basque nationalists have called for the picture to be moved to Bilbao.

created a monochrome nightmare of violence and terror, using visual metaphors from his recent work, including the dying horse, the bull and the weeping woman. To those shocked at this explosion of anger and outrage, he responded: *'Painting is not done to decorate apartments; it is an instrument of war against brutality and darkness.'* The artist forbade the painting to be moved to his native country until the republic had been restored. When the painting finally arrived in Madrid in 1981, one national newspaper announced: *'The war has ended!'*

hypothetical bombardment of a small town'. Eventually their foreign press bureau settled on the story that the Republicans themselves, desperate for a sensational propaganda coup, had sent '*Asturian miners to dynamite Guernica and set fire to its buildings'* and had then blamed it on the German bombers. Nazi propagandists in Berlin also tried to wash their hands of the business by attacking Steer's integrity and denouncing the '*lying Jewish press'* (they noted gleefully that the name of Steer's newspaper, when spelled backwards, became '*semit'*). Naturally enough, Basque propagandists set out to make the opposite case, suggesting that Guernica had no value as a military target at all and exaggerating the number of casualties, which they put at 1654 dead and 889 wounded.

For decades after the end of the civil war, interested parties battled over the facts behind the distortions of propaganda. For the defeated Basques, living with the calumny that the destruction of their cultural heartland had been the work of their own '*arsonists and dynamiters'* was just one among many cruel indignities heaped upon them by the victorious Francoist regime. In Spain itself, it was only after Franco's death in 1975 that the full truth began to emerge. The fact that the bombing was carried out by bombers and fighters of the Condor Legion, a supposedly 'volunteer' unit of Hermann Göring's resurgent German *Luftwaffe*, supported by Italian planes, was a poorly kept secret that Wolfram von Richthofen, commander of the Condor Legion at the time, made no effort to conceal in his diaries. Later, documents were uncovered that proved what had always been suspected – that the operation was carried out with the full knowledge of the Nationalist high command, including Franco himself. Recent research has also corrected distortions on the Basque side, such as the number of deaths, which is now reckoned to lie in the region of 250.

'THE DEEP, DEEP SLEEP OF ENGLAND'

Many who witnessed the destruction of Guernica and other atrocities of the Spanish Civil War saw them as a harbinger of the horrors that awaited the democracies of Europe if they failed to oppose the ruthless aggression and imperialist ambitions of Germany and Italy. At the end of his account of his own experiences in Spain, *Homage to Catalonia* (1938), George Orwell paints an idyll of England as a nation frozen in time: '*the men in bowler hats, the pigeons in Trafalgar Square, the red buses, the blue policemen – all sleeping the deep, deep sleep of England, from which I sometimes fear that we shall never wake till we are jerked out of it by the roar of bombs'*. Many of the intellectuals who rushed to Spain to join the International Brigades and to fight for the cause of the Republic were driven by the realization that failure to confront Franco in Spain would presently lead to a far more serious encounter with Hitler and Mussolini in the rest of Europe. The struggle in Spain came to symbolize the more general fight against fascism, and the ostrich-like policy of non-intervention in Spain was seen to mirror the greater folly of appeasement in the face of totalitarian aggression.

TIMELINE

14 April 1931 Spanish Second Republic proclaimed

Feb 1936 Left-wing Popular Front comes to power

17 July 1936 Failed right-wing military coup signals outbreak of Spanish Civil War

Oct 1936 Creation of Euskadi (autonomous Basque republic)

31 March 1937 General Mola launches Nationalist assault on Euskadi

26 April 1937 Bombing of Guernica

Aug 1937 Basque army surrenders to Nationalists

July 1937 Picasso's *Guernica* exhibited in Paris

1 April 1939 Franco declares civil war at an end

20 Nov 1975 Death of Franco begins transition to liberal democracy

Sept 1981 *Guernica* arrives in Spain

AFTERMATH

The bombing of Guernica had the desired effect. The defenders' will to resist evaporated, and by the end of April Nationalist forces were in full control of the town. The Basques themselves struggled on for four months, but their forces, starved of support and supplies, eventually surrendered at the end of August 1937. Around 7000 Basques had died in the fighting, but as many as 50,000 were later imprisoned or executed, and some 150,000 followed the Basque government abroad into decades of exile. The sufferings of the Basques mirrored those of Spain as a whole. By the time Franco declared the civil war at an end on 1 April 1939, around a third of a million people had been killed in the fighting or by disease. In the wake of the Nationalist victory, tens of thousands of those who had remained loyal to the Republic were executed and Spain itself remained internationally isolated and in the grip of a military dictatorship for nearly four decades.

'Guernica may be regarded as the most glaring example ... of the full application of the 'totalitarian war' principle in so far as such a war must take no humanitarian considerations of any kind into account. It is also regarded as an experiment in future German warfare, and Guernica is aptly described by a French observer as "Göring's air manoeuvres" – at the expense of innocent Spaniards.'

MANCHESTER GUARDIAN, 1 MAY 1937

On Sunday 7 December 1941 early cloud over the Hawaiian island of Oahu parted, promising a warm and sunny day for the men at the US naval base at Pearl Harbor. Many would have been looking forward to a day at the beach, swimming and surfing. At 7.55 the stillness of the morning, till then broken only by the tolling of church bells, was shattered by the arrival of a dive bomber, the first of more than 350 aircraft that would sweep across the island over the next two hours. Seeing a blast of dirt and smoke as the first bomb smashed into the ground alongside Battleship Row, Logan Ramsey, an officer on duty at the Command Centre, dashed to the radio room and frantically sent off a message: *'Air raid, Pearl Harbor, this is no drill!'* An earthier mix of surprise and urgency was shown by an ensign on board the USS *Oklahoma*, who had just seen a torpedo crash into a cruiser. Running to the soon-to-be-stricken ship's PA system, he bellowed: *'All hands, man your battle stations! This is no s**t, Goddam it! Jap planes are bombing us!'*

PEARL HARBOR
⇥ *7 December 1941* ⇤

A stunning surprise attack brings the USA into the Second World War

As Ramsey's message came through, shock in Washington was no less extreme. *'My God,'* gasped Secretary of the Navy Frank Knox; *'this can't be true, this must mean the Philippines.'* *'No, sir,'* replied Admiral Harold Stark, Chief of Naval Operations, *'this is Pearl.'* The tangled mess of misjudgement, negligence and intelligence failures that underlay the disaster would take decades to unravel, but the consequences of the widespread incompetence were immediately obvious. A major task force of the Imperial Japanese Navy had been allowed to strike a hammer blow at the very heart of the US Pacific Fleet. Six of the eight battleships anchored at the base that day were sunk, the other two damaged; three destroyers, three cruisers and four other vessels were also sunk or disabled. Nearly 300 planes

Sailors in a motor launch rescue a survivor from the USS West Virginia, *hit by seven torpedoes and two bombs while at anchor on Battleship Row at Pearl Harbor. She settled on an even keel and, like most of the battleships sunk in the Japanese raid, was raised and restored to service.*

TIMELINE

Sept 1931 Japanese extend control in Chinese state of Manchuria

July 1937 Start of Second Sino-Japanese War

Sept 1940 Japanese army moves into northern Vietnam (part of French Indochina)

Sept 1940 Germany, Italy and Japan become allies in Tripartite Pact

July 1941 Japan completes its occupation of Indochina, prompting imposition of US sanctions

7 Dec 1941 Japan launches a surprise attack on the US naval base at Pearl Harbor

8 Dec 1941 US Congress declares war on Japan

11 Dec 1941 Germany and Italy declare war on the USA

25 Dec 1941 The British colony of Hong Kong falls to Japan

15 Feb 1942 Fall of Singapore completes Japanese occupation of Malaya

8 March 1942 Allies in Dutch East Indies (Indonesia) surrender

6 May 1942 US forces in the Philippines surrender

June 1942 Japanese naval strength terminally weakened by defeat at Midway

were hit, most of them while still parked on the ground and more than half damaged beyond repair. Among military personnel, there were over 3400 casualties, more than 2300 of them killed. And the price the Japanese paid for delivering this juddering blow? The loss of 29 aircraft, six submarines (five of them midgets), and fewer than 100 men.

At least, that was the *immediate* price the Japanese paid. For the very next day US president Franklin D. Roosevelt made perhaps his most famous speech before Congress, declaring that 7 December 1941 would be '*a date which will live in infamy*'. On that same day Congress, previously sharing the American people's general aversion to getting embroiled in a 'foreign war', united behind the president and voted to declare war on Japan. And within days, in accord with their Tripartite Pact with Japan, Germany and Italy had declared war on America. '*We are all in the same boat now,*' Roosevelt observed to British prime minister Winston Churchill. And the latter had no doubt of the impact his new ally would make: '*Hitler's fate was sealed. Mussolini's fate was sealed. As for the Japanese, they would be ground to powder.*'

EASTERN MENACE

During the 1930s Japan had grown into an ever more menacing presence in eastern Asia. At the beginning of the decade, Japan's imperial and expansionist ambitions were evident in the so-called Manchurian incident, when the huge, resource-rich northern Chinese region of Manchuria was occupied, turned into the puppet state of Manchukuo and subjected to rapid economic exploitation. By 1937 local conflicts and border incidents had escalated into a full-scale war between China and Japan, and over the next few years Japanese forces conquered a large part of northern China. Tokyo's hunger for raw materials, lacking at home and essential for its war economy, prompted covetous glances towards British, French and Dutch possessions in the Far East. Emboldened by the fall of France to Hitler in June 1940, Japan occupied northern Vietnam in September. In the same month the Tokyo government signed the Tripartite Pact with fascist Germany and Italy, a move that was specifically intended (according to the German foreign minister von Ribbentrop) to deter the '*American war-mongers*', by showing them that '*if they enter the present struggle, they will inevitably have to contend with the three great powers as adversaries*'.

In his 'infamy' speech of 8 December, Roosevelt spoke of Japan's '*unprovoked and dastardly attack*', but in the eyes of the Japanese there had been no lack of provocation. In the grip of the Great Depression, the USA had initially been slow to react to Japan's project of expansion, doing little more than supplying limited aid to the beleaguered Chinese. America had enormous leverage, however, as resource-starved Japan was dependent on its neighbour across the Pacific for much of its imports of vital materials, including oil and steel. From early 1940 the USA began to restrict exports, and following Japan's occupation of the rest of Indochina in July 1941,

Japanese assets in the USA were frozen and a full embargo on trade in oil, scrap metal and other strategic goods was put in place. Throughout 1941 diplomatic negotiations aimed at a peaceful resolution were conducted between Tokyo and Washington, but there was little trust or common ground, and by November talks had reached a virtual deadlock: the Japanese demanded a free hand in China and exports to be restored to former levels; the Americans insisted on complete withdrawal from China and Indochina.

PLANNING FOR 'GREATER EAST ASIA'

Convinced that diplomacy was bound to fail and that war with the USA was now inevitable, the Japanese military planners set about devising a strategy that would allow them to improve and consolidate their position in Asia while securing an independent supply of raw materials. With the Dutch already defeated by Hitler and Britain in danger of suffering the same fate, there seemed every chance that a co-ordinated advance southwards could rapidly seize British Malaya and Singapore and the Dutch East Indies (Indonesia), which were weakly defended, and the American Philippines. Around their newly acquired territories the planners envisaged establishing a fortified

Japanese troops raise their arms in triumphant salute near the city of Nanjing, then the Chinese capital, in 1937. When they took the city in December of that year, they conducted a series of terrible atrocities against its citizens, massacring up to 300,000 people.

perimeter, extending from Burma to the Marshall Islands and comprehending Southeast Asia and most of the western Pacific. The huge resources of the conquered territories could then be exploited to feed the mighty military-industrial complex that would be needed to defend them against counterattacks from the defeated imperial nations. Repulsed, the latter would eventually tire and sue for peace, allowing Japan to retain its newly won empire.

As matters stood in 1941, the one clear obstacle to Tokyo's strategy to create what it euphemistically called a 'Greater East Asia Co-Prosperity Sphere' was US power in the Pacific. And it was one man in particular – Admiral Isoroku Yamamoto, commander-in-chief of the Combined Fleet – who unwaveringly saw what had to be done: *'Japan must deal the US Navy a lethal blow at the outset of the war. Only thus can she fight with any reasonable prospect of success.'* Delivering that 'lethal blow' would be fraught with risk, but Yamamoto had (in the words of a colleague) a 'gambler's heart'. He had no doubt where the blow must fall: Pearl Harbor.

Admiral Isoroku Yamamoto, the brilliant Japanese naval strategist who masterminded the attack on Pearl Harbor. His death in 1943, when US fighters shot down his plane over the island of Bougainville, dealt a devastating blow to the Japanese war effort.

OPERATION HAWAII

Yamamoto's plan, codename Operation Hawaii, was to use a powerful naval task force as a platform to launch a massive aerial attack on the US base in Hawaii. The minimum objective was to knock out the US fleet for long enough to allow the southern advance through Southeast Asia and the Philippines to be completed and the Japanese positions to be consolidated. Under the command of Vice Admiral Chuichi Nagumo, the task force, including all six of the navy's regular aircraft carriers, sailed from Hitokappu Bay in the Kurile Islands on 26 November and had reached a point some 270 miles (432 km) north of Hawaii by 6 December. With strict radio silence observed, they evaded detection all the way.

At 6.00 on Sunday 7 December the first wave of 183 planes, including torpedo planes, bombers and fighters, took off from the carriers. *'It was like the sky was filled with fireflies,'* one Japanese pilot recalled. Just under two hours later they reached Oahu. Commander Mitsuo Fuchida, leader of the first wave, gave the prearranged signal – *'Tora! Tora! Tora!'* (*'Tiger! Tiger! Tiger!'*) – indicating that complete tactical surprise had been achieved. The dive bombers and the slow-moving torpedo planes – sitting ducks if the anti-aircraft gunners had been waiting – swooped down to attack the ships moored along Battleship Row, while fighters split off to strafe the US planes neatly lined up on the Hickam and Wheeler

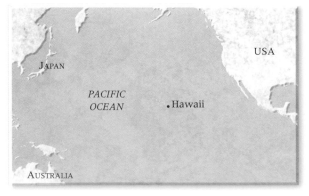

airfields. The first phase of the assault lasted little more than half an hour, but most of the damage was done in that time. Most spectacular of all, the USS *Arizona*, hit in the magazine, exploded with a terrible 'whoosh!', as a huge sheet of flame engulfed the forward section and shot hundreds of feet in the air. The second wave of 168 planes, all bombers and fighters, arrived at 8.40 and carried on the mayhem for a further hour.

Japanese A-6M ('Zero') fighter-bombers warming up on the deck of the aircraft carrier Shokaku *before the raid on Pearl Harbor.*

THE SLUMBERING GIANT

Japan's 'sneak attack' at Pearl Harbor had caught the US forces (as one sailor recalled) *'in a state of complete nonreadiness'*. The systemic failures in both Oahu and Washington were in many ways hard to excuse. At the beginning of 1941 a high-level US Navy report had highlighted the strong possibility, in the event of war with Japan, that *'hostilities would be initiated by a surprise attack upon the Fleet or the Naval Base at Pearl Harbor'*. Less than two weeks before the attack, on 27 November, a 'war warning' sent to all bases, including Hawaii, advised that diplomacy had broken down and that *'hostile action was possible at any moment'*. In spite of these and other warnings, the commanders on Oahu persisted in the

BACK DOOR TO WAR?

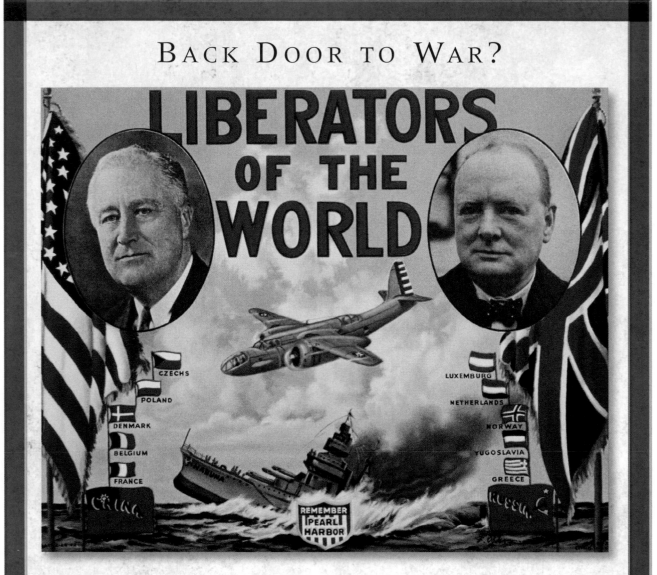

E ra-defining events in history are a magnet to revisionists and conspiracy theorists, and Pearl Harbor is no exception. Roosevelt – so the theory goes – was desperate to enter the war in order to prevent a German victory in Europe and to save Britain but was inhibited by public opposition to direct involvement in a foreign war. To open a 'back door' to war, therefore, he imposed trade embargoes and obstructed negotiations in the full knowledge that such moves would provoke a Japanese attack and thereby transform public opinion. Much of this is not in dispute. Roosevelt made little effort to hide

This US propaganda poster shows Roosevelt and Churchill and urges all the Allies to 'Remember Pearl Harbor'.

his sympathy for Britain and was quite willing to stretch the notion of neutrality to breaking point, declaring that America must be '*the great arsenal of democracy*' and introducing measures that made the USA a belligerent in all but name. And no one denies that the path to war was opened up by the Japanese attack. What is lacking is any firm evidence that the president and his advisers deliberately manipulated events to cause such an outcome.

view that the main threat lay in sabotage and allowed normal Sunday routine to continue. Just hours before the attack, the first strike wave of aeroplanes was picked up on radar and one of the Japanese midget submarines was spotted, but the warnings were misread and the scale of the danger not properly understood. Yet the commanders on the ground were themselves very poorly served by their superiors in Washington, who failed to pass on vital messages that had been intercepted and deciphered and included many clues that the Japanese planners were envisaging an aerial attack.

It is often said that Pearl Harbor was a tactical triumph that proved to be a strategic disaster – that Japan, in the very act of winning the battle, lost the war. Yet the triumph, such as it was, could and should have been more emphatic. It was pure chance that the three aircraft carriers assigned to the Pacific Fleet were not at the base on the day of the attack and thereby escaped. And if the cautious Nagumo had decided to launch a third strike against the shore facilities and oil reserves (as his more audacious subordinates urged), far greater and longer-lasting damage might have been inflicted on the US position in the Pacific. Yet the attack in fact achieved what Yamamoto had predicted: a six-month window in which the forces of Japan rampaged through Southeast Asia and the Pacific, sweeping aside weak opponents to capture Hong Kong, Malaya, Singapore, the Philippines, the Dutch East Indies and most of New Guinea within just five months. Yamamoto never supposed that Japan could prevail in the long term against the vastly superior US economy, set on a proper war footing. His mistake was to suppose that the USA would not have the stomach for the long fight and would wish to reach an accommodation with the new 'Greater Japan'. What he had actually done, as Nagumo feared, was *to wake a slumbering giant and fill her with a terrible resolve*.

ANOTHER PEARL HARBOR

The physical damage caused on 7 December 1941 was quickly made good. Not so the psychological trauma. On the following day Roosevelt vowed that the USA must *'make very certain that this form of treachery shall never endanger us again'*, and the cries *'Remember Pearl Harbor!'* and *'Never again!'* have informed US foreign and defence policy ever since. Most recently and controversially, parallels were immediately drawn between Pearl Harbor and the 9/11 attacks in New York and Washington, and the subsequent 'war on terror' was explicitly premised on the 2001 attacks as 'another Pearl Harbor'.

'Yesterday, December 7, 1941 – a date which will live in infamy – the United States of America was suddenly and deliberately attacked by naval and air forces of the Empire of Japan... Always will we remember the character of the onslaught against us. No matter how long it may take us to overcome this premeditated invasion, the American people in their righteous might will win through to absolute victory... I ask that the Congress declare that since the unprovoked and dastardly attack by Japan on Sunday, December seventh, a state of war has existed between the United States and the Japanese Empire.'

PRESIDENT FRANKLIN D. ROOSEVELT, SPEECH TO CONGRESS, 8 DECEMBER 1941

'Troops without ammunition or food. Effective command no longer possible. 18,000 wounded without supplies or dressings or drugs. Further defence pointless. Collapse inevitable. Army requests immediate permission to surrender in order to save lives of remaining troops.' This desperate radio message, sent to Hitler by General Friedrich Paulus from his HQ in Stalingrad on 24 January 1943, elicited a stern reply from the Führer: *'Surrender is forbidden. Sixth Army will hold their positions to the last man and the last round and by their heroic endurance will make an unforgettable contribution toward the establishment of a defensive front and the salvation of the Western world.'*

STALINGRAD

⤛ *31 January 1943* ⤜

The bloody struggle that terminally reversed Hitler's fortunes on the Eastern Front

Paulus obeyed the order to save the Western world – for another week, at least. By the end of January 1943 the German Sixth Army, which had begun its assault on the city of Stalingrad on the Volga river nearly five months earlier, had been reduced from nearly a third of a million men to just over 90,000. The meagrest of rations, supplemented by the odd rat and some horsemeat, had dried up completely with the loss of the last airfield, while the temperature had fallen as low as –30°C (–22°F). The emaciated and frostbitten remnant, squeezed by advancing tanks and infantry and pounded from all sides by a relentless barrage of guns and mortars, had been split into two small pockets in the shattered ruins of the city. On the last day of the month Soviet forces finally overran the pocket in which Paulus had set up his headquarters. Slumped on his bed and utterly dejected, Paulus – a field marshal of one day's standing – more or less silently acquiesced in the surrender. The soldiers in the second pocket fought on until 2 February.

The battle that had finally come to an end was one of the bloodiest in human history. Exact figures are not known, but it is estimated that the Soviet Red Army suffered over 1.1 million casualties, of whom 480,000 were killed. On the Axis side, the Germans are believed to have lost around 150,000 dead and wounded, while their allies – Romanians, Italians and Hungarians – lost many tens of thousands more. Of the 91,000 taken prisoner after the battle, only a small fraction – little more than 5000 – ever returned home; the rest died of their wounds or perished in labour camps. But the impact of the Battle of Stalingrad went far beyond physical loss and trauma. Used to winning quick victories and inflicting massive casualties, the Wehrmacht had been stopped in its tracks and its Blitzkrieg tactics blunted. The *'whole rotten structure'* which Hitler had predicted would come crashing down with a single kick had suddenly acquired an air of unexpected solidity. The Red Army, accustomed to chaotic retreats and stratospheric casualties, had shown astonishing tenacity and stamina under a new generation of competent officers. Above all, the Soviet

Soviet troops cross a moonscape of blasted buildings in the beleaguered city of Stalingrad. Every building and street was bitterly fought for.

TIMELINE

Aug 1939 Germany and the Soviet Union sign the Non-aggression Pact

22 June 1941 Axis forces begin invasion of Soviet Union (Operation Barbarossa)

Aug 1941 Siege of Leningrad begins (ends in Jan 1944)

Sept 1941 Fall of Kiev opens up the Ukraine

28 June 1942 Launch of the summer campaign on the Eastern Front (Operation Blue)

Sept 1942 Battle of Stalingrad begins

19 Nov 1942 Zhukov launches massive Soviet counteroffensive (Operation Uranus)

Dec 1942 Attempt to relieve Stalingrad pocket (Operation Winter Storm) fails

31 Jan 1943 Field Marshal Paulus surrenders German Sixth Army

people had demonstrated an almost limitless willingness to make sacrifices in the cause of resisting the German invaders. Many further sacrifices lay ahead in the Great Patriotic War, but the tide had turned. And the writing was on the wall for Hitler and the Axis powers.

OPERATION BARBAROSSA

In August 1939 the German and Soviet foreign ministers, von Ribbentrop and Molotov, signed a non-aggression pact. From the start it was an unholy marriage of convenience, an alliance of two totalitarian regimes which for different reasons needed to buy time. Stalin was desperate to avoid war at a time when his armed forces were weak and unprepared, while Hitler, with matters in the east put on hold, would have a free hand to turn his attention to Poland and to matters on his western frontier. But for Hitler, who had never hidden his detestation of Soviet communism, an agreement that ran counter to every ideological principle – *'a stain on our reputation'*, as propaganda minister Joseph Goebbels later called it – was never meant to last. A basic tenet of National Socialism (Nazism), outlined in *Mein Kampf* (1925), was that large tracts of territory in eastern Europe and western Russia should be occupied, the Slavic inhabitants evicted or enslaved, and their land colonized as *Lebensraum* ('living space') for the Nazi 'master race'. Stalin had always been in the cross-hairs, so it was no surprise (except, bizarrely, to Stalin himself) when, following the fall of France in June 1940, Hitler turned his gaze eastwards.

Delayed by failure to defeat Britain, the German invasion of the Soviet Union, codenamed Operation Barbarossa, finally got underway on 22 June 1941. It was a colossal undertaking. According to the ambitious plan, over three million troops from Germany and its allies, divided into three Army Groups (North, Centre and South), would employ huge Blitzkrieg pincer movements to destroy the bulk of the Red Army along the long German–Soviet border. When this had been achieved, Leningrad, Moscow and the Ukraine would be occupied.

Starting off with a string of swift and stunning victories against the ill-prepared Soviet forces, the campaign very nearly succeeded. By the autumn the Axis drive had penetrated deep into Soviet territory; Leningrad had been encircled and some German tanks had approached within 20 miles (32 km) of Moscow. In the south, however, the Axis forces soon ran into difficulties caused by stiffer Soviet resistance and lines of communication stretched to breaking point by the vast distances involved. A month into the campaign, Hitler diverted panzers (mobile armoured units) from their drive on Moscow, ordering them south to reinforce the assault on Kiev. In its immediate goal the redeployment worked well – Kiev fell in September, with heavy losses, and opened up the Ukraine – but the momentum of the campaign as a whole had been lost. The advance on Moscow, renewed at the end of September, made stuttering progress before being halted by the onset of winter and a partially successful Soviet counterattack.

OPERATION BLUE

Bolshevism, according to Goebbels, was supposed to *'collapse like a house of cards'* and to take Stalin and the Soviet state with it. But Barbarossa, scheduled to be over in a matter of months, had not quite followed the Führer's script. True, staggering losses had been inflicted on the Red Army – over three million of its soldiers were dead and as many again had been taken prisoner – and vast tracts of Soviet land had been captured. But nearly a million of the invading force had been killed or injured too, and crucially, the *'whole rotten structure'* may have creaked horribly but it hadn't quite fallen down. With the USA now beginning to flex its huge industrial and military muscle in the Allied cause, it was imperative to tidy things up on the Eastern Front in 1942.

The basic objective of the 1942 campaign, codenamed Operation Blue, was to starve the Russian war economy of fuel and so bring the Red Army to a standstill. To this end the Führer shifted his focus south, directing the bulk of his forces against the oilfields of Baku, east of the Caucasus Mountains. Beginning in late June, one force pushed south into the Caucasus, while another moved east towards the Volga. By cutting the Volga, Hitler aimed to block communications (including movement of oil) between north and south of the Soviet Union, but just weeks into the campaign he chose to complicate matters by insisting on the capture of Stalingrad (modern Volgograd), supposedly to prevent a Soviet counterattack being launched from east of the Volga. Just as in the previous year, the campaign made a brilliant start, as

A German armoured column advancing through western Russia during Operation Barbarossa. Initial gains were impressive, but the German thrust foundered on dogged Soviet resistance and the sheer manpower available to Stalin.

PAVLOV'S HOUSE

One man and one house in particular came to symbolize the heroic struggle of the Soviet forces in Stalingrad against the Nazi invaders. On 27 September 1942 Yakov Pavlov, a sergeant in a machine-gun unit, led a small band of men who occupied a four-storey apartment block overlooking 9 January Square that stood squarely across the German line of advance to the Volga. *'They bombarded us from the air,'* Pavlov later recalled. *'Our house was assaulted by heavy tanks, we lived under heavy artillery fire. Machine guns were firing without stop. Sometimes we ran out of ammunition. We didn't have enough water and food. We couldn't breathe, because of dust and ashes.'* Yet Pavlov and his men held on for an astonishing 58 days before being relieved on 24 November, lifting Soviet spirits and sapping the morale of the Germans.

the German mechanized units, supported by the *Luftwaffe*, rolled hundreds of miles across the vast and unending steppe. *'The Russian is finished,'* cried a jubilant Hitler – prematurely.

THE BATTLE FOR STALINGRAD

By late August Paulus's Sixth Army had reached the outskirts of Stalingrad. Following a hail of incendiary bombs that reputedly left some 40,000 civilians dead, the German troops moved through the smouldering city, with the object of taking control of the Volga and so preventing supplies and reinforcements reaching the Soviet defenders. But the defending forces, principally the Soviet 62nd Army under Lieutenant General Vasily Chuikov, were not ready to roll over. *'There is no land across the Volga,'* Chuikov beseeched his men – a message that was no doubt reinforced by Stalin's infamous Order Number 227, which demanded that every inch of Soviet soil be defended on pain of death.

Troops of Paulus's Sixth Army in a ruined factory in Stalingrad. As winter and hunger set in, some German soldiers even resorted to cannibalism.

Accustomed to taking whole cities in days, the German soldiers suddenly found themselves fighting against desperate men (and women) who measured their lives in hours, not years, and turned *'every trench, every pill box, every rifle pit, every ruin'* into a fortress. The masters of Blitzkrieg had been reduced to fighting in factories, cellars and sewers, *'not for individual buildings and shops, but for every step of a staircase'*. As the grisly stalemate dragged on, Hitler diverted armoured units from the Caucasus, leaving the southern advance too weak to make further headway. The oilfields remained in Soviet hands, subverting the main purpose of the campaign.

The first frosts and snows of winter in Stalingrad settled on Axis soldiers who were exhausted, hungry and demoralized. As more and more of the best troops were sucked into the urban fighting from outside, the job of guarding the flanks fell increasingly to the inferior armies of Germany's allies, mainly Romanians and Italians. Stalin's talented military deputy, General Georgy Zhukov, saw an opportunity to launch a counteroffensive. Undetected by German intelligence, a huge force of a million men, 900 tanks and 1100 aircraft was brought together to execute Operation Uranus. Starting on 19 November, two massive armoured strikes were launched to the north and south of the city, driving into the weak flanks, which quickly gave way. Just four days later, the two pincers of the attack linked up west of Stalingrad, completing a classic encirclement that trapped nearly 200,000 German troops. An Axis attempt to break the cordon (codename Winter Storm) was made in December, but Paulus was expressly ordered not to break out and the operation came to nothing. As food, fuel and ammunition began to run out, the noose tightened around the Sixth Army. Paulus was well aware that he and his men were doomed: '*You are talking to dead men,*' he numbly observed to a liaison officer flown in by Hitler.

BIG MOTHER

Named Tsaritsyn till 1925 and Stalingrad till 1961, Volgograd is today an important industrial town of over 1 million inhabitants that extends for 50 miles (80 km) along the west bank of the Volga. On the Mamayev Kurgan, a hill rising in the centre of the city, a massive statue of a female warrior was erected in 1967 to commemorate the events of 1942–3. Weighing 7900 tons, the 'Motherland Calls' statue measures 85 metres (280 ft) from the plinth to the tip of the huge sword she holds aloft.

A POISONED CHALICE

On 30 January 1943 Hitler promoted General Friedrich Paulus to field marshal, observing as he did so that no German of that rank had ever surrendered or been taken alive. Ignoring the hint to fight to the death or take his own life, Paulus surrendered the next day and was taken prisoner. '*What hurts me most,*' Hitler commented afterwards with regard to the promotion, '*is that … I wanted to give him this final satisfaction … He could have freed himself from all sorrow and ascended into eternity and national immortality, but he prefers to go to Moscow.*' Paulus himself, who spent ten years in Soviet captivity, contemptuously dismissed the Führer's lofty bombast: '*I have no intention of shooting myself for that Bohemian corporal.*'

'*From storey to storey, faces black with sweat, we bombard each other with grenades in the middle of explosions, clouds of dust and smoke, heaps of mortar, floods of blood, fragments of furniture and human beings … Stalingrad is no longer a town. By day it is an enormous cloud of burning, blinding smoke; it is a vast furnace lit by the reflection of the flames. And when night arrives, one of those screeching howling bleeding nights, the dogs plunge into the Volga and swim desperately to gain the other bank. The nights of Stalingrad are a terror for them. Animals flee this hell; the hardest stones cannot bear it for long; only men endure.*'

LIEUTENANT WEINER, GERMAN OFFICER AT STALINGRAD

'I saw piles of glasses for little children. That is what the Nazis were like – when they murdered the children they didn't even throw away their broken glasses. They kept them all and stored them away meticulously … It wasn't only glasses and shoes and clothes, of course. There were also enormous bundles of women's hair. At first I didn't realize what it was, then somebody told me – one of the intelligence officers: the hair of women killed by the Germans. And I asked, "How many women do you have to murder to get that much hair?" It's a horrible thing even to think about and a terrible thing to see … I had tears in my eyes. The atrocities I saw there, committed by the Germans, were terrible, dreadful, the worst thing you could imagine.'

RUSSIAN GENERAL VASILY PETRENKO

AUSCHWITZ
27 January 1945

The site of the greatest mass murder in history is discovered by the Red Army

It took something special – specially dreadful – to move a Soviet officer to tears: a young colonel who had witnessed many atrocities and become battle-hardened in some of the most appalling fighting of the Second World War. *'I had seen hanged people and burned people. But still I was unprepared for Auschwitz.'* More than half a century later, Vasily Petrenko was still haunted by the memory of the horrors that met the eyes of the Red Army soldiers who liberated the biggest and most terrible of the Nazi death camps on 27 January 1945.

At the end of 1944, as Soviet troops were closing in, SS officers who administered the Auschwitz-Birkenau extermination and slave-labour camp did all they could to cover their tracks. The gas chambers and crematoria were blown up, incriminating documents and files were burnt. From the middle of January 1945 the 'death marches' began, in which over 60,000 prisoners – those still able to walk – were evacuated westwards, away from the fighting, to the already overcrowded, filthy and typhus-infected concentration camps within Germany. Half-starved, frozen, dressed in rags, shoeless, thousands of those on the marches dropped dead on roads

The main entrance to the Auschwitz-Birkenau camp after liberation in 1945, showing the railway lines that brought train-loads of deportees directly into the facility. Once arrived, they were segregated for immediate execution or slave labour in work details.

'*paved with corpses in the snow*' or were shot as they failed to keep up.

Around 7500 wretches, most of them ridden with disease and near death, remained in the camp when the Soviets arrived at the end of the month. Most of the storerooms had been burnt by the fleeing Nazis, but the liberators still discovered a staggering horde of loot stripped from the victims: over a million suits, coats and dresses; mountains of shoes, spectacles, toys and children's clothing; innumerable sets of teeth (valued for the gold fillings and bridges); and some seven tons of human hair, shaved from the victims before they were murdered and destined for use in the manufacture of mattresses and carpets. Such were the pathetic relics of one of the most sickening crimes in history.

THE IDEOLOGY OF RACE AND HATE

The extreme anti-Semitism that found its final grotesque expression in the Holocaust was central to National Socialist ideology from the outset. The most distinctive and sinister aspect of this ideology, developed by Adolf Hitler in his book *Mein Kampf* (1925), was the conception of Jews not solely as a religious group but as a racial category. Regarded as *Untermenschen* ('subhumans'), Jews were portrayed as an evil race that had conspired to bring about Germany's defeat in the First World War and now strove to dominate the superior 'Aryan' race of which Germans were the prime exemplars. Backed up by a great deal of bogus but popular science, the Nazi racial theory informed a whole ideology of Aryan blood purity and of struggle against and subjugation of inferior races. The grisly logic of this ideology led the Nazis to exclude and ultimately murder those who did not conform to their Aryan ideal. This extended beyond Jews to other 'foreign races', including Roma (Gypsies), Slavs and blacks. And concerns for the nation's 'racial hygiene' led to sterilization and later extermination of various groups within Germany who were defined as 'congenitally sick' and 'asocial', including homosexuals and those suffering from mental illness or physical disability.

In Hitler's Germany, and all the territories overrun by Nazi forces, propaganda was spread to persuade people that a 'Jewish conspiracy' controlled the world and was responsible for both capitalism and Bolshevism. In this Serbian poster, an evil Jewish puppeteer manipulates Stalin and Churchill (who is dressed as a freemason).

Hatred and demonization of Jews was neither new nor limited to the Nazi faithful, so when Hitler came to power in January 1933, he found a receptive audience for the repressive anti-Semitic measures that he immediately began to introduce. Within months Jews had been legally excluded from employment in education and in the law and from holding any kind of public position. Under the Nuremberg laws of 1935 Jews were defined according to supposed racial criteria and stripped of their rights as German citizens, and marriage between Jews and non-Jews was forbidden. From 1938, by which time Hitler and his party

felt popular and secure in power, there was a marked radicalization in the treatment of Jews. The so-called Aryanization (basically, legalized theft) of Jewish businesses and assets was stepped up and accompanied by a series of organized riots and demonstrations through the summer that culminated on 9 November 1938 in *Kristallnacht*, or the 'night of broken glass'. In this massive pogrom, Nazi activists burnt down hundreds of synagogues and looted thousands of Jewish houses and shops throughout Germany and Austria, while more than 90 Jews were murdered and over 20,000 rounded up and sent to concentration camps.

TERRITORIAL SOLUTIONS

As persecution of Jews living within the German Reich escalated through the 1930s, more and more of the victims fled abroad. The Nazi authorities were happy to encourage the exodus, provided they could control it, which basically

In April 1933, soon after Hitler came to power, brownshirt thugs of the Nazi SA (Sturmabteilung) round up Jews in the city of Chemnitz in Saxony and force them to whitewash a wall. It was but a short step from such discrimination and ritual humiliation to systematic murder on an industrial scale.

193

TIMELINE

30 Jan 1933 Hitler comes to power as German chancellor

March 1933 First concentration camp built at Dachau, mainly for political opponents; Hitler calls for boycott of Jewish businesses

Sept 1935 Nuremberg laws strip Jews of German citizenship

9 Nov 1938 Jews and their businesses attacked in *Kristallnacht*

1 Sept 1939 Nazi invasion of Poland marks beginning of the Second World War

Oct 1939 Segregation of Polish Jews in ghettos begins

May 1940 Auschwitz established as concentration camp for Polish political prisoners

March 1941 Construction of Birkenau (to hold Soviet POWs) ordered by Himmler

June 1941 Mobile death squads (*Einsatzgruppen*) get to work in occupied Soviet territory

Dec 1941 First mass killings of Jews by gas, at Chelmno camp in Poland

20 Jan 1942 'Final Solution' discussed at Wannsee conference

May 1942 Opening of Sobibor death camp, where 250,000 will eventually die

July 1942 Opening of Treblinka death camp, where 870,000 will eventually die

18 Jan 1945 Evacuation of Auschwitz begins (death marches)

27 Jan 1945 Red Army liberates Auschwitz-Birkenau

meant offering a passport and exit visa in exchange for an emigrant's property and wealth. Thus, by the outbreak of war in September 1939, the Reich had already been 'cleansed' of about a quarter of a million German Jews and many more from German-occupied Czechoslovakia and Austria. The start of the war obliged the Nazis to rethink their policy, however, as forced emigration became more problematic just at the moment when the occupation of Poland brought more than 1.5 million additional Jews under Nazi rule. The long-term plan was to settle ethnic Germans in the newly conquered territories, and to this end the order was given to concentrate the Jewish populations of Polish towns and cities into the poorest slum areas. Many thousands ended up dying of starvation and disease in the filthy, cramped ghettos.

Barbaric as they were, the ghettos were never intended to be a permanent solution to the 'Jewish problem'. In the early years of the war, a succession of more or less unrealistic 'territorial solutions' were considered. The first such scheme, dreamt up in late 1939, involved setting up a 'Jewish reservation' – a kind of super-ghetto in the Lublin area of eastern Poland, to which Jews from Poland and elsewhere in the Reich would be deported. Following the fall of France in June 1940, this plan was shelved in favour of an even more grandiose conception: the so-called Madagascar Plan. This piece of vicious whimsy, involving the transportation of upwards of four million European Jews to the French (Vichy-administered) island colony in the Indian Ocean, foundered on the small matter of the German navy having signally failed to wrest control of the seas from the British Royal Navy. The prospect of a third variant on the territorial theme opened up in late 1940, when Hitler finally turned his attention to the invasion of the Soviet Union. The vast wilderness of (supposedly) soon-to-be-conquered Siberia offered a suitably bleak spot where the hated Jews could be dumped to rot, freeze or starve to death.

The Nazi planners' more ambitious schemes were partly thwarted by Stalin and the Red Army, but the war against the Soviet Union nevertheless presented an opportunity to test and perfect the methods of mass

murder that would soon be used more widely. Nazi orthodoxy insisted that Bolshevism was itself a product or facet of the grand Jewish conspiracy, so the Soviet campaign was conceived from the beginning as an ideological war of extermination aimed at establishing a new 'ethnic order' in the conquered territories. From June 1941, SS-administered mobile death squads known as *Einsatzgruppen* operated behind the front lines, rampaging through newly occupied villages and towns and rounding up and shooting Jews and Soviet commissars (communist party officials). The mass slaughter was keenly supported by many local collaborators, notably in Latvia and the Ukraine, who also initiated a wave of murderous pogroms. Surviving Jews were rounded up and confined in concentration camps and ghettos. By the end of the year the death toll of Jews murdered on Soviet soil had risen to around half a million.

THE FINAL SOLUTION

There is no extant document that indicates when and in what circumstances Hitler and the Nazi leadership took the decision to move from widespread but sporadic mass murder to a systematic programme of extermination of all

Clutching bundles containing all their remaining worldly possessions, deportees from Hungary are herded off a train at Auschwitz-Birkenau in 1944. Jews from all over Europe were transported on gruelling journeys to the death camps.

THE AUSCHWITZ-BIRKENAU COMPLEX

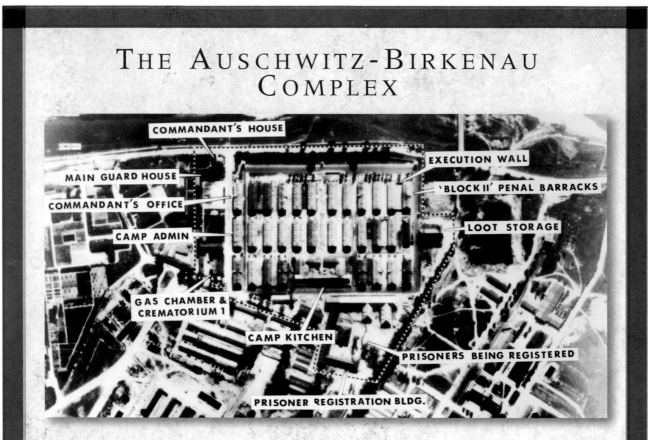

COMMANDANT'S HOUSE

EXECUTION WALL

MAIN GUARD HOUSE

'BLOCK II' PENAL BARRACKS

COMMANDANT'S OFFICE

LOOT STORAGE

CAMP ADMIN

GAS CHAMBER & CREMATORIUM 1

CAMP KITCHEN

PRISONERS BEING REGISTERED

PRISONER REGISTRATION BLDG.

The largest of the six death camps set up by the Nazi regime in occupied Poland, Auschwitz (German for Oswiecim, a small Polish town nearby) was in fact three camps in one. The oldest part, Auschwitz I, was originally established in late spring 1940 as a detention centre for Polish political prisoners. A year later the camp was extended into nearby Birkenau, initially to accommodate Soviet prisoners of war. This part later became Auschwitz II, the extermination centre. The first mass killings using the insecticide gas Zyklon-B were carried out in spring 1942 in makeshift huts. From March 1943 the slaughter was conducted on an industrial scale in four huge purpose-built gas chambers and crematoria, each capable of processing 2000 bodies a day. The killing reached a peak in the summer of 1944, when nearly half a million Hungarian Jews were deported to the camp. The third part, Auschwitz III (Buna-Monowitz), was a slave-labour camp

An American aerial reconnaissance photo of Auschwitz, taken in August 1944.

and the centre of a large network of outlying labour subcamps.

Herded into cattle trucks, Jews and other 'undesirables' were brought to the complex from all over Europe. On arrival the young and the able-bodied were selected for labour on piteous rations till their strength gave out. They then usually suffered the same fate as most new arrivals (the old, the sick, young children and their mothers), who were deemed unfit for work and sent straight to the gas chambers. Thousands of prisoners (especially twins) were also used as subjects for barbaric medical experiments by the camp doctor, Josef Mengele , the 'Angel of Death'. It is thought that over 1.1 million people died at Auschwitz. Ninety percent of these were Jewish, but tens of thousands of Roma (Gypsies), Poles and Soviet prisoners of war were also killed.

European Jews. The lack of such a document proves nothing, as vast quantities of paperwork were deliberately destroyed in the final years of the war – though it has given rise to one of the most heated of all historical debates. The best-known event in this connection is the Wannsee Conference, a meeting of top Nazi officials, chaired by Himmler's deputy, Reinhard Heydrich, which took place on 20 January 1942 in a lakeside retreat in the Berlin suburbs. At Wannsee Heydrich announced that all territorial solutions were unworkable and that henceforth all European Jews would be deported 'to the east', to be worked to death or killed, but the focus of the meeting was more on finalizing the details of an agreed policy than on the policy itself. Remarks made by Himmler in the summer of 1941 suggest that annihilation of European Jewry was already an established policy by that date, and he and other SS officers had been researching more discreet and efficient killing methods for some months. The mass killings that had become routine on the Soviet front spread through Poland in October 1941, as local ghetto commandants massacred tens of thousands of Jews in anticipation of a huge influx of German and Austrian Jews whose deportation Hitler ordered at that time. It is likely in any case that the *'Final Solution of the Jewish Question in Europe'* was being put into effect on the ground, by many local actions and initiatives, some time before any formal policy was adopted.

The fruits of Himmler's gruesome research were first seen in December 1941 at the Chelmno camp in Poland, where *Gaswagen* – 'gas vans' – pioneered in the Nazi compulsory euthanasia ('T4') programme were used for the mass murder of Jews from the Lodz ghetto. In March 1942 mass killings in fixed gas chambers began in the Belzec camp, southeast of Lublin. Just a few days later makeshift gas chambers were operating at Birkenau, and by the end of July the Sobibor and Treblinka camps had opened, which between them accounted for over a million deaths. Altogether, the Nazi regime constructed six sites with gas chambers and crematoria, specifically for the purpose of wiping out the Jewish population of Europe. By the time the killing finally ceased, around six million Jews – roughly two-thirds of Europe's pre-war Jewish population – had been slaughtered.

HOLOCAUST OR SHOAH

The term 'Holocaust' comes from the Greek *holokauston*, meaning a burnt sacrifice offered whole to the gods. Its application to Germany's systematic extermination of six million Jews and others was inspired by the Nazis' use of pyres and crematoria to dispose of their victims' bodies. Given its etymology, many Jews find the term deeply offensive and prefer to use the Hebrew word Shoah, meaning 'calamity'.

'The Führer has ordered that the Jewish question be solved once and for all and that we, the SS, are to implement that order ... The Jews are the sworn enemies of the German people and must be eradicated. Every Jew that we can lay our hands on is to be destroyed now during the war, without exception. If we cannot now obliterate the biological basis of Jewry, the Jews will one day destroy the German people.'

SS LEADER HEINRICH HIMMLER, SUMMER 1941

At 8.15 on the morning on 6 August 1945 the first atomic bomb to be used in anger, nicknamed 'Little Boy', exploded some 550 metres (1800 feet) above the centre of the Japanese city of Hiroshima. The huge blast, equivalent to the detonation of more than 15,000 tons of TNT, flattened every wooden structure within a radius of 1.2 miles (2 km) of ground zero, leaving only a few reinforced-concrete structures as skeletal remains in the blasted landscape. In the first microseconds a massive fireball was created, which emitted an intense blast of lethal radiation and heat. In the ensuing firestorm over two-thirds of the city's buildings were destroyed and an area of some 13 square kilometres (5 sq mi) was reduced to ash.

HIROSHIMA

⊰ *6 August 1945* ⊱

The US atomic attack on Japan heralds the beginning of the nuclear age

On the ground the suffering was immense. Such was the heat in the immediate vicinity of the explosion that birds in flight literally burst into flames and almost every human was killed instantly. Days later thousands of corpses, immolated and charred black, were still to be found welded like lumps of burnt jam to the streets. Further from the centre, the savage force of the blast and the intense heat left the injured in torment, with skin lacerated by shards of glass and burnt, blistered or torn away from the underlying tissue. Many managed to escape the immediate inferno, only to die in the coming days and weeks, coughing up and urinating blood. Estimates of the immediate and short-term casualties of the attack have never been firmly established. A survey carried out by Hiroshima City estimated civilian deaths within a year of the blast at close to 120,000, with perhaps another 20,000 military deaths on top. Among the survivors, the long-term effects of mental trauma and high-level exposure to radiation, including cancers and birth abnormalities, are incalculable.

Two days after the Hiroshima attack, Stalin declared war on Japan and a powerful Soviet army invaded Manchuria, rapidly sweeping aside Japanese resistance. And the day after that, a second US atomic bomb was dropped on the port of Nagasaki, raising the death toll from the two bombings to over 200,000. The causal connection between these three shattering blows and the Japanese offer of surrender made just days later has been the subject of heated debate ever since. Whatever the ultimate motivations, on 15 August the Japanese emperor Hirohito urged his people to *'endure the unendurable'* and so brought an end to the Second World War. The means that US president Harry S. Truman chose to use in order to hasten that end ushered in the nuclear age. The apocalyptic horrors that had been visited on two Japanese cities cast a deep shadow over the following half century: a period of Cold War, in which peace between the two global superpowers, the USA and the Soviet Union, was marked by profound distrust and unease and preserved only by the threat of 'mutually assured destruction' and a nuclear Armageddon.

TRUMAN'S CALL

In planning the final stages of the Pacific war in early summer 1945, the factor that was uppermost in the minds of Truman and his military advisers was the cost in lives (principally, though not exclusively, American lives) that would be

Amid the flattened ruins of the surrounding city, the Hiroshima Exhibition Hall was one of the few buildings to remain standing after the dropping of the first atomic bomb. It has been preserved and now functions as a Peace Memorial.

TIMELINE

Aug 1942 Manhattan Project set up to develop atomic bomb

12 April 1945 Truman becomes president on the death of Franklin D. Roosevelt

Feb–March 1945 US Marines suffer nearly 30,000 casualties in capturing island of Iwo Jima

April–June 1945 Island of Okinawa taken by US forces, at cost of nearly 50,000 casualties

16 July 1945 Atomic bomb successfully tested near Alamogordo in New Mexico desert

26 July 1945 Potsdam Declaration calls on Japan to surrender unconditionally

6 Aug 1945 First atomic bomb dropped on Hiroshima

8 Aug 1945 Soviet Union declares war on Japan and invades Manchuria

9 Aug 1945 Second atomic bomb dropped on Nagasaki

15 Aug 1945 Hirohito makes radio broadcast urging acceptance of US surrender terms

incurred by launching an invasion of the Japanese mainland, a step that most experts considered necessary to defeat Japan. Military thinking at the time was heavily influenced by the high price recently paid by US forces in capturing two small islands, Iwo Jima and Okinawa, where fanatical Japanese resistance, by soldiers and civilians alike, had led to nearly 80,000 American casualties. Truman's fears that invasion of the Japanese mainland would turn into '*another Okinawa ... from one end of Japan to another*' appeared to be confirmed by the estimates he received from his planners. Even relatively conservative projections suggested that conquest of Japan would take a year or more and cost well in excess of 200,000 US casualties, a quarter to one-third of which would be deaths. In other words, it was anticipated that there would be at least as many casualties in the final months of the war as there had been in the previous three and a half years of fighting put together.

Faced with this grim scenario, there was nevertheless one ray of hope for Truman. At the end of April 1945, less than two weeks after he had taken over the presidency following Roosevelt's sudden death, Truman was handed a detailed report on the top-secret Manhattan Project, a mammoth scientific enterprise whose object was to develop an atomic bomb (see 'Fat Man' and 'Little Boy', p.202). The report opened with the ominous words: '*Within four months, we shall in all probability have completed the most terrible weapon ever known in human history.*' In spite of vehement opposition to unfettered military use from several leading scientists, a high-level committee of respected politicians and scientists, appointed by the president to consider the proper use of the still untested new weapon, recommended that it should be used against Japan and that in order to maximize its shock value it should be used without prior warning. Truman had set off in mid-July for the Potsdam Conference in Germany fearful that a swift conclusion of the war with Japan depended on drawing the Soviet Union into the conflict, but on 16 July, the eve of the conference, he received word that the first atomic bomb had been successfully tested near Alamogordo in the New Mexico desert. Unburdened of the necessity of kowtowing to Stalin, ten days later Truman, in conjunction with Britain and China, issued the Potsdam Declaration, in which the Japanese government was called

A SIMPLE DILEMMA?

The underlying logic of Truman's decision to launch a nuclear attack on Japan was neatly summed up by the pilot who dropped the first bomb, Paul Tibbets: *'Yes, we're going to kill a lot of people, but by God we're going to save a lot of lives.'* It was a simple dilemma – atomic bomb or land invasion – and till his dying day Truman does not appear to have been much troubled by the choice he made. American public opinion generally sided with the president, but there nevertheless emerged a fierce revisionist tendency, gathering pace in the dark days of the Cold War, that built up a stern critique of Truman's actions in August 1945 and the motivations that lay behind them.

The inevitability of the central dilemma – bomb or invasion – was questioned on both sides. Shortly after the war the US Army Air Force published a report claiming that strategic bombing alone had already brought Japan to the point of capitulation, while the US Navy claimed that a state of near-starvation caused by its submarine blockade would have swiftly led to surrender. Apparently damaging evidence also emerged that Truman's administration had grossly exaggerated its casualty projections for a land invasion and that Japan had already approached the Soviet Union with a request to broker a peace; this latter initiative, known to the Americans through intercepts, had been stymied by US insistence on unconditional surrender and refusal to guarantee that the emperor would not be removed. The central allegation based on these strands of evidence was that the atomic bombs had been dropped not to induce Japanese capitulation (which would have happened anyway, without an invasion) but to pre-empt Soviet entry into the Pacific war or to

Colonel Paul Tibbets stands beside Enola Gay, *the plane from which he dropped the world's first atomic bomb.*

issue a warning to Stalin not to challenge American hegemony in the postwar world. Recent research using data from formerly inaccessible Soviet archives has provided a corrective to such extreme positions, although most historians today would agree that Truman's motivation was considerably more complex than a simple desire to save American lives.

'FAT MAN' AND 'LITTLE BOY'

'We have spent two billion dollars on the greatest scientific gamble in history – we won.' The gamble President Truman was referring to was the Manhattan Project, a top-secret 'race of discovery' which began in mid-1942 to develop an atomic weapon before scientists working in Nazi Germany could beat them to it. The project was under the direction of theoretical physicist Robert Oppenheimer, based at his secret headquarters at Los Alamos, New Mexico, and at its peak employed over 120,000 people at numerous installations in the USA and elsewhere. On 16 July 1945 a plutonium implosion bomb equivalent to nearly 20,000 tons of TNT was successfully tested at Trinity Site, Alamogordo, New Mexico; the flash produced by the explosion was visible for 250 miles (400 km), while the 'strong, sustained, awesome roar which warned of doomsday' could be heard up to 50 miles (80 km) away. The bomb dropped on Nagasaki, nicknamed 'Fat Man', was of the same type as the Trinity bomb, while the one dropped on Hiroshima ('Little Boy') was a simpler bomb with a fissile core of uranium-235. The latter, though less powerful, caused more extensive damage because of the flat topography of Hiroshima. Many of the scientists working on the project were ambivalent about its aims, and Oppenheimer himself expressed his awe at the Trinity test by quoting from the Hindu *Bhagavad Gita*: '*I am become Death, Destroyer of Worlds.*'

Oppenheimer (centre) and his colleagues inspect the Trinity test site after the blast.

upon to surrender unconditionally or face *'prompt and utter destruction'*. Staring at inevitable defeat, yet unable to countenance the shame of surrender, Japan's military and civilian leaders, hopelessly split, formally rejected the declaration on 28 July. The Japanese people were now inexorably locked on a course to discover the full and terrifying meaning of their enemies' ultimatum.

A RAIN OF RUIN

In the early hours of 6 August 1945 a modified B29 Superfortress, followed by two observation planes, took off from the US airbase on the island of Tinian in the Marianas. The lead plane was piloted by Colonel Paul Tibbets – *'the best damned pilot in the Air Force,'* according to one of his superiors; it was he who had named the plane *Enola Gay*, after his mother. In the plane's bomb bay was 'Little Boy' – a uranium-fission bomb measuring 3 metres (10 feet) long and weighing just under 4.5 tons. Their first-choice target that day was Hiroshima, selected because the busy industrial city had hitherto been spared the attentions of the US conventional bombers and so would show off, both to Japanese decision-makers and to US military assessors, the full extent of Little Boy's awesome power. At 8.15 the bomb was dropped from about 9450 metres (31,000 ft) and exploded less than a minute later over the centre of the city. *'What had been Hiroshima,'* one of the crew reported, *'was a mountain of smoke like a giant mushroom.'* Tibbets's co-pilot merely remarked: *'My God, what have we done?'*

Initially bewildered by the nature and scale of the calamity that had befallen them, the Japanese leaders did not have to wait long before the US president standing in front of the White House disabused them:

> *'Sixteen hours ago an American airplane dropped one bomb on Hiroshima... It is an atomic bomb ... The force from which the sun draws its power has been loosed against those who brought war to the Far East ... If they do not now accept our terms they may expect a rain of ruin from the air, the like of which has never been seen on this Earth.'*

The almost physical revulsion on the part of many Japanese, especially in the military, at the idea of surrender meant that it took a further week of bitter wrangling – not to mention a second atomic bomb, a Soviet attack, a huge conventional bombing raid and a failed military coup – before the utter hopelessness of their situation fully dawned on the Tokyo government. By this time Emperor Hirohito had resolved to *'swallow his own tears'* and to sanction acceptance of the surrender terms (provided that his own removal was not one of them). Attempting in his first-ever radio broadcast to open the eyes of his people to harsh reality, the emperor softened the blow with one of history's most spectacular understatements: *'The war situation has developed not necessarily to Japan's advantage ... '*

'I held my son firmly and looked down on him. He had been standing by the window and I think fragments of glass had pierced his head. His face was a mess because of the blood flowing from his head. But he looked at my face and smiled. His smile has remained glued in my memory. He did not comprehend what had happened. And so he looked at me and smiled at my face which was all bloody. I had plenty of milk which he drank all throughout that day. I think my child sucked the poison right out of my body. And soon after that he died. Yes, I think that he died for me.'

EIKO TAOKA, TRAVELLING ON A TRAM HALF A MILE FROM GROUND ZERO

'There'd been the biggest motorcade from the airport. Hot. Wild … The sun was so strong in our faces … They were gunning the motorcycles. There were these little backfires. There was one noise like that. I thought it was a backfire. Then next I saw Connally [the Texas governor] grabbing his arms and saying, "No, no, no, no, no!" with his fist beating. Then Jack turned and I turned. All I remember was a blue-gray building up ahead. Then Jack turned back so neatly, his last expression was so neat … He looked puzzled, then he slumped forward. He was holding out his hand … I could see a piece of his skull coming off. It was flesh-colored, not white – he was holding out his hand … I can see this perfectly clean piece detaching itself from his head. Then he slumped in my lap, his blood and his brains were in my lap … And I kept saying, "Jack, Jack, Jack!" and someone was yelling, "He's dead, he's dead!" All the ride to the hospital I kept bending over him, saying, "Jack, Jack, can you hear me, I love you, Jack".'

JACQUELINE KENNEDY

DALLAS
⤞ *22 November 1963* ⤝

A youthful and charismatic president and the hopes of a generation die together in Texas

In an interview on Friday 29 November 1963, exactly one week after the event, the former First Lady, Jacqueline Kennedy, expressed these harrowing recollections of one of the most traumatic events in American history: the assassination of John F. Kennedy, 35th president of the United States.

Anxious to end feuding between local Democrats in Texas that might jeopardize his prospects of re-election in 1964, Kennedy embarked on a multi-city tour of the state in November 1963. On Friday 22 November, under a cloudless blue sky, the presidential motorcade was driving from Love Field airport to the Dallas Trade Mart, where the president was scheduled to give a speech. At 12.30 Kennedy and his wife, sitting in the back of the dark-blue open-top Lincoln Continental

Flanked by police outriders and security men, President John F. Kennedy's motorcade passes through Dallas on the fateful morning of 22 November 1963. Seated in front of the president and First Lady is Texas governor John Connally, who was seriously injured in the shooting.

presidential limousine, were moving slowly down Elm Street, acknowledging the cheers of the lunchtime crowds that had gathered on the pavements and grassy lawns of Dealey Plaza. Suddenly Kennedy was struck by two rifle bullets in quick succession. The first passed through the base of his neck, going on to strike and seriously (though not fatally) injure Governor John Connally, who was sitting with his wife in front of the president. The second shot smashed into the president's head above the right ear, blowing away a large chunk of skull and brain. He was rushed to the Parkland Memorial Hospital, where he was pronounced dead at around 1.00 pm. Little more than two hours after the shooting, the visibly distraught widow, still dressed in the same blood-spattered pink wool suit, stood beside Vice President Lyndon B. Johnson on Air Force One as he took the oath of office. In the back of the plane, shortly to leave for Washington DC, was a coffin containing the shattered corpse of her murdered husband. A popular and charismatic figure in life, in death John F. Kennedy was destined to become a national icon, a cherished symbol of hopes and ambitions blown away in a bloody moment of mayhem.

John and Jacqueline Kennedy and their children pose for press photographers after attending church in April 1963. The youthful dynamism of 'JFK' – carefully nurtured by his advisers – perfectly captured the mood of optimism pervading the United States as it entered the 1960s.

A LIFE UNFINISHED

At the time of his death, John Fitzgerald Kennedy had been president for less than three years – just 1037 days. The first president born in the 20th century, at the age of 43 he was the youngest man (and the first Catholic) ever elected to the highest office. Given that his administration was brutally truncated, much that had been promised was inevitably left undone, and the record of actual achievement was relatively modest. But it was the promise of what might have been, as much as the realization of what had been lost, that was the key to Kennedy's enduring appeal. *'We stand on the edge of a New Frontier,'* he had said in accepting the Democratic nomination, and at his inauguration in January 1961 he gave an inspirational speech in which he set out a vision of social justice at home and democratic freedom abroad. The time had arrived in which America would reassert itself and redefine its global mission, under the leadership of a youthful and energetic president:

'Let the word go forth from this time and place, to friend and foe alike, that the torch has been passed to a new generation of Americans – born in this century, tempered by war, disciplined by a hard and bitter peace …'

Inevitably the future that was robbed by a sniper's bullet came to be compared with what actually followed. The gleam of hope and idealism that sparkled in the Kennedy years came to appear ever more brilliant as the country, under an increasingly unpopular Johnson, stumbled into the escalating horrors of Vietnam and a period of unprecedented civil unrest. Race riots and the assassination of civil rights leader Martin Luther King, hopes renewed, only to be dashed by the murder of President Kennedy's younger brother Robert, Richard Nixon's corrupt administration: all conspired to add a retrospective lustre to what had been lost in Dallas in November 1963.

But there was more to Kennedy's 'magic' (the word that his wife used of him) than youth and a promise for the future left tragically unfulfilled. Though born into privilege – he was the second son of a wealthy Irish-American family that was to become virtual royalty in Massachusetts – Jack Kennedy (or 'JFK', as he was commonly known) had a popular touch that allowed him to connect with ordinary people. After the death of his older brother in the Second World War, Jack, a hero of the war himself, became the focus of the family's political aspirations. In a stellar political career that progressed from the House of Representatives to the Senate and finally to the White House, he acquired a distinctive aura, a special élan that combined with a quick wit to produce a

On 28 August 1963, the US civil rights movement organized a mass 'March on Washington for Jobs and Freedom'. The highlight of the event was an address ('I Have a Dream …') by Martin Luther King, Jr. Five years after Kennedy's murder, King was also struck down by an assassin's bullet.

TIMELINE

29 May 1917 John Fitzgerald Kennedy born in Brookline, Massachusetts

July 1960 Kennedy wins Democratic presidential nomination

Nov 1960 Kennedy beats Nixon to become 35th US president

20 Jan 1961 Kennedy sworn in as president

April 1961 Bay of Pigs invasion fails to depose Cuban leader Castro

Aug 1961 Alliance for Progress initiative begins in Latin America

15–28 Oct 1962 Cuban Missile Crisis sees nuclear stand-off between USA and USSR

Aug 1963 Limited Test Ban Treaty prohibits nuclear testing above ground

1 Nov 1963 Kennedy backs military overthrow of South Vietnamese president

22 Nov 1963 Kennedy assassinated; Lyndon B. Johnson sworn in as president

24 Nov 1963 Lee Harvey Oswald killed by Jack Ruby

July 1964 Civil rights legislation introduced by Kennedy is passed into law

Sept 1964 Publication of Warren Report on Kennedy's assassination

4 April 1968 Assassination of Martin Luther King, Jr in Memphis, Tennessee

5 June 1968 Fatal shooting of Robert F. Kennedy at Ambassador Hotel, Los Angeles

beguiling radiance and warmth. Among the first to recognize and exploit the new medium of television, Kennedy was blessed with good looks, a glamorous wife, model children and a natural poise in front of the camera that were soon to become familiar in millions of American households. Consciously or not, he at once helped to define and became the apogee of the so-called 'Kennedy style'. By the time he beat Nixon to the presidency in 1960 (by the narrowest of margins), all the elements were in place to create the myth of the 'Camelot on the Potomac' that has continued to hold America in its spell ever since.

A NEW FRONTIER

In domestic politics Kennedy's 'New Frontier' legislative programme was supposed, in the words of his campaign slogan, to *'get America moving again'* – to energize by means of a range of tax cuts and incentives an economy that had flagged under Eisenhower. His social programmes were essentially in the mould of Roosevelt's New Deal, including federal aid for education, increases in the minimum wage and social security benefits, and medical care for the elderly, though in practice many of his initiatives were blocked by an unsympathetic and conservative Congress. In the area of civil rights Kennedy was at first diffident in pushing for serious change, and it took the mass demonstrations against racial inequality led by Martin Luther King to finally galvanize the president into decisive action. In June 1963 Kennedy delivered a televised speech in which he deprecated a state of affairs in which the heirs and grandsons of the slaves freed by Lincoln were not yet fully free:

> *'They are not yet freed from the bonds of injustice. They are not yet freed from social and economic oppression. And this Nation, for all its hopes and all its boasts, will not be fully free until all its citizens are free.'*

Having infused the issue of the treatment of black Americans with greater moral urgency, Kennedy proposed major new civil rights legislation which was passed by Congress in the year after his death.

DIPLOMACY AND DEFENCE

It was on the treacherous ground of foreign policy that Kennedy most conspicuously and eloquently staked his claim to greatness. The central insight in his analysis of the USA's international relations and obligations was articulated in a number of important speeches, perhaps most clearly in his inaugural speech of January 1961 and his 'Long Twilight Struggle' address made at the end of the same year. In an age where nuclear weapons threatened global destruction, it was imperative, he argued, to achieve an effective balance between diplomacy and defence. Instinctively and fervently anti-communist, Kennedy stressed the need to defend basic

democratic values and to actively resist oppression wherever it might occur – to '*pay any price, bear any burden, meet any hardship, support any friend, oppose any foe to assure the survival and the success of liberty*'. Yet strength must be tempered by flexibility. He recognized that there must be a limit to concession ('*while we shall negotiate freely, we shall not negotiate freedom*'), but he castigated those who saw no space for compromise and for whom everything was black or white: '*appeasement or war, suicide or surrender, humiliation or holocaust… Red or dead.*' In the end – and always starting from a position of strength – there must be a place for principled diplomacy: '*Let us never negotiate out of fear. But let us never fear to negotiate.*'

In practice, Kennedy's tough but flexible approach to foreign policy met with mixed results. Judging that the Soviet Union presented a real and imminent global threat (he spoke more than once of the approach of '*the hour of maximum danger*'), the president pressed for more military spending and pitched a newly confident America into the front line in a number of confrontations. His first attempt to reverse the communist tide, in Cuba in April 1961, ended disastrously in the Bay of Pigs fiasco, where a botched invasion by US-trained Cuban exiles handed the communist leader Fidel Castro a considerable

Kennedy addresses the nation on live television during the Cuban Missile Crisis of 1962, the sternest test of his short presidency. He emerged from this tense stand-off with his reputation for firm but deft leadership enhanced.

'DALLAS IN WONDERLAND'

In September 1964, ten months after the assassination of John F. Kennedy, any lingering doubts over the circumstances of the killing were apparently laid to rest by the publication of the findings of an investigative commission chaired by US chief justice Earl Warren. This hefty report, running to 888 pages plus 26 volumes of supporting documents, concluded that Lee Harvey Oswald, a 24-year-old New Orleans native who was arrested within 90 minutes of the murder, fired three shots from the sixth storey of the Texas School Book Depository. The first shot missed; the second struck Kennedy in the neck and then hit Governor Connally; the third struck the president's head from behind and proved to be fatal. Two days after the shooting, while being moved from a cell in the basement of the Dallas police headquarters, Oswald was shot and killed by Jack Ruby, a local nightclub owner with shady connections. Neither Oswald nor Ruby, according to the report, was *'part of any conspiracy, domestic or foreign, to assassinate President Kennedy'*.

However, for most Americans, the Warren Report failed adequately to explain Kennedy's assassination. Opinion polls taken since the 1960s have consistently shown that between 70 and 80 percent of them believe that Oswald did not act alone and that there was some sort of official cover-up. This suspicion has been fuelled by hundred of books, papers and websites produced by dedicated conspiracy theorists (known as 'Warren critics').

The most complete recording of the assassination is the so-called 'Zapruder film', a 27-second sequence of home movie shot by Dallas dressmaker Abraham Zapruder, the 486 frames of which have been pored over diligently by official investigators and

Lee Harvey Oswald in custody, moments before his assassination by Jack Ruby (left).

Warren critics alike. Warren scepticism reached a peak in 1991 with the release of Oliver Stone's fanciful movie *JFK*, aptly dubbed *'Dallas in Wonderland'* by the *Washington Post*. While no detail of the assassination has escaped scrutiny, the most intense attention has focused on the alleged impossibility of the second shot (sarcastically referred to by Warren critics as the 'magic bullet') and on the theory that the fatal shot was fired by a second gunman from the celebrated 'grassy knoll' in *front* of the presidential limousine. The most common suspected culprits are right-wing dissidents inside or outside the government and the Mafia, enraged by Kennedy's crackdown on American organized crime.

Much of the scepticism is driven by a refusal to believe that the killing could have been the work of a 'lone nut' – a mentally disturbed misfit with no obvious political agenda. But this central irony seems to have been accepted by the president's wife, who on hearing of Oswald's Marxist leanings remarked that her husband *'didn't even have the satisfaction of being killed for civil rights … It had to be some silly little Communist.'*

propaganda victory. Significantly, though, Kennedy learned from this debacle and espoused the 'Alliance for Progress' initiative, which used economic and social incentives, initially with some success, to encourage pro-US regimes in Latin America.

For Kennedy's presidency, the hour of maximum danger truly did arrive in October 1962, when US intelligence discovered that Soviet intermediate-range ballistic missiles had been secretly deployed on Cuba, which lies just 90 miles (144 km) from the coast of Florida. Blockading the island, Kennedy demanded that Nikita Khrushchev, his Soviet counterpart, withdraw the missiles. For 13 agonizing days the world seemed to teeter on the brink of nuclear conflict, but at last Khrushchev backed down, agreeing to remove the missiles and dismantle the bases in return for a pledge that the USA would not invade Cuba. US Secretary of State Dean Rusk pithily summed up the tense situation: *'We're eyeball to eyeball and the other fellow just blinked.'* The terrifying proximity of catastrophe brought about a partial thaw in US–Soviet relations, which resulted in the signing of a nuclear test ban treaty in August of the following year.

AS GOOD AS HIS WORD

The mystique surrounding Kennedy could only be enhanced by the fact that the boldest promise he ever made – perhaps the boldest promise that *anyone* has ever made – came true, precisely on schedule. In May 1961 the president declared before Congress that *'this Nation should commit itself to achieving the goal, before this decade is out, of landing a man on the Moon'*. Sure enough, on 20 July 1969 – within the decade – Apollo 11 commander Neil Armstrong became the first person to set foot on the Moon.

FUTURE IMPLICATIONS

The nostalgia with which succeeding generations have looked back at the Kennedy era is inevitably inspired by hypotheticals, none greater than the question of the administration's stance on Vietnam. Determined to arrest the global spread of communism (which Kennedy's predecessor Dwight D. Eisenhower termed the *'falling domino effect'*), Kennedy authorized increased US support for the efforts of the pro-American government in South Vietnam to resist communist insurgents and by the time of his death over 15,000 US military advisers and trainers had been sent to Southeast Asia. Then, in the autumn of 1963, he backed a coup to overthrow Saigon's unpopular president, Ngo Dinh Diem (1901–63), but the change in regime only increased instability in the region and virtually guaranteed that US forces would get sucked into the worsening conflict. No one knows, of course, whether Kennedy would have managed (as many believe) to extricate himself from the unfolding catastrophe or if he would have presided over the kind of escalation pursued by his successor. In any event, Kennedy's efforts in Vietnam suggested the limitations of his global vision and began to reveal the limits of US power that he himself failed to fully recognize and which would be painfully exposed over the succeeding decades.

'Ask not what your country can do for you;
ask what you can do for your country.'

KENNEDY'S INAUGURAL ADDRESS, JANUARY 1961

At 1.23 in the morning on Saturday 26 April 1986 reactor number 4 at the Chernobyl nuclear power plant on the border of the Soviet republics of Ukraine and Belarus exploded. A combination of faulty design and human error had conspired to send the reactor out of control, causing a huge power surge and a massive build-up of steam that blew off the 2000-ton upper plate covering the reactor. With the reactor core exposed, graphite blocks surrounding the nuclear fuel within caught fire, sending a torrent of radioactive particles spiralling into the atmosphere. Over the next nine days clouds of toxic fallout would be blown across Europe, bringing devastation and misery at the whim of wind and rain.

CHERNOBYL
26 April 1986

The world's worst nuclear accident hastens the demise of the Soviet Union

Unaware at first of the scale of the catastrophe, the world looked on in horror as firefighters, helicopters and engineers struggled to tame the deadly inferno. Long in the habit of secrecy and accustomed to controlling the presentation of events, the floundering Soviet authorities at first kept quiet. It was not until the following Monday evening – after their hand had been forced by high radiation levels detected over Sweden – that Moscow officials issued the following brief statement: '*An accident has occurred at the Chernobyl atomic power plant as one of the atomic reactors was damaged. Measures are being taken to eliminate the consequences of the accident …*'

Seasoned Soviet-watchers in the West guessed that the bland statement hid a darker secret. Their suspicions were soon confirmed as the worst nuclear accident in history gradually played out on news bulletins across the world. A huge human tragedy unfolded as hundreds of thousands of people were evacuated from their homes, leaving behind fields, farms and factories that would be contaminated for generations to come. A far more insidious and intangible misery would soon visit many in the form of illness and death – or a life sentence to the fear of illness and

Shortly after the catastrophic accident at the Chernobyl nuclear power station, a scientist holds a Geiger counter out of the open door of a helicopter hovering above the shattered main reactor hall to test levels of radiation.

death. And alongside the countless stories of personal suffering, there was an epoch-making tale of geopolitical change. For the sad story of Chernobyl – the shoddy design and mismanagement that caused it and the bureaucratic bungling and insensitivity with which it was handled – became a metaphor (and eventually an epitaph) for the whole bankrupt Soviet system. The wind of change that had just begun to blow in Moscow became in time an irresistible hurricane that would sweep away 70 years of corrupt and oppressive rule.

CRISIS IN REACTOR NUMBER 4

On 26 April 1986 reactor number 4 at the Chernobyl nuclear plant was scheduled to close down for routine maintenance. The crew working the night shift were asked to use the shutdown to run a test to see how the reactor's cooling system could cope with a loss of emergency power. To carry this out, the power output of the reactor had to be stepped down to about a quarter of its full operating capacity and a number of safety features had to be temporarily disabled. As the reactor was being prepared, the power level fell sharply and unexpectedly to less than 1 percent of normal output, so the operators removed most of the control rods to compensate and restore power to the required level. At first this appeared to have worked, but suddenly there was a power surge, and as the emergency

Engineers in the control room of reactor number 3 at Chernobyl. Although the design of the reactors at the plant is now widely regarded as unsafe, several such facilities still operate within Russia, Ukraine and Lithuania.

A FATAL FLAW

In power stations, electricity is generated by spinning turbines. In fossil-fuel power plants, the turbines are driven by steam created by burning coal, oil or gas, but in a nuclear station the heat that turns water to steam is produced by energy released during the fission (splitting) of unstable nuclei of radioactive elements such as uranium. The neutrons emitted from the disintegrating atoms must be slowed down (or 'moderated') in order that they bombard other nuclei and set off a chain reaction, and the whole process is regulated by control rods, which can be lowered between the fuel rods to absorb neutrons.

In the type of reactor most commonly found in Western countries, water, pressurized to prevent boiling and contained in a closed circuit, circulates through the core to extract heat, which is then transferred to a secondary circuit, where steam is created to turn the turbines. In this type of design, the closed (primary) water circuit also acts as the moderator, and if there is any loss of pressure in this circuit, the moderating function is reduced and the reactor slows down.

This self-regulating feature was absent at Chernobyl – with disastrous consequences. Instead, in the Chernobyl-type reactor, found only in the Soviet bloc, the circulating coolant water was allowed to boil and supply steam direct to the turbines and moderation was performed independently by graphite (carbon) blocks placed around the enriched-uranium fuel rods in the reactor core. Experts regard this design flaw as one of the main causes for the reactor failure.

shutdown procedure failed, within a split second the power level and temperature of the core had rocketed. As the reactor ran out of control, there was a massive build-up of steam within the system, which caused a violent explosion that exposed the reactor core. As oxygen from outside was sucked into the core and the temperature soared to thousands of degrees, the fuel rods began to fracture and melt and graphite blocks that formed the moderator caught fire, throwing radioactive particles, including isotopes of iodine, caesium, strontium and plutonium, from the molten core into the atmosphere.

There is still confusion surrounding the exact causes of the accident, though it is clear that serious flaws in the reactor design were exposed during the test and compounded by mistakes made by the human operators, who were poorly trained and working under pressure. The lack of the benign moderator feedback mechanism, which would have slowed the reactor down automatically (see A Fatal Flaw, above), was probably the main cause, but other factors contributed. The severity of the accident was certainly increased by the lack of a separate concrete containment structure built around the reactor core, while the large quantity of graphite in the core was responsible for the inferno that raged for nine days and cast radioactive material far and wide.

CONTAMINATION SPREADS

The wreckage of Chernobyl reactor number 4, now entombed in a crumbling concrete sarcophagus, lies in Ukraine, close to its northern border with Belarus. Independent today, in 1986 these countries were the two westernmost

TIMELINE

1978 First reactor at Chernobyl comes on stream

1983 Reactor number 4 comes on stream

26 April 1986 Chernobyl reactor number 4 explodes

27 April 1986 Evacuation of Pripyat settlement for power-plant workers

5 May 1986 Evacuation of 19-mile (30-km) zone around reactor completed

6 May 1986 Fire extinguished, release of radiation halted

15 Nov 1986 Concrete sarcophagus enclosing stricken reactor completed

1989 Second phase of major resettlement from contaminated areas

April 1989 Construction work on reactors 5 and 6 at Chernobyl halted

Oct 1991 Reactor number 2 permanently closed following fire

Dec 1991 Collapse of the Soviet Union

Dec 2000 Chernobyl nuclear complex finally shut down

republics of the Soviet Union. Precisely which areas would be blasted by the malignant touch of radioactive fallout, most of which was released within the first ten days of the accident, was decided by a grim game of chance. The most significant factor was the direction of the prevailing winds, but the level of contamination was also highly dependent on local soil conditions and rainfall. Large tracts of northern Ukraine and of Russia's western border were seriously contaminated, but worst affected was Belarus, where more than half the radiation settled and nearly a quarter of the total land area was polluted. Altogether, in the three most seriously damaged countries, Belarus, Ukraine and Russia, over 142,000 square kilometres (55,000 sq mi) of land – an area nearly as large as England and Wales put together – were subjected to dangerous levels of radioactive contamination. The radioactive plume did not, of course, respect national borders, and in these early days generally smaller, though still serious, amounts of radiation were spread over much of Scandinavia, Poland and the Baltic states, into southern Germany, Switzerland and northern Italy, and as far afield as northern France, the United Kingdom, Greece and Turkey.

Wind and rain were not the only ways that the radiation spread. The power station was located on the Pripyat river, a tributary of the Dnieper, whose basin was the main source of drinking water for 30 million people. Infiltration of groundwater was an immediate concern and monitoring of drinking water and milk was started within a week of the accident. Over longer periods, forests in particular would concentrate radioactive materials, and animals dependent on forest plants, such as wild boar and reindeer, would show high levels of contamination. Livestock and human food chains were also badly affected. Much of the population living in polluted areas was dependent on subsistence farming and restrictions on hunting and fishing proved hard to enforce. As a result, stopping the spread of contamination was almost impossible.

A MODERN EXODUS

The Soviet nuclear programme was both secretive and centralized, so the immediate response was co-ordinated from Moscow. Kremlin bureaucrats liked to create their 'Heroes of the Soviet Union', and there was certainly no shortage of candidates in the immediate aftermath of the

A FLOUNDERING SYSTEM

At the time of the accident Mikhail Gorbachev had been Soviet leader for just over a year. Later he recalled his hastily improvised response to the totally unforeseen crisis: '*I was astounded: how was such a thing possible? Nuclear scientists had always assured the country's leadership that our nuclear reactors were completely safe ...*' Moscow's often inept handling of the crisis – secretive, slow to respond, ineffective in protecting citizens and 'liquidators' alike – was a key factor driving *perestroika* ('political restructuring') and *glasnost* ('openness'), policies espoused by Gorbachev that helped end the Cold War and heralded the demise of the Soviet Union.

A SOVIET GHOST TOWN

The town built to accommodate the power-plant workers, Pripyat, was (in the words of Soviet premier Mikhail Gorbachev) a *'beautiful model city'*. On the sunny spring day on which the accident occurred, the red smouldering core and the column of black smoke rising from the stricken reactor, just a couple of miles distant, would have been clearly visible from the town. Abandoned for good 36 hours after the explosion, it is today an eerie ghost town: a fossilized relic, now vandalized and looted, of the Soviet era, a town of crumbling apartment blocks complete with communist iconography, including massive hammer-and-sickle emblems and images of Politburo worthies. Particularly poignant is a large ferris wheel, due to be opened a week later on the day of the official Soviet May Day celebrations but never used: a rusting testament to a moribund system.

The derelict, irradiated city of Pripyat, built in the 1970s, was once home to 47,000 technicians, workers and their families.

Chernobyl explosion. Over the first nine days much of the emergency effort was channelled into attempts to smother the intense graphite-fuelled fire and to slow the escape of radiation. To this end some 30 military helicopters made around 1800 runs, dropping around 5000 tons of sand and lead on top of the blazing corpse of the reactor. The probable effect of this frantic endeavour, however, was to trap heat inside the reactor and so exacerbate what rapidly became the experts' chief concern: that the white-hot core would burn down through the base of the reactor building and plunge into water that had accumulated below, initiating a second explosion even greater than the first. In the end no such explosion occurred, and by 6 May both the fire and the radioactive emissions were under control – though it appears now that this outcome had little to do with the emergency crews' valiant but largely ineffective efforts.

At the same time, in the country around the stricken reactor, a human drama that would last decades was beginning to unfold. The exodus started in Pripyat, a model Soviet town which had been built a couple of miles from the power station specifically to house the plant operators. Leaving virtually everything behind, Pripyat's 47,000 inhabitants were bussed out on the day following the explosion, never to return. Over the next week and a half they were joined by another 80,000 or so who were evacuated from some 75 settlements in a 19-mile (30-km) exclusion zone surrounding the power plant. Since 1986 nearly half a million people have been resettled or moved out of the heavily contaminated areas – though over five million have stayed on to face an often bleak and uncertain future.

INVISIBLE AND UNTOLD DANGER

As in other aspects of the Chernobyl disaster, opinion is sharply divided over the impact it has had – and will continue to have – on health. It is clear, at least, that immediate casualties were heaviest among those (staff and firefighters) who were on site at the time of the accident and shortly afterwards. Of the 600 or so people in these categories, about a quarter received massive doses of radiation and were exposed in a few hours to between 1000 and 10,000 times the annual safe limit for an individual in the general population. Around 50 of those exposed in this way died within weeks of the accident. More controversial is the prognosis for about 800,000 so-called 'liquidators' – mainly soldiers – who were engaged in clean-up operations in the three years following the accident. Mainly working within the exclusion zone and inadequately protected, all or most of these were exposed to high doses of radiation. The casualties were deliberately downplayed at the time by the Soviet authorities and have been exaggerated – according to proponents of nuclear energy, at least – in more recent official reports published by the three most heavily affected countries, which suggest that around 25,000 have died so far.

Most contentious of all is the situation of those living in the contaminated areas who were exposed to lower doses of radiation. That their general state of health is poor is not in doubt, but the causes are fiercely contested. Pro-nuclear lobbyists tend to emphasize psychological factors such as

A SEALED SARCOPHAGUS

In 2007 a French company was contracted by the Ukrainian government to build a huge arch-shaped steel canopy, which will slide over the crumbling concrete 'sarcophagus' that has shrouded the reactor since November 1986. This 200-metre (650-ft) long structure is expected to take five years to build and to cost $1.4 billion.

depression and uncertainty over the risks of ill health for themselves and their children – a sort of health fatalism that has been inculcated by nuclear doom-mongers and which has exacerbated recognized social factors such as poverty, inadequate diet and poor living conditions. The only area where there is anything approaching agreement is in the case of thyroid cancer, which has shown a marked increase among those who were children or adolescents at the time of the accident. Even here there is a wild disparity in actual estimates across all age groups, ranging from a few thousand to around 100,000. And there is no sign of any consensus at all in the case of other diseases, including cancers such as leukaemia and a wide variety of other illnesses and conditions, such as immune deficiencies, diabetes, heart disease and birth abnormalities. A host of special interests have obscured the picture: the stark truth is that nobody really knows.

An abandoned village in the 19-mile (30-km) safety cordon (known as the 'Zone of Alienation') set up around the crippled Chernobyl reactor. Despite the risk of contamination, some elderly people refused to leave their homes in the zone or returned there illegally after being evacuated.

Fearful that their chance to peer into the fairytale world of the West might vanish as fast as it had appeared, East Berliners hurried towards the wall in their tens of thousands. The cordon of police in front of the Brandenburg Gate, showing little appetite to resist, gave way as revellers from East and West linked arms in the wall's notorious death strip, singing, dancing and shedding tears of joy. Many clambered up onto the wall itself: 24 hours earlier they might have met a hail of bullets but now they found only fellow party-makers, lighting sparklers and spraying champagne over the onlookers gathered below. Some alert individuals even came armed with hammers and pickaxes, all set to hack out lumps of concrete and make a start on the work that would soon be entrusted to bulldozers.

BERLIN
9 November 1989

The Berlin Wall, symbol of the Cold War and a divided Europe, is breached

Fittingly, the fall of the Berlin Wall started in chaos and confusion. At a live press conference on the evening of 9 November 1989, a spokesman for the East German communist government announced that all travel restrictions to the West would be lifted, adding – prematurely – that the suspension would come into force with immediate effect. Suddenly faced with jubilant crowds demanding passage through the wall, at 11.00 pm bemused sentries opened access points that they had guarded (and in some cases killed for) for the past 28 years. *I did not free Europe, or release my people, or any of that nonsense,'* one guard recalled. *'It was that crowd in front of me and the hopeless confusion of my leadership that opened those gates.'* Easing travel restrictions was in truth just one of several desperate moves made by the floundering communist leaders to catch up with the liberalizing movements elsewhere in the Eastern bloc and to win back some measure of popular support; in fact they were merely bowing to the inevitable. Having experienced the bright lights of West Berlin, the revellers were not about to give up their new-found freedom. Those gates would never be closed again, and the communist regime that had

On the night of 9–10 November 1989 thousands of ecstatic Berliners gathered around and on top of the wall to celebrate the opening of the border that had divided the city for 28 years. The official East German term for the hated wall was the 'anti-Fascist protective rampart'.

neurotically guarded them for nearly three decades would be swept aside in a tide of popular protest, to become an unpleasant footnote in European history.

Since its erection in August 1961 the Berlin Wall had been an ugly scar running through the centre of the former German capital, cutting through the arteries that bore the life blood of the city; an impenetrable blockage that split up families and separated friends. A divided city in a divided country in a divided Europe, Berlin had become a symbol of the Cold War, a physical reminder of the irreconcilable differences between two ideologies – West and East, capitalism and communism, democracy and state control. Just as the wall had held back the tide of history, blocking progress and holding minds in prejudice and distrust, so its removal brought a torrent of change, carrying Germany towards reunification and integration into Europe and sweeping aside outmoded Cold War assumptions, alliances and allegiances.

TORN CURTAIN

Soon after the end of the Second World War, a deep ideological fault line – the 'Iron Curtain' of which Churchill had warned in March 1946 – formed across Europe. To the west of the line were the capitalist democracies of Western Europe; to the east a communist bloc comprising those countries in Eastern Europe that the Soviet Union had occupied by the end of the fighting in May 1945. And right in the middle, straddling the line and taking centre stage in the Cold War that developed between the two opposing alliances, were the remnants of defeated Germany. Divided into four zones of occupation by the victorious powers, in 1949 Germany split into two separate countries: the three western zones (US, British and French) formed the Federal Republic of Germany (FRG) or West Germany, while the Soviet zone became the German Democratic Republic (GDR) or East Germany. Through the 1950s the larger, democratic FRG underwent its fabled 'economic miracle', in which industrial production and living standards rose sharply, establishing it both as a capitalist powerhouse and as a frontline member of the US-led NATO alliance that confronted the allies of the communist Warsaw Pact across the Iron Curtain. By contrast, the GDR, though presented by communist propagandists as an economic prodigy, was in fact industrially backward, socially repressive, religiously intolerant and politically in thrall to Moscow.

In view of their many privations and often drab way of life, it is no surprise that many East Germans were drawn by the growing affluence of West Germany, and from its creation in 1949 there was a steady exodus from the GDR to its prosperous western neighbour. In 1952 the communist authorities sealed the border between the two Germanys, but there was still an escape hatch: Berlin. Although completely surrounded by East German territory, the former capital had been divided into four sectors (mirroring the zones into which the country as a whole had been divided) and retained a special status under 'Four Power' control. Throughout the 1950s there was no physical barrier between the Soviet sector (which had become the capital of the GDR) and the three Western sectors which together formed West Berlin. Taking

'THE WEST'S TESTICLES'

Berlin presented a thorny problem for successive Soviet leaders. The constant haemorrhaging of refugees to the West was not only an embarrassment, demonstrating the weakness of the communist system, but gravely undermined the economy of a key Warsaw Pact ally. At the same time, both Stalin and his successor Khrushchev saw Berlin as an opportunity – a vulnerable point that could be exploited to wring concessions from the West. Berlin was, as Khrushchev graphically put it, *'the testicles of the West; every time I want to make the West scream, I squeeze on Berlin'*.

In 1948–9 Stalin had tried to force the Western powers out of Berlin and prevent the formation of a West German state by blockading the city, only to be thwarted by a massive airlift. And from 1958 Khrushchev again began to apply pressure, demanding that East Germany be recognized by the West as a sovereign state and that Berlin be declared a *'free city'* from which foreign troops should be withdrawn. It was only the

Watched by West Germans, East German troops repair a section of the wall that was damaged during a daring escape in 1963.

hope that West Berlin might thus be prised away from the West and absorbed into the Soviet bloc that had prevented the erection of a containing wall before 1961. Khrushchev's strategy reached a climax at the Vienna Summit of June 1961, where he hoped he could bully the newly elected US president John F. Kennedy into caving in over the status of Berlin. But Kennedy saw firmness over Berlin as critical to the USA's credibility as guarantor of European security and freedom against communist aggression, a stance most famously enunciated in his *'Ich bin ein Berliner'* speech of June 1963. The building of the Berlin Wall just two months after the Vienna meeting presented, paradoxically, a defeat of sorts for both sides, yet one that worked in the interests of both, reducing tension and paving the way for a long period of uneasy stalemate.

'Something is wrong. We are in a rapid descent ... we are all over the place ... We are flying low. We are flying very, very low ... Oh my God, we are way too low.' The voice of flight attendant Amy Sweeney broke off, and seconds later, at 8.46 a.m., the Boeing 767, with 92 crew and passengers (including five terrorists) on board, crashed into the side of the north tower of the World Trade Center in New York City. The horror had begun half an hour earlier, as the hijackers attacked and stabbed two flight attendants and cut the throat of a passenger. After forcing their way into the cockpit and taking control of the plane, they issued a warning to the terrified survivors, which was inadvertently relayed to air-traffic controllers in Boston: *'Nobody move. Everything will be okay. If you try to make any moves, you'll endanger yourself and the airplane. Just stay quiet.'* Laden with fuel for the flight from Boston to Los Angeles, American Airlines Flight 11 exploded on impact in a massive fireball, instantly killing all on board and unknown hundreds in the tower.

NEW YORK

⋖ *11 September 2001* ⋗

The worst terrorist attack in US history brings on a global conflict of civilizations

For 17 agonizing minutes rush-hour commuters and others on the streets of Manhattan stared into a brilliant azure autumn sky, frozen with horror and confusion: had they witnessed a dreadful accident, or was it something even more horrible and sinister? As millions around the world became transfixed by TV images of the stricken tower, any doubts evaporated at 9.03 precisely, as a second airliner ploughed straight through the south tower, producing a second, even more violent explosion. Even now, as black smoke came billowing out of the twin towers, the full extent of the catastrophe was not apparent. Just before 10.00 the south tower began to collapse, killing those still trapped inside and crushing those who had rushed to rescue them. The north tower followed half an hour later, adding to

One of the most shocking and iconic news images of all time captures the moment, at 9.03 on the morning of 11 September 2001, when United Airlines Flight 175 slammed into the south tower of the World Trade Center. To the right, the north tower is already ablaze from the first attack.

the blinding pall of smoke, dust and debris that rolled through the streets of Manhattan. As news of further hijacks spread – including a successful strike against the Pentagon in Arlington, Virginia, the nerve centre of the US military – it suddenly seemed as if no one, anywhere, was beyond the terrorists' reach.

The shock and revulsion of the American people at the attacks of 11 September 2001 – soon shortened to '9/11' – were matched by a collective outpouring of sympathy from around the world. A similar level of support was given, initially at least, to the US government's swift and dramatic response: a 'war on terror' which, President George W. Bush declared, *'will not end until every terrorist group of global reach has been found, stopped and defeated'*. Over time, however – and especially after the focus of this novel form of war had moved to Iraq – questions began to be raised, at first in Europe and then increasingly in the USA itself, about the precise aims of that war and about the controversial means used to pursue it. As positions became ever more polarized, the war against terror took on the appearance of a clash of civilizations and of irreconcilable world-views, with the USA and its allies on

102 MINUTES OF HELL

8.46 a.m. American Airlines Flight 11 (Boeing 767 flying from Boston to Los Angeles) crashes into the north tower of the 110-storey World Trade Center (WTC), striking between the 95th and 103rd floors; all 92 on board are killed.

9.03 United Airlines Flight 175 (Boeing 767, Boston to Los Angeles) hits the south tower of the WTC, striking at about the level of the 80th floor; all 65 on board are killed.

9.37 American Airlines Flight 77 (Boeing 757, Washington to Los Angeles) crashes into the Pentagon in Arlington, Virginia, killing 64 on board and 125 in the Pentagon; a section of the five-sided complex collapses.

9.45 The White House and the Capitol in Washington are evacuated.

9.59 The south tower of the WTC collapses.

10.03 United Airlines Flight 93 (Boeing 757, Newark to San Francisco) crashes in a field near Shanksville, Pennsylvania, after a group of passengers and crew, alerted by cellphone calls recounting the earlier incidents, tries to overpower the hijackers; all 44 on board are killed. The probable targets are thought to be the White House or the Capitol in Washington.

10.28 The north tower of the WTC collapses.

one side and Islamic fundamentalists on the other. In the space of less than two hours, in cloudless blue skies over the eastern United States, any lingering optimism that had followed the end of the Cold War disappeared, to be replaced by a new and uncertain era in which the surviving global superpower, self-professed guardian of freedom and democracy, would be pitted against a ruthless, dedicated, elusive and indefatigable enemy.

At Ground Zero

Especially at Ground Zero – the site of the collapsed towers – the devastation was so complete that it took months to pick through the wreckage, to piece together the human and other physical remains, and to assess the extent and cause of the destruction. An exact casualty figure will never be known. Not counting the 19 hijackers, all of whom were killed in the attacks, the official figure (considerably lower than initially feared) stands at just under 3000: 246 on board the four hijacked planes; 125 at the Pentagon; and just over 2600 in New York City. This last figure includes both those who were trapped in the twin towers themselves and just over 400 emergency workers, the majority from the New York City Fire Department.

Almost all of those who died in the twin towers were caught at or above the impact points of the two planes, both of which had nearly full fuel tanks and were in effect massive incendiary missiles. Among the most poignant of the day's countless ghastly details were the many 'phone calls made by doomed victims to loved ones in the moments before the towers collapsed; one of the most haunting images was the plight of the so-called 'jumpers' – the 200 or so

OPPOSITE: Firefighters pick their way through a sea of rubble at Ground Zero after the collapse of the twin towers; the skeletal remains of one of the skyscrapers looms out of the dust. Officers of the New York City Fire Department paid a terrible price for their bravery in trying to rescue people from the buildings; 341 firefighters and two paramedics lost their lives.

poor wretches who chose to plummet to their deaths on the streets below rather than be consumed by the searing inferno within the skyscrapers.

THE PRICE OF FAILURE

It was not until the publication of the extensive report by the government-appointed 9/11 Commission in July 2004 that the full official account of the circumstances of the attacks was given. By that date all the most significant strands of the story had been unravelled.

The co-ordinated suicide attacks were the fruit of years of careful planning by terrorists associated with al-Qaeda, a loosely affiliated network of extremist Islamist groups fundamentally opposed to Western (and especially US) influence and activities in the Muslim world. The hijackers were broadly following injunctions issued by al-Qaeda's leader, Osama bin Laden and others to pursue a *jihad* (holy war) against the West and Israel and specifically *'to kill the Americans and their allies – civilian and military – and to plunder their money wherever and whenever they find it'*.

One week after 9/11, a New York policeman, wearing a mask to protect him against the dust that still drifted over Lower Manhattan from the destroyed twin towers, stands by a poster of America's – and the World's – Most Wanted.

Bin Laden appears to have been personally involved in the planning for 9/11, especially in providing funds and recruiting volunteers – 15 of the 19 hijackers were, like bin Laden himself, Saudi nationals. The principal architect of the plot, however, was probably not bin Laden himself but Khalid Sheikh Mohammed, a senior al-Qaeda associate who is thought to have devised the essentials of the plan in 1996. Preparations for the attacks included extensive training at al-Qaeda camps in Afghanistan and at flight schools in the USA.

While the 9/11 attacks were clearly the result of meticulous planning, the fact that they could probably have been, but were not, prevented has been called the greatest failure in the history of the US intelligence services. As the Commission report pointed out, al-Qaeda's activities and intentions towards the USA were nothing new to either the Federal Bureau of Investigation (FBI) or the Central Intelligence Agency (CIA). Osama bin Laden himself had been on the FBI's 'Ten Most Wanted' list since 1998, when he and his organization were implicated in devastating

simultaneous car bombings of the US embassies in Tanzania and Kenya, which killed over 200 people. Two years later they were involved in a suicide attack on the guided-missile destroyer USS *Cole* while the vessel was docked in Yemen. Al-Qaeda links had even been established with an earlier attempt in 1993 to destroy the World Trade Center with a truck bomb detonated in an underground garage. Prior to the 9/11 attacks, suspicious movements on the part of some of the future hijackers were known to US intelligence agencies, and just weeks before, on 6 August 2001, a briefing document entitled 'Bin Laden determined to attack inside US' (one of many such reports and briefings on the subject) was sent to President Bush.

In the final analysis, however, the intelligence agencies involved had failed to co-ordinate their activities and the Bush administration (like Clinton's before it) had failed to develop a coherent and focused strategy to tackle the recognized threats posed by al-Qaeda. The shocking price of those failures was paid on 11 September 2001.

US tanks roll past Saddam Hussein's grandiose monument to the Iran–Iraq War in Baghdad soon after they captured the city in April 2003. The US-led invasion fomented Islamist violence in a country where it had previously been insignificant.

TIMELINE

Feb 1993 Bomb detonated beneath World Trade Center kills six and injures over 1000

Aug 1998 Al-Qaeda sponsor bombings of US embassies in Nairobi and Dar-es-Salaam

Oct 2000 USS *Cole* attacked by al-Qaeda suicide bombers, killing 17 sailors

11 Sept 2001 9/11 terrorist attacks kill close to 3000 in USA

20 Sept 2001 Bush delivers *'war on terror'* speech before Congress

7 Oct 2001 Start of war against Taliban regime in Afghanistan

Jan 2002 Bush condemns *'axis of evil'* in State of the Union speech

19 March 2003 Invasion of Iraq by US forces and *'coalition of the willing'*

July 2004 Publication of report on 9/11 by National Commission on Terrorist Attacks

THE WAR ON TERROR

Nine days after the 9/11 attacks President Bush made a seminal speech, delivered before Congress and broadcast to the nation, that set out the agenda that was to define his presidency and influence US foreign and domestic policy for years to come. After implicating both al-Qaeda and bin Laden in what he described as an *'act of war'*, Bush in effect declared a *'war on terror'*, in which those behind the 9/11 attacks would be brought to justice and al-Qaeda and other terrorist groups would be eradicated. In this *'lengthy campaign, unlike any other we have ever seen'*, Bush vowed that the US government would *'direct every resource at our command – every means of diplomacy, every tool of intelligence, every instrument of law enforcement, every financial influence, and every necessary weapon of war – to the disruption and to the defeat of the global terror network'*. Crucially, in this new form of war, measures would be taken not only against the terrorist groups themselves but against any nation that harboured or supported them. For every nation, Bush now laid down a stark choice: *'Either you are with us, or you are with the terrorists.'*

Trauma followed by anger within the USA demanded swift action, and in his speech of 20 September Bush delivered a stern ultimatum to the Taliban regime in Afghanistan, an extreme and repressive Islamist movement that was linked to and providing support for al-Qaeda. Just weeks after 9/11, the Taliban's refusal to hand over al-Qaeda leaders or to close down their training bases prompted decisive US military action ('Operation Enduring Freedom') in support of Afghan opposition groups. The Taliban soon collapsed under the military pressure and was forced into hiding, although many al-Qaeda and Taliban leaders escaped and began a long guerrilla campaign to destabilize the new US-backed government in Afghanistan.

A COSTLY DIVERSION?

The Afghan initiative attracted widespread international sympathy and the full support of the United Nations and NATO, which had immediately declared that *'an attack on one is an attack on all'*. But before long concerns arose over the aims and direction of the US administration's war on terror. Hackles were raised by Bush's unfortunate characterization of the war as a *'crusade'*, which lent support to the claim that the West was waging war against the whole Muslim community. Moreover, his elucidation in January 2002 of the notion of an *'axis of evil'*, consisting of *'rogue states'* such as North Korea, Iran and Iraq, did nothing to allay anxieties in France, Germany and other countries (later satirically dubbed the *'axis of weasels'*) that believed in a more measured response to the threat.

Opposition reached a crescendo in spring 2003, when the US government – supported by the UK and a handful of other countries in a *'coalition of the willing'* but lacking a clear UN mandate – launched a massive assault on Iraq. Although the brutal Iraqi dictator Saddam Hussein was swiftly overthrown, no link between his regime and al-Qaeda was ever established and the main justification (or pretext) for the attack – his possession of 'weapons of mass

The 2003 invasion of Iraq prompted mass rallies around the world against the war. Thousands took part in this demonstration in Washington on 25 October of that year. Even many in the intelligence community took the view that the Iraq adventure had been a distraction from the vital struggle against terrorism.

destruction' (WMDs) – was soon shown to be illusory. Before long the country, beset by a fierce Islamist insurgency, had descended into a state of chaotic violence and instability. As US casualties and costs escalated, the invasion of Iraq aroused increasingly strident opposition within the USA. Many critics were also deeply alarmed by a steady erosion of civil liberties and an apparent disregard for human rights, as witnessed, for example, in the abuse and torture of prisoners by US military personnel at Abu Ghraib in Iraq and the detention and treatment of so-called 'enemy combatants' at Camp X-Ray in Guantanamo Bay, Cuba.

Bush had promised that the war on terror – *'civilization's fight … the fight of all who believe in progress and pluralism, tolerance and freedom'* – would bring on *'an age of liberty, here and across the world'*. By 2008, with support for the president and his policies inside and outside the USA crumbling, that promise was looking desperately forlorn.

'TO PLUNDER THEIR MONEY …'

On top of the human cost, the 9/11 attacks have had a massive economic impact both on the USA and on world markets. The New York stock exchanges remained closed for six days following the attacks and opened to see some of the biggest one-day losses in history. By 2008 the centrepiece of the war on terror – the Iraq war – had run up a direct cost to the US Treasury close to 1 trillion dollars; Nobel prize-winning economist Joseph Stiglitz has put the true cost at three times that figure.

INDEX

FURTHER READING

Thermopylae 480 BC Paul Cartledge *Thermopylae: The Battle that Changed the World* (Macmillan, 2006)

Rubicon 49 BC Adrian Goldsworthy *Caesar: The Life of a Colossus* (Phoenix, 2007)

Bethlehem 4 BC Mark Allan Powell *The Jesus Debate: Modern Historians Investigate the Life of Christ* (Lion Hudson, 1999)

Teutoburg Forest AD 9 Adrian Murdoch *Rome's Greatest Defeat: Massacre in the Teutoburg Forest* (The History Press, 2006)

Jerusalem AD 70 Karen Armstrong *History of Jerusalem: One City, Three Faiths* (HarperCollins, 2005)

Rome AD 410 Peter Heather *The Fall of the Roman Empire: A New History* (Macmillan, 2005)

Yarmuk AD 636 David Nicolle *Yarmuk AD 636: The Muslim Conquest of Syria* (Greenwood Press, 2005)

Tours AD 732 J.M. Wallace-Hadrill *The Barbarian West 400–1000* (Basil Blackwell, 1989)

Rome AD 800 Roger Collins *Charlemagne* (Macmillan, 1998)

Hastings 1066 Frank McLynn *1066: The Year of the Three Battles* (Jonathan Cape, 1998)

Ain Jalut 1260 Reuven Amitai-Preiss *Mongols and Mamluks: The Mamluk–Ilkhanid War, 1260–1281* (Cambridge University Press, 2005)

Constantinople 1453 Roger Crowley *Constantinople: The Last Great Siege* (Faber and Faber, 2005)

Bahamas 1492 William D. Phillips and Carla Rahn Phillips *The Worlds of Christopher Columbus* (Cambridge University Press, 1993)

Tenochtitlán 1521 Ronald Wright *Stolen Continents: 500 Years of Conquest and Resistance in the Americas* (Mariner Books, 2005)

Plymouth Hoe 1588 Neil Hanson *The Confident Hope of a Miracle: The True Story of the Spanish Armada* (Corgi Books, 2004)

Jamestown 1607 Benjamin Woolley *Savage Kingdom: The True Story of Jamestown, 1607, and the Settlement of America* (HarperCollins, 2007)

Culloden 1746 Bruce Lenman *The Jacobite Risings in Britain, 1689–1746* (Scottish Cultural Press, 1995)

Botany Bay 1770 Richard Hough *Captain James Cook: A Biography* (Coronet Books, 1995)

Philadelphia 1776 Robert Middlekauff *The Glorious Cause: American Revolution, 1763–1789* (Oxford University Press, 2007)

The Bastille 1789 J.M. Roberts *The French Revolution* (Oxford University Press, 1997)

Waterloo 1815 Gunther E. Rothenberg *Napoleonic Wars* (Weidenfeld & Nicolson, 2001)

Galapagos Islands 1835 Paul D. Stewart *Galapagos: The Islands that Changed the World* (BBC Books, 2006)

Gettysburg 1863 Hugh Bicheno *Gettysburg* (Cassell, 2001)

Sarajevo 1914 James Joll and Gordon Martel *The Origins of the First World War* (Longman 2006)

Dublin 1916 Charles Townshend *Easter 1916: The Irish Rebellion* (Allen Lane, 2005)

The Somme 1916 Martin Gilbert *Somme: The Heroism and Horror of War* (John Murray, 2007)

Petrograd (St Petersburg) 1917 Sheila Fitzpatrick *The Russian Revolution* (Oxford University Press, 2008)

Guernica 1937 Nicholas Rankin *Telegram from Guernica: The Extraordinary Life of George Steer* (Faber and Faber, 2003)

Pearl Harbor 1941 John Toland *Infamy: Pearl Harbor and its Aftermath* (Berkley Publishing Group, 1991)

Stalingrad 1943 Antony Beevor *Stalingrad* (Penguin, 2007)

Auschwitz 1945 Martin Gilbert *The Holocaust: The Jewish Tragedy* (HarperCollins, 1989)

Hiroshima 1945 Stephen Walker *Shockwave: The Countdown to Hiroshima* (John Murray, 2006)

Dallas 1963 Robert Dallek *John F. Kennedy: An Unfinished Life* (Penguin, 2004)

Chernobyl 1986 Piers Paul Read *Ablaze: The Story of Chernobyl* (Mandarin, 1994)

Berlin 1989 Frederick Taylor *The Berlin Wall: 13 August 1961–9 November 1989* (Bloomsbury, 2007)

New York 2001 Lawrence Wright *The Looming Tower: Al-Qaeda's Road to 9/11* (Penguin, 2007)

PICTURE CREDITS

For Geraldine, Sophie, Lydia and Pippa

First published in Great Britain in 2008 by

Quercus Publishing Plc
21 Bloomsbury Square
London
WC1A 2NS

Copyright © Ben Dupré 2008

A CIP catalogue record for this book is available from the British Library

Cloth case edition: ISBN-978 1 84724 833 6

Printed case edition: ISBN-978 1 84724 255 6

Printed and bound in China

10 9 8 7 6 5 4 3 2 1

Designed and edited by BCS Publishing Limited, Oxford.